ANDANDO CAMINOS

Andando Caminos

Teaching Spanish in Waldorf Schools

Elena Forrer

Lindisfarne Books | 2014

2014
Lindisfarne Books
An imprint of SteinerBooks / Anthroposophic Press, Inc.
610 Main Street, Great Barrington, MA 01230
www.steinerbooks.org

Copyright © 2014 Elena Forrer. All rights reserved. No part of this book may be reproduced, stored in a retrieval system, or transmitted in any form or by any means, electronic, mechanical, photocopying, recording, or otherwise, without written permission from SteinerBooks.
Design by William Jens Jensen

Publication of this work was made possible by a grant from the Waldorf Curriculum Fund.

Library of Congress Control Number: 2014936234

ISBN: 978-1-58420-159-5 (Paperback)
ISBN: 978-1-58420-160-1 (eBook)

CONTENTS

Foreword by Elena Forrer vii

1. The Essence of Waldorf Education by Joan Caldarera 1
2. The Language Teacher 8
3. The Language Lesson 14
4. From Storytelling to Reading, Speaking, and Writing 27
   Stories for the Lower Grades 61
   Stories for the Middle Grades 78
   Narrative Paragraphs and Stories for Upper Grades 90
5. Integrating a Vocabulary Topic into a Story or Context . . . 120
6. Teaching Grammar: From the Picture to the Concept 149
7. Poetry and Recitation through the Grades 187
8. Other Resources 266

Bibliography 313

This book is dedicated

to the memory of

Santiago Muelas Medrano

FOREWORD

I am pleased to present *Andando Caminos*, a work that I see as a continuation of *Senderos*. When *Senderos* was published, Spanish had little history as a modern language taught in a Waldorf curriculum. Our wish was to offer inspiration and practical support for Spanish language teachers who were new to this work, and to schools for whom Spanish was a new subject. Since that time, most Waldorf schools in the United States have incorporated Spanish as one of the languages in their curriculum, and many teachers have benefited from its publication.

Andando Caminos offers further support in all aspects of the Waldorf Spanish lesson, based on the developmental levels as the child moves through the grades, and on the corresponding indications from Rudolf Steiner. For the language teachers, it is just as important to understand children in each stage of their development as it is to cultivate balanced and artistic lessons. *Andando Caminos* does not intend to bring a lesson plan to teachers, but to provide support for this task.

There are ample materials available from the Hispanic culture, and although countries in Latin America and Spain often share songs and customs, others are distinctive to each region or country. The Spanish language offers a wealth of materials for our lessons. At the same time, it leaves us free to express what is in our hearts and what we perceive our students need through our individual creativity and artistic teaching. *Andando Caminos* offers a practical perspective on planning the lesson, as well as encouragement for each teacher to find his or her own artistry and gifts.

From the folk tale «*El Gallo Kiriko*» to Nicolás Guillén's «*Los Abuelos*», from the Mexican legend of *Los Volcanes* to the shadow play of the ballad *Conde Olinos*, I have tried to bring pieces suitable for all of the grades. Each piece is introduced with explanatory text for the teacher and is arranged according to the grades, from first to eighth. All the pieces included in this book have been presented in the classroom. Due to copyright restrictions, much of the material I would like to have shared with you has had to be removed. Particularly absent is a wider selection of stories, poetry, written music and lyrics for the upper grades. Many of these materials, however, are online, and I have offered ideas and support for finding and working with them.

Language teachers in a Waldorf school need more than strategies for delivering content. The work involves a humanistic approach to learning, creativity, and a path of self-discovery. In the words of the Spanish poet Antonio Machado, «*Caminante no hay camino se hace camino al andar*».

⁂

I wish to offer my gratitude to the following colleagues for their help with *Andando Caminos*: Joan Caldarera was especially instrumental from the beginnings of the book not only with the introduction, but also with editing and advising; Diamela Wetzel for her contribution to the chapter of Grammar, Allison Carroll for her insights and multiple corrections in the English language, Nora Hidalgo for her contribution of some of the Mexican readings, Marcela Mejía for her contribution for grade 3 in the section "Integrating Vocabulary"; Ann Grandin for her keen advises with the English language and editing chapter 2; Alberto Correa for Spanish proofreading; Álvaro Fernández de Córdoba for his work revising, formatting and advising in some of the Spanish selections; Santiago Muelas Medrano, to whom this book is dedicated, for his encouragement and his unconditional help with many of the stories presented; and most special thanks to SteinerBooks for warmly embracing this project.

I

THE ESSENCE OF WALDORF EDUCATION

Joan Caldarera

A Waldorf school can be seen as the home of a values-based education. Chief among the values Waldorf education espouses are those of reverence, trust, and faith in the gradual unfolding of the developing human being. Moral growth is as essential as physical and intellectual growth, and is nurtured in everything, from the smallest consciously formed gesture (watch a kindergarten teacher carefully folding a cloth) to the grandest idea elegantly stated (hear a high school teacher describe the flowerlike pattern formed by tracing the arcs of the orbit of Venus.) The moral component lies in the reverence, whether for things like play-cloths or for scientific truths. In this context I am reminded of my favorite of the verses Rudolf Steiner wrote for use in the schools:

> To wonder at beauty,
> Stand guard over truth,
> Look up to the noble,
> Resolve on the good;
> This leads us truly
> To purpose in living,
> To light in our thinking,
> To peace in our feeling,
> And gives us trust
> In the workings of God,
> In all that there is
> In the width of the world,
> In the depth of the soul.

Here are the three great ideals—beauty, truth, and goodness—coupled with three valiant verbs—wonder, guard, resolve. Together they can be seen as goals. As teachers, we lead our students toward the experience of these goals every day, in the hope that they will continue such striving and bring meaning to our students' lives when they are grown. Further, this verse given by Rudolf Steiner addresses the totality of a human being, in its threefold aspect of doing, thinking, and feeling, which, when developed morally, can lead to purpose, clarity, and peace—guiding powers through which the child grows into a fully human adult.

Wonder, guarding, and resolution also lead our students to recognize and revere all that is a manifestation of the creative force in the universe—all that is holy or divine. Out of this recognition grows trust, a prerequisite for the courage that is necessary for facing the future. The final words of the verse, referring to "width of the world" and "depth of the soul," point to the correlation between our innermost being and the world around us, a kind of microcosm/macrocosm conjunction that suggests a sublime inclusiveness.

The third line, "Look up to the noble," can be seen as a form of advice for leading the moral life, especially for the high school graduates as they head off into their futures as young adults—may they choose wisely the heroes they look up to, so that they admire only those who are noble. It may be that, with the values of Waldorf education to guide them, they may one day become those that others can view as admirable models.

Therefore, it is clear that the purpose of a good education is to help manifest the capacities of children into the world in new ways. In other words, a poor education assumes the purpose of impressing or imposing its "superior" values upon the current order of things. Such an assumption guides standardized testing, imposed by the current body of authority to recapitulate facts; one cannot "test" for the not-yet-known. Nonetheless, virtually every educator trusts the long-term pedagogical value of discovery and learning through experimentation, experience, and even failure. In the end, whether a child is at play in a kindergarten, writing a poem in grade school, or exploring quantum physics in high school, the process is "owned" by the student in its wholeness, it is the capacity to bring an imagination, idea, or ideal into the discipline and gristmill of reality, regardless of outcome, that holds the key for life-long learning and inspiration. These capacities are the building blocks of tomorrow's innovators and entrepreneurs, and it is these that Waldorf schools can strengthen in our children. This is an educational system that does not punish and stigmatize failure, but one that embraces the long-term values of transforming our view of failure into one of successes not yet realized.

In the Origins, a Vision for the Future

After World War I, at the Waldorf-Astoria Cigarette Company in Germany, the visionary director, Emil Molt, enlisted the help of Rudolf Steiner, a philosopher and scientist, and asked him to come up with a new way of educating children—a way that not only prepared them for the academic world, but also enabled them to develop a strong sense of moral values, and the capacity to think for themselves. For, so he reasoned, the best way to keep history from repeating itself was for young people to develop a social conscience, and to become true individuals with the capacity to judge independently.

Rudolf Steiner developed a holistic approach; he recognized that children are not small adults, as was the customary view at that time, but suggested that the curriculum should tie into the natural development of the child's body, mind, and spirit. He created an arts-integrated, developmentally appropriate curriculum. He put his ideas into practice at the factory school, and honed and refined the curriculum over the next few years. In the ninety years since then, Waldorf (or Steiner) Schools around the world have used and developed this curriculum by conditioning it to the culture and needs of the children.

The Waldorf Philosophy: Based on an In-Depth Understanding of Human Development

Waldorf educators view each student as an evolving human being with a body, soul, and spirit, all of which must be nurtured by education. The education places human development along with the liberal arts and sciences at the center of its work and curriculum. Following the indications of Rudolf Steiner (1861–1925), teachers engage the children with the understanding that subjects must be brought to them in different ways at different ages and stages of development. The three "soul capacities" of thinking, feeling, and willing are essential components in Waldorf education. Waldorf teachers address them holistically in every lesson. They are also highlighted sequentially as the children grow and develop: willing dominates learning through imitation in the first seven years through activities and play; feeling is prominent in the grade school years, approximately ages seven to fourteen; *thinking* is the primary focus of high school.

Between birth and age seven, the child learns mainly through imitation. The atmosphere surrounding the child is filled with beauty, morality, and role models worthy of imitation. At this age the children need warmth and protection to develop their capacities in a natural, supportive, non-competitive, and free atmosphere for creative play and work.

Children between the ages of seven and fourteen learn best from loving and consistent authorities who embrace the world with interest. At this age academic subjects are presented artistically in order to engage the children's feelings so that they will value the world and *want* to master the basic academic, artistic, practical, and physical skills they will need for life. This is achieved through the combined efforts of a lead class teacher, who ideally accompanies the children from first through eighth grade, and a number of specialist teachers who bring a range of subjects to the class on an ongoing basis.

High school students learn best in an atmosphere of challenge and enthusiastic expertise in which they can exercise their independent thinking. At this age, students deepen their understanding of the world through challenging intellectual study as they begin to develop real mastery of their artistic, scientific, literary, historical, and physical capabilities.

On Cultivating Imagination in the Waldorf School

One of the fundamental goals of Waldorf education is to educate students "who are able, of themselves, to give purpose and direction to their lives," as characterized by Rudolf Steiner, the founder of Waldorf education. To do this requires a pedagogy that allows for the greatest independence and flexibility of thought. Within the context of the capacities of thinking, feeling, and willing lies the imagination, which can be seen as a mediator between and integrator of the three.

One of the key aims of the Waldorf method of education is to help the child toward developing the faculty of an open and disciplined imagination. Thus, for example, the teachers generally tell stories to the young children without offering printed pictures; words provide the raw materials and the child must enliven the story with his or her self-generated images.

The students produce their own artistic workbooks, called "main lesson books," which are the students' "textbooks" and record the courses. Playfulness is encouraged in them, because Waldorf teachers believe that imaginative explorations can be just as educational as objective facts and conclusions, if not more so.

"Age of Exploration" Student in grade 7
San Francisco Waldorf School

Grade 4 Spanish book

Educating as an Art

As a beginning, imagine the students happily at work: first graders singing their counting song in the rosy glow of their first classroom; fifth graders eagerly raising their hands, fully engaged in their Spanish lesson; sixth graders repeating the eurythmy form, however self-consciously, because they are challenged to get it right; high school students bending over microscopes in pairs, viewing the blood circulating through the fish they have raised; kindergarteners in the playground, digging all together, marveling at how deep they can go as a team. Then remember that at each stage—the active physical learning stage of the youngest children, the feeling and imagination-centered learning of the grade school classes, the search for both inner and outer truth as the thinking matures in the high school—the teachers aim to build the capacities of their students, helping them to love to learn, even as they practice skills and guide the discovery of knowledge. This is the sacred task of teaching, which needs constant renewal.

Schooling as a Process of Self-Development

To begin to understand the development of children it is necessary to note the central place of love in their growth, especially their moral growth. When the child is very young, she receives the world and all its gifts with open arms. The world is good to the young child as she basks in the love of her parents, in the care she must receive, unable as she is, initially, to care for herself. As the young child grows through the first seven or so years, a foundation for life is firmly laid if she can be filled with a mood of gratitude toward, for example, the light of the sun, the fruits of the earth, or the nurturing of the adults around her. Then the foundation for later life is established in the healthiest way.

In the middle part of childhood, this thankfulness gives rise to love. Gratitude does not disappear, just as plant roots remain even after stems grow from them, and it must continue to be cultivated, but the "stem and leaves" of the growing child's moral life are now ready to be tended. When he visited grade school classes in the first Waldorf school in Stuttgart, Rudolf Steiner reportedly asked the children, "Do you love your teachers?" If they answered with an enthusiastic yes, then he was sure the education was proceeding as he'd hoped, for it is out of love that children from around seven to fourteen learn. One of the things they learn is to love learning, and another is to seek and love beauty in the world, in all its forms.

Out of love grows the blossom of adolescence: responsibility. Responsibility to oneself, to others, and to the world manifests in the heartwarming idealism of youth. If our young people feel it is their duty to right the wrongs they see around them as they seek the truth, then they have discovered duty. The great German man of letters, Johann Goethe, defined duty as what arises "when one loves what one commands oneself." When the point is reached that the young person can say he loves what he commands himself, then his moral education has blossomed into fruition. Gratitude-Love-Duty. In this metamorphosis, love is the center, the turning point.

With this outline of a path as a guide, we can begin to look at how children learn in the holistic way found in the Waldorf schools—through the path of inner development. Effective long-term learning occurs when the topics presented resonate with the students' need to know, and when that knowledge builds upon memory, experience, and active engagement with increasing sophistication. One could say that the imaginative and eminently practical play Waldorf schools encourage in the kindergarten is transformed through the twelve-year curriculum to the imaginative, disciplined, and practical thinking of the high school graduate. Just as the love of language and stimulation of imagination are the building blocks for reading and self-expression in the kindergarten, imaginative learning in the grade school leads to understanding and connecting to the world in the high school. I am reminded of the oft-quoted phrase of Rudolf Steiner's that many Waldorf schools use to describe their mission in working with children from early childhood through high school: "Receive them in reverence, educate them with love, let them go forth in freedom."

From the vantage point of having completed college, alumni look back on their Waldorf education with appreciation for how they were recognized for who they are. They were given the support and opportunities to shine through their strengths and engage with their weaknesses, to understand that the basis of a healthy social life is the appreciation of difference and a respect for individual freedom exercised with responsibility, and to value their own perspective and capacity to change the world. This is evidenced in the remarks from one eloquent alumnus, a Waldorf "lifer" from a pioneering high school graduating class, who spoke with unusual clarity about education and the need for change in the world. He ended his remarks by referring to the gifts he and his classmates received from their education, and then he, too, echoed the importance of the values of reverence, love, and freedom:

"As my classmates from the pioneering class prepare to graduate college, to pursue our dreams, to go out into the world and put this ideal education to work, the high school is truly spreading its wings. While we may soar miles away, and perhaps miles apart as well, we cannot and will not forget our teachers, and this community that fostered our intellects, nurtured our imaginations, facilitated the growth of rare and special friendships, and through passion, caring, and understanding gave us the tools to truly prepare us to take on the world. So, bring it on with reverence, let's truly practice the love we learned, let's respect and steward our cherished freedom. These are our gifts, our inheritance, and the tools for our future."

The four-year high school experience is both an outward and inward journey. It is intended to prepare developing adolescents to meet the world and engage themselves in it. At the same time, the curriculum and faculty guide the students in coming to know themselves, their gifts, and their capacities. The hope is that students may grow into being as much at home in the world as they are in themselves. Although Waldorf high school education seeks to extend the students' capacities for feeling, willing, and thinking, which were first addressed in the grade school, the emphasis at the high school is on strengthening the adolescent's capacity for imaginative and critical thinking. Academic accomplishment is a goal, as is the development of social responsibility. Both are also means for a meaningful, purposeful, and inspired life. These, in the end, are the aims of Waldorf education.

2

THE LANGUAGE TEACHER

As René Querido says in his book *Creativity in Education*, "In the Waldorf schools, we recognize that all the children are born with capacities for wonder, gratitude, and responsibility." Throughout the Waldorf curriculum, these capacities are nurtured along with academic development. This is all possible if we hold the child, asking ourselves the question of what is needed during the lesson. This question allows for new possibilities to open for an imaginative transformation in the lesson. When teaching the students, we need on the one hand, to consider how to engage and bring forth the capacities of the children, and on the other, to acquire a sense of reverence and enthusiasm for what is needed in the classroom. If we look at these aspects, we must consider the following "golden rules" by the Pedagogical Section[1] when talking about the teacher:

1) Connect everything to the human being.

In the language class, the teacher strives to bring meaningful materials that connect the students with people and real life situations. We also strive to bring stories and legends that emulate the folk soul and the character of the different Hispanic countries (see chap. 4 or 5).

2) First the doing, then the understanding.

The students need the experience first, then the rules. This principle certainly applies to grammar. (Having first had the experience of how, for instance, an imperfect tense sounds in a particular situation, they are then asked to distinguish why this verb operates this way in this particular situation.)

3) Lead from the whole to the parts.

The students need to feel the language as a whole and not in parts. The story content is at the center of the lesson as a point of departure instead of for instance, practicing a drill out of context (see chapter 4 or 5).

---

[1] Kellman, et al., *Working Materials for the Class Teacher: Forming the Lessons of Grades One through Eight* (tr. Mel Belenson).

4) *Imply that the world is beautiful.*

The teacher brings beauty in her presentations, so children can strive to develop beauty in what they are doing and learning. Imagination and clarity are paramount components in these language presentations.

5) *Bring everything into a picture.*

Presenting the stories, vocabulary, dialogues, etc. in a vivid representation instead of through dry intellectual concepts with grammatical rules is essential. The lesson needs to flow more "from the heart to the head and less from the head."

6) *Infuse activity with rhythms.*

The child needs alternation between movement and rest, or listening and activity. The key is to be able to read the students and find a good balance, giving them what they need. In the intellectual activities the ego connects with the body. In the activities that are more imaginative and pictorial, the ego releases itself from the body.

7) *Have practical life in mind.*

Our teaching also needs to have a practical purpose. As language teachers, we also need to provide the students with situations in which everyday practical vocabulary is necessary.

8) *Journey from knowledge to knowing.*

It is in high school that students discover who they are and begin to explore and channel their calling into a profession or vocation.

Steiner viewed language study as an essential part of the curriculum and a vehicle for listening, comprehending, and speaking that cultivates feeling, thinking and willing in the students. Two language lessons are woven into the curriculum to carry a distinctive folk soul into the class, which nurture developmentally the students through their hearts, heads and hands. As the students grow, these capacities are embodied in the lesson with different emphasis, as it has been mentioned in the introduction: until age seven, the children learn through imitation with their hands and though doing. From seven to fourteen, the students apply their feelings as they acquire new knowledge through engaging activities prepared to ignite the child's interest. After age fourteen, in high school, students exercise independent thinking and are taught by experts in their fields. The end result is to provide the students with a foundation needed to develop into free and moral individuals. For the language teacher, it is essential to understand these stages as the child moves through the grades and to prepare the lessons accordingly.

New Waldorf language teachers need to have ample knowledge of the Waldorf curriculum, an understanding of child development through the grades, and knowledge of the best way to address the children's development in the language lesson. Schools may be able to support a Waldorf training program, but language teachers need one or more mentors to navigate the eight grades taught during the week. It is even more important in this subject to support and slowly introduce new teachers to the grades. For instance, during first week a teacher might simply observe the lower grades and only gradually handle one's the lessons on one's own. This provides an opportunity to connect with the children gradually at the beginning of the teacher's journey in a school. A well-planned transition for newcomers is vital, particularly for full-time teachers, because language teachers will need not only to take responsibility for the lesson, but also seek out and observe unfolding capacities in the children. Ultimately, a successful lesson depends on the teacher's individual connection to the material and students and an ability to recognize unique capacities for development in each child.

A key consideration today is to assess whether the role of the language teacher has been recognized and valued at the same level as the other subject and class teachers. Language teachers do not hold the same responsibility as a class teacher, but they certainly hold a picture of most of the grades by having a sense the whole school each week. Often this role is not well understood, and language teachers do not feel integrated into the community. Schools need to embrace their new colleagues with support by making a viable plan through a mentor and a training program to guide newcomers as equals in all the school's aspects. This transition is essential for establishing continuity and strengthening the whole language program. This is also essential for the teacher's connection to the students and the life of the school. Eventually, language teachers need to become well acquainted with the state of the school and the pedagogy by attending meetings, conferences, and events. Faculty meetings are the heart of the school and become the door for new teachers to Waldorf education, the children, the faculty, and the community. Faculty meetings are fully planned with not only school business but also pedagogical studies, child and class studies, festival celebrations, and artistic activities. Language teachers can become active participants of this organ, even when they are new.

Active committee work and attending conferences with parents, parent evenings and other events are also key aspects of the language teacher's work. Parents get to establish a relationship with the subject teachers when they give presentations to the parents about course objectives and how they meet their child's developmental needs. Frequent and warm communication between class teachers and language teachers is extremely valuable, because language teachers will often be part of a special relationship between the class teacher, parents, and the students. Class teachers and language teachers are partners for many years. However, there is also another aspect in our collaborative work. When the first Waldorf school opened, Rudolf Steiner gathered the teachers to remind them of their work in full consciousness for the spiritual reality concerning the child and the school. He wanted those teachers to be aware that

The Language Teacher

they do not stand alone in the work of supporting the children. During their first gathering, Steiner said, "In the evenings before your meditation, ask the angels, archangels, and archa to help you in your work the next day. In the morning, after the meditation, you may feel yourself united with the beings of the third hierarchy."[2]

For this work, teachers act in freedom and depend on their own personal disposition to take up the meditations given to help teachers in their endeavors. It will be up to the language teachers to show interest and desire to cultivate this private aspect of one's teaching.

The following is a verse that Rudolf Steiner gave to Maria Rosch, who taught classic languages in the first school (contemplation, reflection, or in the words of Christof Wiechert, "a conversation with the soul").

INTRODUCTORY VERSE FOR THE CLASSICAL LANGUAGE LESSONS

> To the one who understands the meaning of language,
> The world reviles itself in pictures.
>
> To the one who can hear the soul of language,
> The world unlocks itself as a being.
>
> To the one who experiences the spirit of language,
> The world bestows its strength of wisdom.
>
> To the one who can love language,
> Language will grant his own power.
>
> So would I turn my heart and mind
> To the spirit and soul of the word;
>
> And in my love for the word
> Fully experience my self.
>
> *Given to Maria Rosch, November 26, 1922*

---

2 Steiner, *Towards the Deepening of Waldorf Education*.

Verso Para Introducir las lecciones de idiomas clásicos

Para aquel que comprenda el significado del lenguaje,
el mundo se revela en imágenes.

Para aquel que pueda oír el alma del lenguaje,
el mundo se abre como un ser.

Para aquel que experimenta el espíritu del lenguaje,
el mundo le otorga la fuerza de la sabiduría.

Para aquel que pueda amar el lenguaje,
el lenguaje le concederá su propio poder.

Así elevo mi corazón y mente
hacia el alma de la palabra;

Y en mi amor por la palabra
Obtengo la experiencia total del YO.

—Rudolf Steiner (tr. Claudio Salusso)

Steiner spoke about the following principles in September 1919, at the end of the course for teachers. After he talked about connection between the teacher and the hierarchies, he also spoke about the qualities that make teachers capable of teaching children:

> Today I would like to conclude these discussions by pointing out something I want to lay upon your hearts; I would like you to stick firmly to the following four principles....
>
> The teacher must be a person of initiative in everything done, great and small....
>
> The teacher should be one who is interested in the being of the whole world and of humanity....
>
> The teacher must be one who never compromises in the heart and mind with what is untrue....
>
> The teacher must never get stale or grow sour.[3]

---

3 Steiner, *Practical Advice to Teachers*, pp. 187–188.

Working Materials for the Class Teacher

As we do our work in the school, we strive to bring love to all the children, not turning away from difficulties, but seeking, changing inwardly in order to meet any adversity. We strive to build sympathy with the nature of the children, understanding what they bring through each step of their development instead of using an educational guide. For this work, cultivation of imagination is a source of inspiration in teaching through artistic work. We offer beauty and order so the children will attempt to do their work with sensibility, thus acquiring a sense of organization with clarity. We bring a joyful attitude and humor to our lessons, even when we encounter hardships, remembering that a teacher is not a teacher but a guide. As Steiner said about our task with children, "Receive them in reverence, educate them with love, let them go forth in freedom."

3

THE LANGUAGE LESSON

3.1. THE THREEFOLD LESSON

WALDORF EDUCATION includes a foundational aspect of pedagogy that separates this method from others. It is built on knowledge of the human being and human development. The needs and development of the children's physical bodies, soul life, and spiritual nature are addressed through educational activities that engage the head, heart, and hands. We aim to build our lessons so that each of these aspects of the human being are integrated and engaged through rhythm and artistic content to meet fully the children at their individual developmental levels.

Language teachers, as well as class teachers and other subject teachers, need not only an understanding of their subject matter, but also the ability to work from an understanding of the *whole human being*.

Looking at a baby, we see that the baby's first action is to connect to life by breathing. Through breath, a child learns to receive and to connect with the environment. This rhythm of inhaling and exhaling takes place first in the chest. Rudolf Steiner refers to this as *the feeling life,* or the heart region, where we first encounter the outer world.

The air we breathe in is carried by the blood (circulatory system) to our limbs and then from the nervous system to the brain. The first response children experience through breathing is movement of the legs. These movements, according to Steiner, produce the contours of speech. Then the more delicate movements of the arms and hands determine the inflection and plastic form of the words. This means that our physical movements are transformed into the inner movements of speech. Moreover, as children imitate their surroundings and learn to speak through inhaling and through exhaling, they learn to transform the spiritual into the physical.

There are three centers where this rhythm interacts: *the head,* in the interplay of nerves and blood and where memory arises, and in the metabolic system, where the nerve function is connected to *thinking* and the *life of consciousness;* the area of *chest,* which is connected to speech, is the central section of the organism and involves the rhythmic organization—blood circulation and lymph system and what Steiner calls *the feeling life;* and *the lower body,* where *the will* is grounded in the metabolism.

At one level, we consider the *physical body* and its perception through the senses. At another level, not physically, we equally consider the *soul* and the *spirit* of the child, where the *life of pictures* is critical for interactions with the world. We teach in pictures formed from sympathy and develop concepts that work in the will and in the whole person. Waldorf teachers consider not only a particular way of *rhythmic teaching,* but also the content, which is rich with imagery for nurturing the children's soul and spirit.

When forming the lessons, Waldorf teachers keep in mind this threefold aspect of the human being—feeling, thinking, and willing—while also developing an understanding that the nature of the human being breathes in the picture-form, thus planting seeds in the children that will ripen into healthy and free individuals.

> The shaping of language is primarily dependent upon the rhythmic and metabolic-visceral systems within the human organism, and only secondarily, insofar as it is re-shaped, as a reflection in waking consciousness, upon the nervous system. The more archaic levels of language, then, are closely connected to the life of sensation and movement.[1]

Thus the question for the language teachers is this: What is really needed in the language lesson so that it addresses and engages all aspects of the human being?

We must form the lesson so that it allows precise support for breathing and a natural way to nurture the soul and spirit of the children. We create a rhythm in our lesson through poetry, music, and movement; we also incorporate imaginative material to evoke mental pictures so that the children "breathe in" a picture form. We can bring this pictorial element in many ways throughout the lessons, as will be explained later. These formative qualities of the language explained here enrich the children in their own being, cultivating their speech and nourishing their souls.

When planning the lessons, teachers face the question of how to integrate vocabulary and organize the language lesson, as well as how to bring about a healthy rhythm of breathing in and breathing out. Often, if the lessons have not been planned in an imaginative or rhythmic way, teachers find themselves lost both in the planning process and in the classroom and left with this question: How can I bring living pictures and rhythm for the different age groups into the lesson?

---

1 Kiersch, *Language Teaching in Steiner Waldorf Schools.* p. 21.

3.2 Beginning steps: forming a Repertoire

In the beginning of the lesson, through movement and rhythmic repetition, the students live into the feeling life of the lesson. René Querido used to refer to this section of the foreign language lesson as "selecting a repertoire." He explained that a "repertoire" could be a choice of themes—not only poetry and songs, but also rhythmic actions and speech.

During the first lesson, only a few minutes are dedicated to "the repertoire," but over time teachers introduce more lines or add sections from a chosen topic. A good selection of poems, actions, commands, songs, movement, and speech at the beginning of the lessons contributes to the process of language acquisition. Steiner emphasizes the importance of movement and the rhythmic system in connection to language:

> Every nuance of speech is derived from the organization of movement; life to begin with all gestures and gesture is inwardly transformed into speech.... First, there are the outer movements of the legs—these produce the contours of the speech; the more delicate movements of the arms and hands determine the inflection and plastic form of the words. In short, outer movements are transformed into the inner movements of speech.[2]

> It is also important to cultivate the element of reflex action in connection with language, that is, to give the children orders—do this, do that—and make sure they carry them out. In this exercise what the teacher says is not followed by reflection on what has been said or by a slowly spoken answer, but by action. In this way the will realm, the element of movement, is cultivated in language lessons.[3]

Starting in the early years, children need to experience the highest expression of the language and its genius. Language teachers, as René Querido points out in his book *Creativity in Education,* do not stress the difficulties of vocabulary or grammar. From an early age, the children will absorb language by "instinct out of habit" and over time we will teach grammatical and vocabulary, not concepts.[4] Poetry is an excellent way to acclimate children to the genius and beauty of language and can easily be included in the repertoire for all of the grades.

Waldorf teachers memorize poems and recite them in a lively manner rather than read them from a book. First we begin by reciting a few lines, and then we have the children repeat them out loud in the next lesson; little by little, the entire poem can be recited by the class in chorus.

---

2 Steiner, *The Art of Education,* pp. 110–111.
3 Steiner, *Practical Advice to Teachers,* p. 139.
4 See chapter 6, "Teaching Grammar: From the Picture to the Concept."

Rather than giving translations of our poems, we offer an image of an introduction in the middle and upper grades, and in the lower grades, the children will understand the content of the poem through perception of the images through our gestures and the sounds, much as it is perceived when learning their mother tongue.

Many actions and vocabulary words can be incorporated in the "repertoire," starting in the early grades. For instance, if the children are learning new words or actions, rather than pointing to the objects in the classroom, we can say, "With my hands I work," or "With my eyes I see," or "With my ears I hear" (as we describe later in the grammar section). When teaching verbs, the "I" of the children joins in the gestures with the physical body, thus experiencing the gestures as joining with them instead of separating them from the environment. As the children learn new expressions or new vocabulary, often these can be incorporated during the "repertoire" portion. Body geography, clothes, actions, expressions, adverbs, prepositions, reflexive verbs, and so on can be easily choreographed and added, as well.

If we wish to have success with our "repertoire" in every grade, teachers need to be familiar with the curriculum, so that age-appropriate material is brought into the context of the particular culture we bring. We need to be able to create materials that meet the children's developmental levels and be able to connect with what we are teaching with our whole body. We also need to cultivate attention to our voices and gestures and the intonation of the songs.

When preparing a lesson for the lower grades, it is helpful to reconnect with our own experiences from childhood, so that we can tap into insights and ideas that have personal meaning. Through this process, we will research and create (and at times recreate) material appropriate for each class. Several aspects are confluent: on the one side, our own soul experiences from our past, on the other, our connection to the spirit of the language. Our imagination, voice, and gestures will be the main tools in our presentations.

Teachers should always open the class with a warm greeting, followed by a sequence of songs, an age-appropriate poem, then rhymes with movements of the limbs, such as clapping and stamping, moving in a circle or just around the desk, and finally by other recitations with gentle and meaningful movements, such as counting or playing a dialog with their fingers.

Particularly in the lower grades, all these movements need to contain imagination. Thus, rather than saying, "Move your hand up,'" or "Stand straight," or "Count numbers," we bring an image such as "Reach out to the sun," or "We are standing like tall trees," or "We are going to climb the stairs," or "We are gnomes digging in the mine with our shovels and counting our jewels."

Poems are usually carefully choreographed, especially in the lower grades; the movements are not improvised but arise from inner pictures. Inner pictures and repetition of the prepared movements provide a strong rhythm for the children and more consistent "breathing."

This segment of the lesson can be repeated in the following lessons, but the repetition of each element should be short—only a few minutes. Speech, movement, and musicality are imbued with a dynamic participation and the involvement of the children with their whole body while we give an appropriate image. Steiner says in this regard, "Until nine or ten, children bring with them enough imaginative imitation to enable us to teach a language so that it will be absorbed by their whole being, not just by their forces of soul and spirit."[5]

In the Middle grades the teacher can expand all the new vocabulary learned through actions with more complex movement. For instance, if the students are practicing months or days of the week, the students can anticipate without help the days in question, stepping forward while speaking the answer or backward using this command: "If today is Friday, then tomorrow is..." (step forward) "And yesterday was..." (two steps back).

Prepositions and adverbs can be acted out with movement of the feet and hands. After grade 3, the students become more grounded and develop a growing awareness of their environment and themselves. Therefore, our repertoire will change accordingly. Poems are also recited, but the movements will transform into something more natural—almost an extension of our speech (coordinating our limbs while learning prepositions or reciting months will be very different from the inner gestures created by the images of the poem).

New vocabulary can be added easily. For instance, if the students are learning about the formation of plural, when pointing out objects around the classroom, it is very helpful to add the plural—"This is the door; these are the doors." "That is the window, and those are the windows." "This is my hand; these are my hands."

Another way to do this could be to act out what we do in the morning:

Por la mañana me levanto, me la lavo la cara, me peino, me visto, como mi desayuno, me lavo los dientes, salgo hacia la escuela. Entro en la escuela, subo las escaleras, abro la puerta y entro en mi clase.

After grade 3, bringing verb conjugation through rhythmical clapping or stamping with choreographed movements allows the children to remember the verb endings at a feeling level.

---

5 Steiner, *A Modern Art of Education*, p. 139.

Songs are also going to be selected according to the children's age level. Perhaps we can bring a folder with songs to offer to the class. Many of the songs will be sung in parts; therefore, if the teacher needs help, it is always good to get advice from the music teacher.

In the upper grades the portion of the lesson from the "repertoire" can be much shorter and contain rhythmic conjugation and vocabulary with appropriate movement and speech work. If the children are learning new verbs and their conjugation, offering them with a rhythm together with clapping or tapping can be helpful. For instance:

Yo canto (tap, tap)	Nosotros cantamos (clap, clap, clap)
Tú cantas (tap, tap)	Vosotros cantáis (clap, clap, clap)
Usted canta (clap, clap)	Ustedes cantan (clap, clap, clap, clap)
Él canta (clap, clap)	Ellos, cantan (tap, tap, tap)
Ella canta (tap, tap)	Ellas, cantan (tap, tap, tap)

If the class is learning conjugation, some rows of children can recite the verb in present tense and another section can do the same or a different verb in the simple past tense. The poem can be recited not only by everyone together, but also by rows or by assigning individual parts. The children will experience the beauty of the language through the sound and the rhythm, while taking in the image given from the different stanzas.

Incorporating vocabulary from the stories read or learned during class can be very helpful. We can use expressions such as *tengo frío* or *tengo prisa*. Also, act out sentences: *Pedro baja deprisa por las escaleras. Él saluda a su madre, toma su abrigo y sale de casa caminando rápidamente.*

Practicing vocabulary words, giving commands, singing different parts, and adding instruments to the song or reciting different verb tenses are other activities that can be rhythmically added to the lesson to help students reinforce their vocabulary and gain a feeling for the language.

Teachers have a lot of freedom in their lesson preparations. Therefore, the allocated time for this section of the lesson will vary, because much depends on the grade, the class, and the topics added. For instance, language teachers need to sense what is appropriate each week and move on to the next section only when the students are ready. If "the repertoire" has not worked out in the context of the lesson, the teacher has to review the reason and make adjustments accordingly.

It is important to memorize a sequential repertoire thoroughly, including poems and to live fully into what we do. Our speech, intonation, singing, articulation, gestures, and movement must be well prepared and executed. It is critical that teachers actively prepare for each and every class. Seeing the students is also essential; teachers always need to take an interest in knowing the students and their capabilities and never assume that they know the lesson content.

3.3 Recalling a Topic and Presenting New Content

Usually, once the students have been seated after the "repertoire," they are extremely attentive and receptive to learning. However, before we present any new content, we must always bring back was has been experienced before. This is a moment to awaken their consciousness and their memory of concepts already learned. If we have guided the students through the right images in our teaching, we will be able to bring back these concepts and images. Throughout this process, we work with what has been "captured" by their memory through the process of "recalling." For many students, this will be a time to consolidate and review material learned previously.

We want the children to think inwardly, so we guide them with what they can remember and what has been "captured" in their memory. If the children are unable to do this, then we lead them through the image again, so that they arrive at a picture and then a concept. In our process of "recalling" with the students, teachers work with the question of memory. This issue has to do with the activity of antipathy. After a picture has been formed, antipathy (if *antipathy* is strong enough) forms the concept arising from memory. This process takes place in the head as the interaction of blood and nerves. If the children have been exposed to imaginative pictures (streaming from *sympathy* and arising from *imagination*), those pictures work in the children's will; if the antipathy is strong enough, the pictures become memory. "That we perceive chalk as white, for instance, arises out of the use of the will, which through sympathy and imagination becomes a living picture."[6]

Another important technique in Waldorf education is the story recall. Stories are told and then retold from previous days, together with the children's input. Retelling a story allows the children to sequence mental pictures imaginatively. With the help of the language teacher, the children learn to express these images in the foreign language. The images from the stories have not been forced (or "taught") but are allowed to be "forgotten" and then "remembered." The rhythm of "forgetting/remembering" creates a healthy balance. The children's "I" is also awakened by developing an inner movement with the story, or "participating" in the speech, thus awakening their will.

---

6 Steiner, *Foundations of Human Experience*, p. 56.

The Language Lesson

The recall allows us to move further ahead with each topic presented. It is important in every class we teach that students feel that something new has been presented. It does not mean we have to present a new topic each time, but rather it could be that the same topic can be approached from different angles. As teachers, we need to find a good balance with grammatical aspects and story content. Grammatical points are illustrated separately from the stories the students read or tell. Therefore, it is the responsibility of the teacher to guide the students though an appropriate grammatical progression from grade 4 on.[7] If we bring too many abstract concepts to our students, we activate the production of carbonic acid in the blood. If we bring the students the right pictures at the right time, we active the production of oxygen and enhance their learning.

New content is the aspect of the lesson whereby the students are going to breathe in the pictures through our narration or discover the peculiarities of the language as they get older and become more conscious of the grammatical rules.

Now let's look at how this process can be presented through the grades. In the lower grades, a "magic ball," a doll, or a puppet is the perfect prop to lead our questions and build up their sentences in their recalling of the stories throughout the weeks. We ask questions related to topics such as age, name, color, objects, and number or size. The children should be able to answer our questions in complete sentences: "My boots are red"; "The window is behind the table"; "My teacher is tall"; or "The curtain is pink."

Question and answer is a very important activity that allows the attentive children to respond to questions and their answers serve as a model for the others. Often after the answer, the whole class can repeat the whole sentence again. In addition, guided questions about the story the students have heard helps the children to speak as they create various scenes from a story. If we take the story, «*El burro, el mantel y el palo*», we can for instance begin a recall with the following questions:

> *Pedrito y su madre no tienen comida para comer. ¿Adónde va Pedrito?*
> *Pedrito va al río.* (they all repeat chorally)
> *Pedrito va al río a pescar."— ¿Qué pesca Pedrito?*
> *Un pez de oro.* (they respond)
> *Pedrito pesca un pez de oro.* (all chorally) *¿Qué dice el pez a Pedrito?*
> *El poderoso genio del río soy, si tú me liberas un premio te doy.*
> (all chorally, and so on)

---

7 See chapter 6, "Teaching Grammar: From the picture to the Concept."

If we follow the recall with illustrations, it becomes easier for the children to understand. We should try to get as much information from children as possible, but we must give them the tools to do so successfully. Therefore, good planning utilizing previous vocabulary is essential.

It is the task of teachers to see individual children, asking each one questions and drawing out all the answers that they are capable of giving. It is always good to give the difficult questions to the quick children, so they can model the answers, and pose simpler questions to the students who need more help. Once the class (from grade 3 on) has established a good vocabulary for different topics, we can give them a challenge by saying something like this: "Let's see how many sentences the class can form without my help."

After the recall has been concluded in the lower grades, perhaps we could retell the story from the beginning, but then add a new illustration or just enhance the image of the story, not only by repeating the same words but also by adding a new vignette.

A basket containing objects to support a story or the experiences of a chosen character is always helpful. Simple questions regarding color, size, or number are certainly important when reviewing the work, but telling and retelling the story will be the main activity. A gnome that goes to school in the lower grades, for instance, can ask the students who have already been acquainted with the objects in our story (while we cover them with a silk and carefully remove one), "What is missing?" One boy, after raising his hand, may respond, "The hat." We then move on in the same way until all the objects have been named again. I can ask, "What does Martin have?" They respond, "He has an apron and a shovel." Now, "What does Martin have?" "He has his boots, his hat, a shovel, and an apron."

In grade 3, simple props for activities can be helpful if the questions are guided. For instance, the teacher could ask, "Is the farmer Pedro watering the garden, or is he cutting the hay?" Story topics from the grade-three curriculum, such as farming, housing, cooking, or building, may also be used for our images to enhance our vocabulary. Many of the topics can be repeated over the following days by adding to the stories as suggested in the following sections.

We can also guide the students through various activities with props or illustrations for a story. If, for instance, we take the story *Pelle's New Suit*, we can prepare all the activities from the story such as "carding the wool," "dying the wool," "spinning the thread," "weaving the thread," "cutting the fabric," and so on. All these activities can be brought in an imaginative way into the lesson for the children to form sentences and recall the story (see chapter 4).

In the middle grades, more questions regarding grammatical aspects can be included. For instance, we may add plurals with a basket of vegetables and/or fruits, asking the students to formulate sentences about colors and sizes. Now the students need to pay attention to sentence agreement, which can serve as a review to others. For example, the teacher can tell a student to form a sentence with the word *apple* and to form the plural: "Las manzanas son rojas y los sombreros son blancos." Then we ask why this sentence has this particular agreement in Spanish. We can also ask the students to observe the differences in gender of naming words and the preceding articles.

We can bring illustrations or a real basket with carrots, potatoes, tomatoes, strawberries, bananas, oranges, and apples and ask for distinctive descriptions. For example, ask the students to form a sentence while we hold a carrot. The student could say, "The carrot is orange," or " The apple is red," or "The banana is long," and we can ask why they formed these sentences in this way. This step can serve as a reminder of how to form the gender and plural of nouns and the agreement with the adjective, and bring to their consciousness something new while moving along with the lesson. We also can recall the story in the same way as explained before, and perhaps the teacher can individualize questions instead of asking students to respond chorally.

When we bring new content in the middle grades—for instance, articles and sentence agreement—we can move ahead and ask a student to change various examples to plural or practice concordance in the sentence. As the sentences unfold, the teacher can write them on the board and then ask the students what has happened. Many will notice how the adjective agrees with the noun in gender and number, and a rule can be established. We also can bring a story to underscore these concepts (see chapters 4 and 6).

After we finish our grammatical review, we can bring a story. In grade 4, we begin with short readings, and by grade 5 the students should be able to follow a good amount of content. Stories such as «*Francisco en la Misión*» or «*El Gallo Kiriko*» help the students first with their choral reading and then with their vocabulary development as they begin to describe the story in their own words, forming sentences.

In the upper grades, this portion of the lesson this is a very important part, because here we can see if the concepts brought in the past lessons are clear. We can ask students a question in their mother tongue with a particular verb tense and have them translate it into Spanish. This is an effective way to bring consciousness to their grammar. We can also incorporate in our sentences the vocabulary covered during the lesson before in our sentences. Another example for grades 6 and 7 may be: "I would like you to form one sentence with the verb *comer* in the past," and "I would like you to change it to present tense," and vice versa.

Taking this same sentence, we can say "Let's change *we* to *they*," and so on. After the students have completed a few examples and they seem to have understood the changes for the conjugation, the teacher is ready to move forward with new material.

If the class has been working with a story or reading, this is also the moment to bring back that content to the class. Many students like to volunteer for summarizing paragraphs while adding their particular descriptions in their own words.

In the upper grades, we can also work in this way and practice forming interrogative and negative sentences orally in class (see chapters 4 and 6). Presentation of new verb tenses—present progressive, past tense or other grammatical topics such as demonstrative adjectives—in different situations can be presented in a living way to the class. We can also refer to our readings from the previous day, bringing back the story content and an analysis of the new vocabulary, and continue the reading.

Bringing stories through the grades is of paramount importance in our teaching. Ideally these stories have been supported by poems, music, or geographical explanations according to their grade level. If, for instance, the students are learning medieval history, the language teacher can bring a ballad and a story from that period. If it is a legend, the teacher will work deeply with the content and the images from those stories, assigning individual parts for reading, followed by working with vocabulary development independently from grammar. The students can concentrate on the images from the story (explained in chapter 4).

We want the students to be able to retell and express themselves as much as possible in the foreign language. Bringing the images without word-by-word translation is essential to keeping the students engaged and learning. From the recollections, students will be able to create and develop sentences and then paragraphs until they can create their own compositions and dialogues, as it is explained and illustrated later with some work from the students.

It is most important that the students are active. In the upper grades, it is vital that teachers understand that the students not only need to relate to the topic, but also need to be conscious of the changes in the language and feel they have learned something new. Thus, it is always helpful to ask ourselves after every lesson, "What did the students learn today?" If we really cannot answer this question, we must review to find insights into what to do differently in future lessons.

Now that the students are ready, we can move on to the next segment of the lesson: practice through individual active work.

3.4 Active Work and Practice

After the new content has been introduced and worked with, allowing time for practice encourages exhalation. Although the lesson develops as a whole, we must allow time for breathing in and breathing out in all the activities. This is the time when the students will practice dialogue, vocabulary, and writing, in their books on their own, with a desk partner, or in groups.

For instance, in the lower grades reenacting the story with costumes, playing games with a lot of interaction—such as *Siete arriba, el anillo, ¿Dónde están las llaves?* or other guessing games—allows for practice and breathing out. Costumes, games, and movement are going to be the main focus during this activity.

When the class has become well acquainted with the objects, we can play another game by calling and asking four students to come to the front and giving them four objects. Then, after forming a circle, I ask them to exchange these objects but not allow the rest of the class to see what is exchanged. You can say, "Heads down and close your eyes." After the objects have been exchanged, we say, "Heads up," and then one of the students asks of the group of four children in the front, "Carla do you have the shovel?" "No, I do not have the shovel," and so forth until the object has been guessed. Then, the students who have guessed these objects can trade places.

In the middle grades the students can work in their lesson book on a topic they have read (as explained in chapter 5), practicing the formation of sentences about a particular vocabulary topic covered or following the teacher in a picture dictation, reading, or retelling a story. Many teachers dedicate a good portion of the lesson to allowing students to draw illustrations arising from the inner pictures of the poems or the stories in their books. Although this is a beautiful artistic activity, the lesson should have a balance in all aspects, and one wouldn't want this portion to overshadow others.

In the upper grades, dialogs, practicing sentences in their books, reading a selection, or acting a dialog or play can take place. For instance, if the students have already reviewed sentences with the ...*er*-ending verbs in the present and the past tenses, and if we have many students in the group, we can then say, "In pairs, let's tell one another..." allowing them to share their sentences. Or they can retell a story in pairs. Then we may ask individual students to report on sentences they have just heard from their partners. In this way, the students need to practice speaking and actively participate with one another or with their individual work. The students need to practice with their own everyday thoughts, but in sentences that use grammar already known, while the sentences themselves can later be forgotten. Practicing dialogs or sentences, reading a story, completing questions, summarizing a story, or writing in their books are just a few suggestions to use during this time.

It is always important to remember that the lesson moves from the whole topic and should flow smoothly. When we bring a new topic, we try to incorporate it in context or through a story in a pictorial way. The children need to experience the vocabulary in images, and these

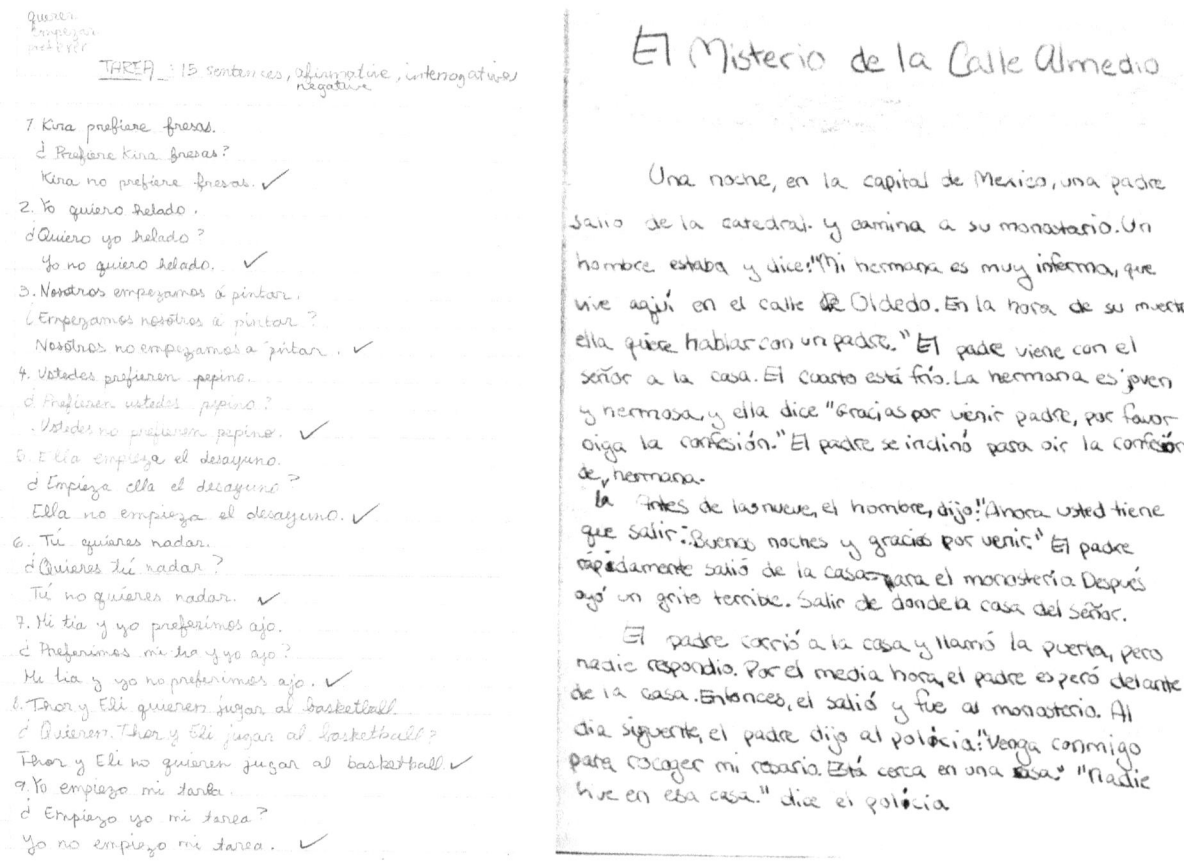

*A practice book from one student in grade 7 (left)
and a summary from a student after reading a story in class eight*

images will flow best if integrated into a situation. As for the teachers, if we have not been trained in Waldorf pedagogy, it is always useful to visit the kindergartens, so we can experience how teachers bring images in stories and create a strong rhythm for the day. This experience can offer new insights into the education and its purpose, leading to better class preparation, particularly for the lower grades. It is also very beneficial for new teachers to visit the main-lesson teachers, so they can also perceive the breathing aspect of a threefold lesson and apply it to their language lessons.

Recognizing breathing in and breathing out (movement and repose, listening and activity, choral and individual work, full wakefulness and dreaming into the pictures) and transforming your rhythm in the lessons as the students get older are key aspects in our preparation.

We tried to connect the children with their reality in feeling by first doing and then understanding. We strive to bring beauty and create situations in which the student will not be taught intellectually but from a practical aspect.

4.

FROM STORYTELLING TO READING, SPEAKING, AND WRITING

Because Waldorf education is based on Rudolf Steiner's all-inclusive philosophy, Anthroposophy, meaning "the wisdom of the human being," human beings are central to the Waldorf curriculum. All subjects are seen in relation to human activity and human understanding, and a strong human connection between students and the teacher is essential to delivering the curriculum. The teacher becomes, among other things, the means through which the students, from the youngest ages, learn about the world and human culture; teachers pass down, orally, whatever wisdom they can "from heart to heart," as was done in past ages. This oral tradition is dependent upon storytelling, and therefore storytelling is one of the most important pedagogical tools aspects of Waldorf education.

In the foreign language lesson, storytelling occupies a paramount position from the earliest grades. Through speech, the teacher gives the children a listening experience, using voice and gesture to create images of a particular content without a translation. Because the experience is multisensory, it creates a deeper understanding at a soul level; feeling connects the students to the sound of the speech and is increased by the accompaniment of gestures, marionettes, and other props.

Teachers enliven the lessons through their free expression, both when choosing the story and when determining the best means of presenting it to achieve the goals of comprehension in their students. Teachers must determine every aspect of the presentation in terms of what is correct for the students' developmental level. The story must be well-prepared, fully penetrated as to its meaning, sound, vocabulary, and syntax, and any props used should be prepared artistically, which nurtures the senses and helps clarify meaning. In addition, the teachers' speech must be clearly articulated and pleasant to the ears, with consciously chosen phrasing to help the students. For example, teachers might identify sections of the story that should be repeated rhythmically, particularly in the lower grades.

In the Foreign Language lesson, rhythm is essential not only for how lessons are structured, but also in the activities that reinforce the lessons. For instance, after frequent telling and retelling of the same story has taken place over several lessons, the children begin to repeat after the teacher. Only then, mirroring acquisition of the mother tongue, does the listening experience transform into speaking. This is a very important step, covering two competencies in language acquisition almost effortlessly and without the use of the written word in the younger grades.

In the early years, students are capable of slowly repeating or chanting with the teacher, in much the same way a young child does after hearing the same story read several times. The rhythmic elements when the story is repeated slowly, encourage the children to participate in the retelling. By doing so, they exercise strong listening and comprehension skills which form the foundation for later incorporation in speech. When experienced in this way, speech is usually imbued with an excellent accent and clear enunciation. In the upper grades, the teacher can choose to approximate the same experience by telling the same story over the course of several lessons and then later giving the students a written copy. This repetition in the upper grades is equally or even more important than in the early grades, because it gives the students confidence to freely render the passage on their own.

4.1 Storytelling in the Lower Grades

In the first grade, the Waldorf curriculum calls for stories containing beautiful images, such as those depicted in fairytales. Language teachers can adapt their choice of stories, telling and retelling them with the help of gestures, puppets, and props. It is our task to prepare stories that can be carried over through several lessons.

Many teachers practice drawing with block crayons or watercolors and direct their efforts to illustrate some of the stories or they bring a felt board. In doing so, the children not only perceive our striving but also receive the fruits of our connection to the content. The result when we bring our own illustrations is always more effective than using a picture book. If a picture book is necessary, we need to find an edition containing artistically rendered illustrations that are developmentally appropriate.

In the process of selecting a story for our students, much will depend on the choice and creativity of the teacher; therefore, there is not one way but many ways to bring a story to the children. When choosing a story for the lesson it can be very effective to select stories with alliteration, onomatopoeia, and repetition of a particular line, such as in the story "The Donkey, the Tablecloth, and the Stick" or "The House that Jack Built."

Teachers begin by telling part of the story with gestures and pointing to the illustrations we bring to the lesson. On consecutive days, we can repeat the story from the beginning, allowing the children to add which animal or vignette, for instance, comes next.

If we take as an example one of the stories previously mentioned, every time the genie speaks, he repeats the same words: «*Burro burrito dame el dinero que necesito*». The second or third time, we can ask the class to join in a choral repetition of this line. As we move along with the

From Storytelling to Reading, Speaking, and Writing

story in subsequent lessons, the children can add more parts while repeating after the teacher. After several lessons, we can see that the children are effortlessly repeating the story. We can even take it a step further by reenacting parts of the story with costumes. The children experience these images deeply through these activities and this part of the lesson becomes a favorite.

I have always found it very helpful to tell stories in rhyme, because this helps the whole class memorize parts unconsciously. The children enjoy hearing the same stories over and over to the point that, if we omit a word, they will correct us. The predictability of the words and the images, and the group repetition, make the students anticipate what will come next and this feeling provides a deep security ("my teachers knows"). Here are some examples of stories offering repetition and onomatopoeia:

In "Three Billy Goats," every time a goat crosses the bridge, we repeat:

Trin, trin

Trin trin" —*Golpeaban las pezuñas.*

Or in "The Sky Is Falling," every time the hen meets a new animal, the hen always answers:

Vamos a decirle al rey
que el cielo se va a derrumbar.

After the children hear a story a second or third time, we can ask questions such as, in the case of "The Sky Is Falling,"

What animal comes next?

And slowly list them all, repeating together:

Vamos a decirle al rey
que el cielo se va a derrumbar.

With this story we can easily use a felt board or our own illustrations. Those of you inclined to draw or paint can create several illustrations or make cut-outs with felt or paper.

Simply telling the story is easy, as the children in a Waldorf school are extremely attentive. However, the language teacher needs to slowly emphasize the repetitive parts as the story unfolds and always use the same words and gestures when displaying the illustrations. One story can last several days (sometimes weeks) and can be used as acting material later. At the end of the story you can always ask questions referring to size, color, or content. Examples of possible questions for the story in "The Sky Is Falling" are as follows:

¿Le cayó a la gallina la piedra en la cabeza o en el pico?

¿Es el pavo más grande que la gallina?

¿Cuántos animales hay en la historia?

¿De qué color es el cielo? ¿Y la nube?

¿Entran los animales en una cueva o en una casa?

¿Es la gallina inteligente?

¿Es la zorra inteligente?

If for instance we take the story «*El burro, el mantel y el palo*», written below, the teacher can bring several illustrations, such as the mother with Pedrito, Pedrito fishing, the genie holding a magic potion, a donkey spitting golden coins, an innkeeper with a "false magic donkey," a tablecloth with a banquet and a stick chasing the innkeeper. You can start the story by pointing to the first illustration[1], with Pedrito and the mother and repeating:

«*Pedrito Pedrito ve al río a pescar*

Pues no hay comidita para cenar».

Then you can display the second illustration and say:

«*Pedrito en el río un pez de oro pescó,*

y el pez dorado de esta forma habló:

«*El poderoso genio del río soy, si tú me liberas un premio te doy*».

Pedrito en el río al pez liberó

y una poción mágica, de él recibió.

Unas gotas de esencia el pez derramó,

Y un burro fantástico apareció.

Y el genio dijo:

«*Burro, burrito dame el dinero que necesito*».

At this point, the teacher can stop the story and during the next class, begin with the narration from the start. The second time the children will join in when the genie speaks or when the donkey speaks. Then the teacher continues to display the innkeeper switching the donkeys and ending when Pedrito happily arrives home with the wrong donkey.

In the next class, we can bring some props that will allow us to reenact the first part, and allow the children to deepen their experience of the story.

---

1 See the illustrations on the following pages.

From Storytelling to Reading, Speaking, and Writing

Reenacting the story

The teacher can bring two donkey hoods, some golden coins, a magic potion, veils for the genie, veils for the water, an apron and scarf for the mother, a fishing pole and hat for Pedrito, a second blue apron with a stuffed belly for the innkeeper, and other items. As you assign parts, there is ample opportunity for the children to learn all the vocabulary related to the costumes as you call out in the foreign language:

> Who wants to be Pedrito? Yes, Pedrito has a fishing pole.
> Who wants to be the mother? Here is the scarf and the apron.
> Here is the river.
> Who wants to be the river? We need two volunteers for the river.
> You will be the innkeeper. Here is the apron and the big belly.
> Here is the magic potion.
> You will be the genie.
> Who wants to be the fantastic donkey?
> Who wants to be the donkey of the innkeeper?

Mother & Pedrito

Fish

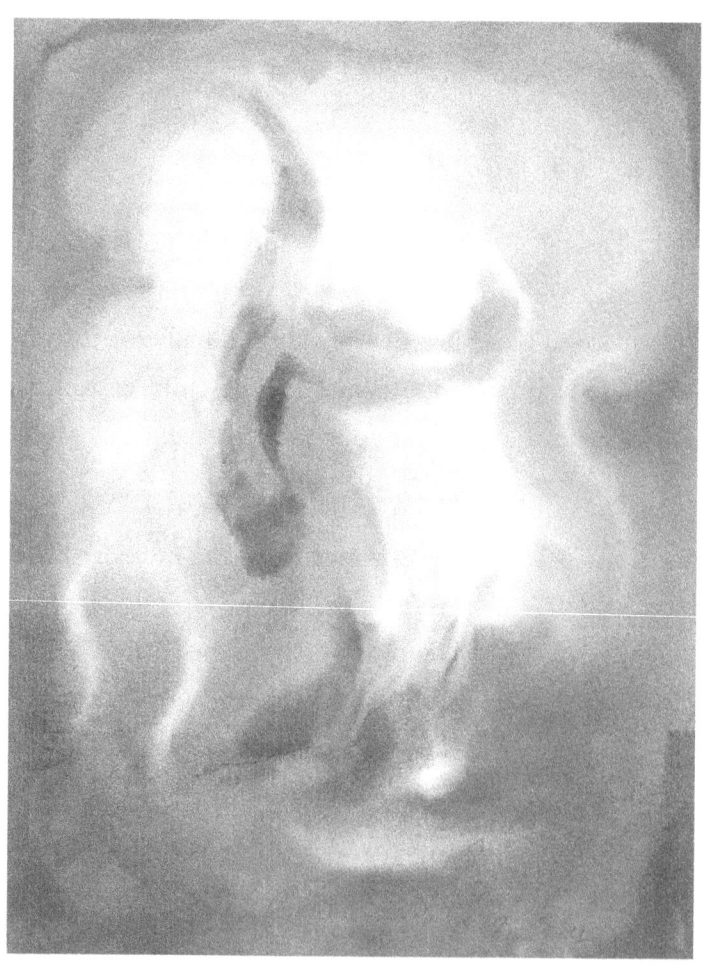
Genie

From Storytelling to Reading, Speaking, and Writing

The Innkeeper

This is one of the children's favorite parts of the lesson. The children love to act out the parts, improvising while the teacher retells the story. We usually move a few desks to allow a bit more space for the improvised stage after the different parts are chosen. Often we play xylophone music during the transitions to maintain a magical mood.

In the subsequent lessons, the teacher can add additional events. After a few weeks, we will finish the story and by then, the children will be able to recite most parts by heart chorally.

In the third grade the stories can continue to be presented in a similar fashion, but the topics will change and connect with the Waldorf third grade curriculum: farming, house building, the Old Testament, etc. Stories like *«La lechera»* (The Milk Maiden), *«La gallina Marcelina»* (The Little Red Hen), *«El nabo»* (The Turnip), *«El traje nuevo de Pedro»* (Pelle's New Suit), or *«El muchachito de mazapán»* (The Gingerbread Man), to name a few, are excellent examples of material for this age.

From this grade on, one can reinforce active listening and comprehension through selected activities. For instance, after the story *«La gallina Marcelina»* has been told and retold, you can do the following exercises with the children.

First, distribute envelopes with five or six blank cards to the children. Have them draw a picture dictation in Spanish (all the instructions are given in Spanish) in the following manner:

1. On the first card: "It is a beautiful day. It is summer, the sky is blue and the Sun shines."
2. For the second card you can say: "In our farm lives a hen. Her name is Gallina Marcelina. Marcelina finds a few grains of corn."
3. "Marcelina wants to plant the corn but she needs help. First she asks don gato."
4. "Then, she asks don perro."
5. On our last card we will draw a delicious bread.

When the children have finished the picture dictation drawings on their cards, they can put them in their envelopes. At the next class you can ask them to display the cards on their desks and then you can begin telling the story in Spanish: "It was a beautiful summer day. The Sun was shining in the blue sky.

When the children hear you say, "The Sun was shining in the blue sky," they should raise the card depicting the blue sky with a Sun and then you move on. "The animals at the farm are peacefully resting and eating, and all of a sudden, Gallina Marcelina finds a few grain of corn." Then the students will hold up the second card. You will continue in this fashion until the story has been completed and all the cards have been held up and shown.

After this story, you can play a game with the cards (see the chapter on games).

In the following lesson you can have the students retell the story to you in this way:

Begin by saying, «*Era un bonito día de verano*». Then, the questions and answers (in Spanish) begin:

TEACHER: *¿Cómo es el cielo?*

THE STUDENTS ANSWER: *The sky is blue and there is a yellow sun.*

TEACHER: *Excellent!* Let's continue: *¿Quién vive en la granja?*

THE STUDENTS: *Los animales de la granja. La gallina Marcelina, el gato, el perro. (etc.)*

TEACHER: *¿Qué encuentra la gallina Marcelina?*

STUDENTS: *La gallina encuentra unos granos de maíz.*

If you see that the students need help with the answers, you can say:

TEACHER: *¿Encuentra la gallina Marcelina unos granos de maíz o encuentra un pan?*
   (We give the students the answer with a dual question.)

STUDENTS RESPOND: *La gallina Marcelina encuentra unos granos de maíz.*

TEACHER: *¿Es el cielo azul o llueve?*

STUDENTS: *El cielo es azul.*

TEACHER: *¿Hay muchos o hay pocos animales en la granja?*

STUDENTS: *Hay muchos animales.*

TEACHER: *¿Hay un perro? ¿Hay un gato? ¿Hay un elefante?* (etc.)

From Storytelling to Reading, Speaking, and Writing

The retelling can continue in this way with a minimum of help. You can then bring real items, such as a few grains of corn, a little sack with flour, husks of corn, a stone grinder, etc., to reinforce the oral comprehension. During the lesson, you can bring the activities of kneading dough, grinding corn, and cutting the husks, preparing your lessons around such activities. You can set up the different stations in order, as you repeat:

1. First we water the plant (you can use a water can).
2. Then we cut the husks (you can draw or bring a sickle).
3. We grind the corn (have a grinder ready with some corn and a bowl).
4. With the flour, we knead the dough (a sack with flour and a roller).
5. We bake the dough and then (a mold and a roller)
6. Now we have delicious bread! (bring real bread or draw a loaf).

We can invite individual students to come to the front and perform these activities. Then we can ask in Spanish:

"What does John do?"
They respond, "John grinds the corn."
"Is John baking the bread?"—"No, John is not baking the bread; he is grinding the corn."

You can continue with a few more examples, invent a game, or bring the song "La bella Hortelana." These activities will reinforce language acquisition by integrating the children's listening and comprehension skills, adding opportunities for speaking, and allowing them to experience the language through real activities.

Another excellent story for grade 3 is the story "Pelle's New Suit," (easily translated in Spanish by using the illustrations from the book). The story begins with Pelle cutting the wool of a sheep. This could be our first illustration. Second, he dyes the wool. Third, his grandmother cards the wool in exchange for his help in the garden. In the next vignette, Pelle brings to his other grandmother the wool for spinning. When the wool is spun he takes it to his mother and she weaves the thread into fabric. Finally he takes the cloth and brings it to the tailor who then sews Pelle a suit. As the group progresses in the retelling, as has been explained earlier, the class is ready for some props.

Some possible props are a bundle of wool, a container with blue cardboard, wool dyed blue, two carders for wool, a spindle (you can always bring an illustration if the item is not found), a little loom often used in third grade and a blue fabric, some scissors, and a needle with thread.

The teacher can then recreate the different scenes or "stations" with the actual activities. When the class has learned all the activities such as "cut the fabric," "weave the thread," "dye the wool," etc., you can play this game. Choose seven students to come to the front. Then ask the class to close their eyes. In the meantime, each of the seven children in the front chooses an activity. The seated children will then open their eyes and guess through the gestures what activity is being done. If they guessed correctly, they can switch places with a child in the front. An example of the type of questions the seated student asks is:

"Is Dimitri sewing the fabric?"
The student standing answers:" No I'm not sewing the fabric."
Student seated asks:"¿Is Anna carding the wool?"
Anna:"Yes, I am carding the wool."[2]

This activity can continue in future classes by having the students retell the story while adding more sentences. Children at this age enjoy challenges, and you can bring this element to the following lesson by saying, "Let me see if you are able to tell me fifteen sentences about the story. You can add anything you want." The children love this part. They become enthusiastic as the teacher tallies on the board each good answer. In the subsequent lessons, you can add all the gestures mentioned in the story to your "repertoire" at the beginning of the lesson. For instance:

—*Corto la lana*
—*Tiño la lana*
—*Cardo la lana*
—*Hilo el hilo*
—*Tejo el hilo*
—*Corto la tela*
—*Coso los pantalones.*

For the story «*La gallina Marcelina*», we can add to our "repertoire":

—*Plantamos el grano*
—*Regamos la tierra*
—*Cortamos las mazorcas*
—*Molemos el grano*
—*Amasamos la masa*
—*Preparamos el pan*
—*Cocinamos el pan.*

After working with this story for several weeks, the children will then be ready for a new story.

---
2 Note: Always encourage the children to speak in complete sentences when answering or asking questions.

From Storytelling to Reading, Speaking, and Writing

Now we will see how the content from stories that have been taught and experienced orally in the lower grades evolves into reading and writing in grades 4 or 5.

4.2 Reading and Writing in the Middle Grades

In the grade 4, the children learn reading in the foreign language through writing, as they did with English in the lower grades. Pictorial stories now become symbols that can gradually be used to form sentences. Poems or stories that have been memorized from the first three grades, now become excellent material for writing and then for reading.

During the first days of the Spanish lesson in grade 4, when leading into reading we bring back to the children their most vivid images from the lower grades. If in the past they have learned by heart poems such as «*A Margarita Debayle*», by Ruben Darío, or «*El sol es de oro*», by Salvador de Madariaga, these poems make perfect reading material to bring in this grade.

As the children begin to write poems and stories, they will soon remember the verses recited many times in the past and begin to read without effort. We can then begin writing sentences to be read out loud. Once the children have acquired a certain level of confidence, then they can have a reader with the printed material that they have learned in the past that contain poems, songs, or short stories. Each class's reader will be unique.

«*El nabo*» (the turnip) is an excellent example of a story that can be part of the written material for this grade. It includes familiar vocabulary and a great deal of repetition. Sometimes, before presenting a story such as this, we might offer a few sentences from the story orally (in this case reviewing the members of the family) or just decide to give the class the story printed in their reader. For instance, if in the second grade the children have listened and reenacted this story, in grade 4, this story can be part of their reading material.

On page 39 is an example of this story and a child's illustration after a picture dictation describing the members of the family. The whole class can read each paragraph in unison together. It is a helpful practice to teach your students to follow each word with their finger to keep their place.

The following page contains illustrations for this poem by a student in grade 4.

El nabo

Un abuelo sembró un nabo. Cuando lo fue a sacar agarró las hojas del nabo y tiró y tiró pero no lo pudo arrancar.

El abuelo llamó a la abuela. La abuela agarró al abuelo, el abuelo agarró las hojas del nabo y tiró y tiró pero no lo pudieron arrancar.

La abuela llamó a su hija. La madre agarró a la abuela, la abuela agarró al abuelo, el abuelo agarró las hojas del nabo y tiró y tiró pero no lo pudieron arrancar.

La madre llamó al padre. El padre agarró a la madre, la madre agarró a la abuela, la abuela agarró al abuelo, el abuelo agarró las hojas del nabo y tiró y tiró pero no lo pudieron arrancar.

Entonces llegó la nieta. La nieta agarró a su padre, el padre agarró a la madre, la madre agarró a la abuela, la abuela agarró al abuelo, el abuelo agarró las hojas del nabo y tiró y tiró pero no lo pudieron arrancar.

Llamaron al nieto y entre todos tampoco lo pudieron arrancar.

Finalmente llegó un ratón. El ratón agarró al nieto, el nieto agarró a su hermana, la hermana agarró al padre, el padre agarró a la madre, la madre agarró a la abuela, la abuela agarró al abuelo el abuelo, agarró las hojas del nabo y de un tirón, ¡sí lo pudieron arrancar!

(from the Russian tradition; adapted by Elena Forrer)

Writing in grade 4

The children in grade 4 begin to write short sentences in their books. And it is not long before they begin to write their own compositions. It is always best to relate to the vocabulary that the students have used in the past, and a composition about themselves

Is a good theme to return to. Since first grade the children have learned to answer questions about their age, their name, their family, the town where they live, their pet, etc., and now in the fourth grade they will be able to describe in writing all these answers. The first example chosen below illustrates the first composition of a fourth grade student. The second example describes the activities and the time, of a clock. These activities have also been practiced orally in third grade; but in grade 4, these sentences are written and read also read out loud to the class.

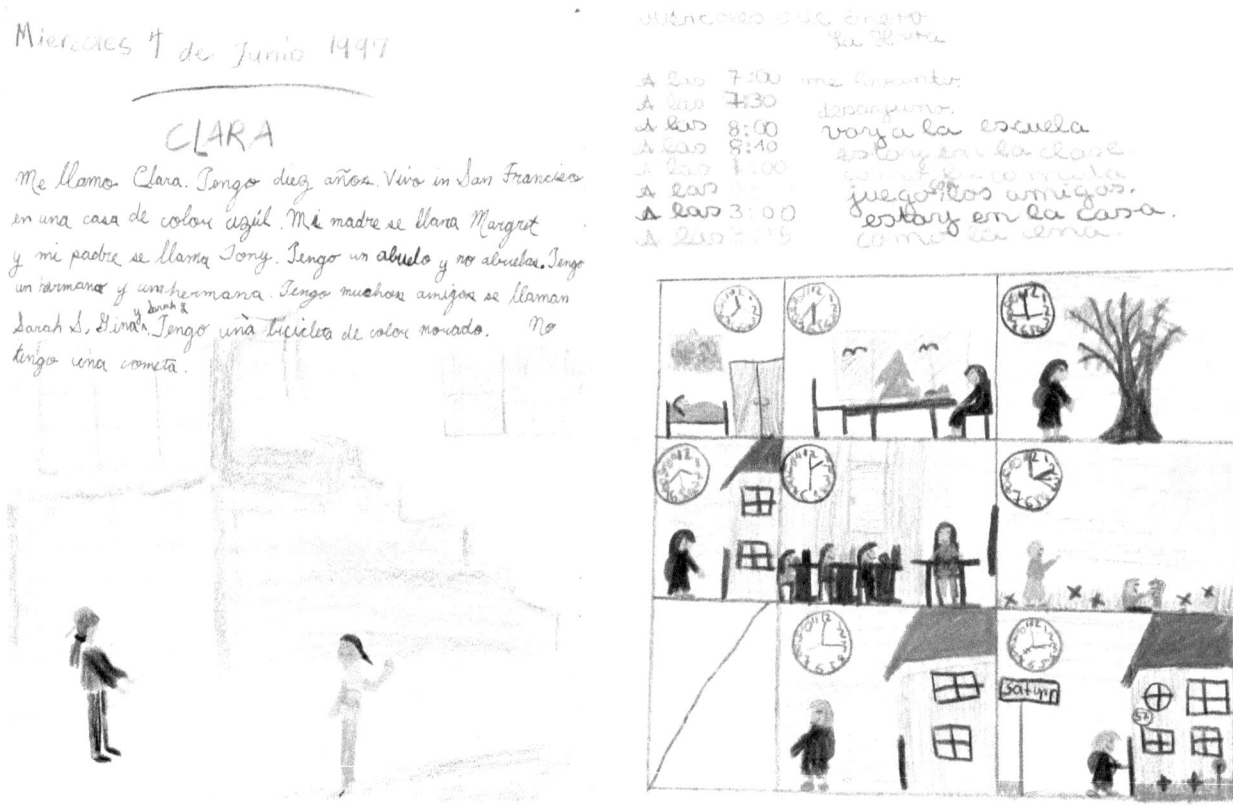

The following could also be a short story for their reader and a follow-up to the composition about themselves. The students can relate to this very simple paragraph about *María and David*. The whole class reads it in unison. The students can easily recall and retell the events after the reading with questions from the teacher to guide them.

From Storytelling to Reading, Speaking, and Writing

DAVID Y MARÍA

David y María están en la clase de la señorita Carmen, en la escuela Waldorf de Madrid. Ellos caminan a la escuela y entran en la clase. María tiene un libro en su mochila. María es morena y tiene los ojos negros. David es castaño y tiene los ojos de color café. Ellos viven cerca de la escuela. María tiene un conejo que se llama Luna. Luna come muchas zanahorias y lechuga. David tiene un perro, su perro se llama Pinto. Pinto corre por el jardín de la casa. Pinto corre detrás de Luna. Todos los días María practica su violín. Pinto escucha a María, ¡María toca muy bien el violín!

A David le gusta pintar y nadar. Él pinta muy bien. En verano David nada en el mar con sus amigos y juega en la playa. El padre de David y María trabaja en una oficina y su madre trabaja en un hospital.

Reading in Grade 5

For the grade 5, many teachers begin to research or write their own stories for the children because it is often hard to find easy reading materials that are interesting and not too difficult for this age. When we finally find a good story, and after the reading has been presented, we let the students freely render the story with their own words. Most of the students manage to understand the story, but some get lost if the reading contains a good amount of new vocabulary or they are not familiar with the story. One way to address this situation is by following Rudolf Steiner's suggestion on how to approach a reading. He suggests that during the foreign language lesson, the teacher could present the material in the form of a story, without a book, from memory, and that the students should listen to it being told. Then, they should try to reproduce what they have heard without first reading it. Steiner speaks about making things understandable by "aural comprehension" rather than visually. After this has been given to the class, we have the children take the text and read after us.

> The right way is for the teacher to relate freely whatever is to be put across to the children or, if a passage or poem is presented verbatim, to speak it by heart without using a book. Meanwhile, the students do nothing but listen; they do not read the text as the teacher speaks. Then, possibly, they are asked to reproduce what they have heard without having read it first. This method is vital for teaching foreign languages.... What matters very much with the foreign language is that the children should understand through hearing rather than through reading.... When this has been accomplished, the children can be allowed to take their books and read the passage.[3]

---

3 Steiner, *Practical Adivice to Teachers*. p. 136.

In the following text from *«Aventuras de aquí y de allá»*, the main character Pablo, when visiting his aunt and uncle in Mexico, discovers a hidden tunnel in the basement. This passage focuses on Pablo finding his way in the house of his aunt and uncle. Through this reading, the student can create an inner picture of Pablo in the house. This story offers a good opportunity to learn or review the parts and rooms in the house while creating interest in a plot.

To engage students in reading, it is necessary to encourage thinking in pictures. One way we can do this is by giving the students little hints about what happens through "verbal comprehension" in your own words and gestures, and as much as possible in the foreign language, in this case, in Spanish. For instance if we take the following example of the reading here from *«Aventuras de aquí y de allá»*, you can explain with your own words the connection between different family members by saying:

> *La familia Brown-García visita México. Ellos van a San Miguel de Allende. La hermana de la señora Brown-García es la tía Julia. Peter, es el esposo de María. Ellos viven en California y tienen dos hijos: Pablo y Ana. Sara es la prima de Pablo y de Ana. Tía Julia y tío Juan son los padres de Sara. Pablo no está contento. Él quiere ir con sus amigos de California. Pablo descubre una puerta misteriosa. La puerta está debajo de las escaleras.*

With this example following the reading chorally and with assigned parts, the students will be now able to understand the connections in the story. It is important to create certain intrigue and mystery in order to maintain the attention and interest of the students. The following is also, from the book *«Aventuras de aquí y de allá»*.

En casa de los tíos

Todos entran en la casa.

Tía Julia: *Sara, Juan, aquí están: Ana, Pablo, María y Peter.*

Sara sale rápidamente de su cuarto y baja las escaleras. Sara está alegre.

Sara: *Hola Ana, hola Pablo. Qué alegría, bienvenidos, ven aquí Ana.*

Pablo está enfadado. Niñas, que fastidio—dice Pablo.

Tía Julia y tío Juan hablan con María y Peter. Pablo ve una puerta debajo de las escalera.

Él camina hacia la puerta, abre la puerta y ve otra escalera pequeña. "Hum."

Pablo mira de lado a lado y comienza a bajar. Él ve una luz al final de un cuarto.

Es un cuarto pequeño, lleno de libros, telarañas, muebles viejos y cajas.

Pablo: *¡Qué interesante!*

Following Steiner's directions, after the reading, the students can retell in their own words what they have understood:

From Storytelling to Reading, Speaking, and Writing

This technique can be applied specifically to the teaching of foreign languages in the following form. You first have the children read aloud, paying attention to proper pronunciation—rather than giving too many pronunciation rules, you read a section and then let the children read after you. Then they retell the passage they have read, forming their own thoughts about it and expressing them in different languages. Quite separately, you teach the lessons on grammar and syntax with rules to be remembered and examples to be forgotten.[4]

After the reading (following the process described by Steiner) and retelling of the story have been completed, we can direct the students to a floor plan of the house in the story. At this point, the students are going to be curious about the rooms in the house, particularly when they read about the "mysterious room" in the basement. Now we can redirect their focus not so much on the story, but more toward the rooms of the house. At the same time, because the teacher has also planned at the beginning of the lesson, and independently from the story, to review the conjugation of the verb *estar* (see chapter 6, "Teaching Grammar"). the students are now practicing the verb *estar* in relation to the location of the rooms. Of course, the mysterious room found in the basement will provide suspense and a desire to read on to the next chapter.

Writing In Grade 5

Now we can focus on a short summary of what the students have read, after the oral rendering. Sometimes if the class is new, we can guide this summary as a class activity on the board. However, the ideal is that every student begins to create his or her own essays.

The following example (top of page 44) illustrates a class rendering after a reading on the topic of "the neighborhood." In this case the student has highlighted vocabulary words and has followed the description with an illustration. The second example is a composition by a ten-year-old student, describing her family and herself after a related reading.

Often when sentences are formed in class, the students can slowly begin discussing the different parts of the sentence. We can ask the students to identify the verbs by highlighting them in red. We use red, because this color embodies activity. Then, we can ask the students to identify the nouns by using the color blue. When we name an object, such as a chair or desk, we separate ourselves from it, and blue embodies this "distance." Finally we can ask the students to use yellow to identify adjectives. The adjectives bring us closer to the quality of the object (see chapter 6, "Teaching Grammar").

---

4 Ibid., p. 129.

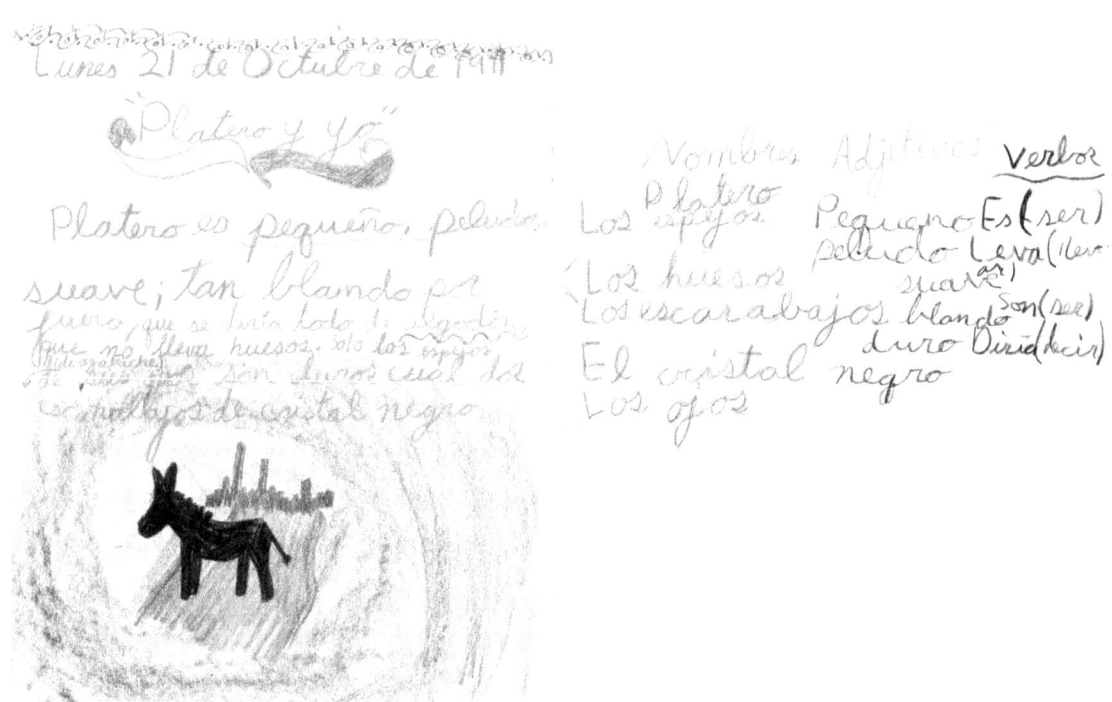

From Platero y Yo, *by a student in grade 5, highlighting in columns nouns, adjectives, and verbs.*

From Storytelling to Reading, Speaking, and Writing

4.3 Reading and Writing in the Upper Grades

Grade 6

As we move through the grades, the teachers now face increasing challenges. For instance, new students who have joined the class widen the gap between the various levels of ability in both written and oral comprehension.

At this age when new students join the group, the result is that the oral and written comprehension ability, can differ greatly from one to another. However, as we also read in the *Faculty Meetings with Rudolf Steiner,* we see that this is not a new problem. When this happens, it is a good idea to divide a large group into two classes so the students are better served. If this is the case, we will face the question of division by ability.

It is also a fact that technology has dominated our adult world. Our students have been affected by our demand for rapid answers and by images that replace inner pictures aroused by their own feelings. Although many of our students have not sought out the use of technology, the reality is their live's have been permeated by it and as a result, supplemented with quick images. In addition, many students this age also experience a hectic life after school with very little time to devote to themselves or to reading. This raises new questions not only for language teachers but also for class teachers: How can we maintain the creation of these inner pictures that arise from frequently longer descriptions? Are translations valuable? How do we present stories in a dynamic way?

As we have mentioned for grade 5, before the students read the passage themselves, we tell a story instead of reading it for "aural comprehension." However, as they get older we ask ourselves: How about translations? Steiner is very clear on this point; he refers to translations as a waste of time in language classes. He clearly places the story at the center of the lesson, allowing the pictures to flow within the listeners and the reader. In both cases, after the students capture the images, they should try to say what they understood without translations in their own words. Steiner explains:

> In the classes when you want to review work and cover new material, it is still good not to require translation but to let the students give a free rendering of the content in the passage they have read...listen carefully for any omissions that might indicate that they have not understood the excerpt. It is more convenient for you, of course, simply to let the children translate, for then you soon see where one of them cannot go on. It is less expeditious to listen for something to be omitted instead of just waiting until the child comes to a stop, but you can nevertheless find out by this means whether something has not been understood, if

a phrase is not rendered correctly in the mother tongue. There will be children who make a very capable rendering of the passage and others whose rendering is much freer in the use of their own words; this does not matter.[5]

From grade 6 on, two new impulses awaken in the students—a wish to grasp and master the language consciously and an increasing need to express their individual thoughts, feelings, and impressions. Stories from the Waldorf curriculum of chivalry of the medieval times, legends, adventures, or even humorous skits can capture the students' interest. Through such readings, the teacher can introduce a particular part of the story by giving students a brief summary in anticipation. Then the class is ready, and individual and group parts are assigned throughout the reading. Often after some paragraphs have been read, we can ask our students to summarize what they have read (not a translation), in Spanish if at all possible, or in English. On the following day, we can ask them to read the same story, taking turns individually or with their desk partners. We can then extract the new vocabulary from the reading and begin to recount the events. Once the story has made an impression, most of the students will be able to express the events in each section. This when the class becomes engaged because they like to express themselves in a foreign language. I often ask students to divide themselves into groups and take active part in the retelling of the story.

If for instance we take the example of the below adapted passage of *El Cid*, it is always good to give the students a broad view of El Cid (see "Narrative Paragraphs and Stories for Upper Grades") as a powerful historical hero and the historical context of this event. If this reading is combined at the beginning of the lesson with a recitation of the ballad «*La vuelta de El Cid*» from el *romancero español* or «*Castilla*», by Manuel Machado, the students will first become imbued with an appropriate historical context through the recitation, and then by the chronological time explained by the teacher. The historical figure of El Cid needs to be explained; for instance, how he was outcast from Castile by King Alfonso after the king is humiliated by El Cid, forcing him to take an oath in front of his vassals, and by demanding King Alfonso to say that he did not take part in the death of his brother Sancho. The vassals of Sancho suspect Alfonso of being an instigator in the sudden death of Sancho. After Sancho's death, Alfonso was crowned king.

When the reading is finally presented, the students can be taken back in time into the historical event, particularly if the content has been previously supported by the poems referring to El Cid and the situation geographically in Spain. At this age, Waldorf students are also learning European geography and medieval history with their class teacher. This is certainly a good grade in which to present this story.

---

5 Steiner, *Practical Advice to Teachers*, pp. 119–120.

From Storytelling to Reading, Speaking, and Writing

The language teacher can have the students illustrate *El Cid* with his horse Babieca, or have them play a medieval melody on their recorders as activities that complement the reading. All these aspects of the lesson—retelling and reciting poems describing this time period—help to create a fuller picture and a deeper understanding of the reading.

After the students have read the story, we can proceed freely to write students' sentences on the board pertaining to the reading. For instance one student might say:

El Cid es un caballero de Castilla.

Another student:

El rey se llama Alfonso.

Then you may ask: *¿Quién es su hermano? ¿Cómo se llama su caballo?*

Su hermano se llama Sancho, su caballo es Babieca.

Then we might move on to recreate the story by retelling more details:

Los vasallos sospechan que Alfonso mató a Sancho.
¿Por qué sospechan sus vasallos que Alfonso mató a su hermano el rey Sancho?
Porque Alfonso quiere ser rey. El Cid humilla a Alfonso en Santa Gadea. (etc.)

This reading can last through several lessons, since we will also include geography, poetry, and music. It can also be retold again in subsequent lessons.[6]

Let's imagine that this is a grade 6 class with mixed levels of ability, and we have prepared a simple reading of a mystery. After we distribute the following reading to the class, we can ask the students to highlight (or underline) key words that they do not understand, while we read the story. This is a moment of complete attention to the reading. The students will not only pay attention to the pronunciation and intonation, but also attentively follow the reading and underline new vocabulary words. Once the teacher has finished, the students are asked to "pull the vocabulary." Let's look at the following example:

---

6 See the complete "El Cid Campeador" in "Narrative Paragraphs and Stories for Upper Grades" and the poems "Castilla," by Manuel Machacho, and "La Vuelta de El Cid," from El romancero español, in "Poetry and Recitation through the Grades."

En la Playa

María y Teresa son muy buenas amigas. Ellas tienen una pandilla en el pueblo y Blas es parte de la pandilla. Ellas llegan a la playa. Es pronto por la mañana y la playa está <u>vacía</u>. Blas está muy <u>contento</u> salta y corre por la arena y el agua del mar. Después, Blas empieza a <u>cavar</u> <u>hoyos</u> con mucha energía. María y Teresa hablan y ríen). De pronto, Blas empieza a <u>ladrar</u>).

—¿Qué pasa Blas? —pregunta María. Teresa se levanta y llama a María.

—¡María, ven! Mira, hay algo en <u>la arena</u> dentro del hoyo. —(Blas continua ladrando).

Teresa empieza a cavar con la ayuda de María y las dos encuentran una caja grande de metal <u>oxidada</u>.

—Es una caja de metal oxidada, parece muy antigua —dice Teresa.

—Vamos a abrir la caja.

Las dos niñas intentan abrir la caja, pero no se abre.

—Está cerrada con llave. ¿Pero, dónde está la llave?

—Vamos a cavar más —dice María—. Las dos <u>buscan</u> en la arena pero no <u>encuentran</u> nada.

—¿De quién será esta caja...?

—Ahora es nuestra. Es nuestro tesoro. Tenemos que encontrar una llave antigua para poder abrir esta caja de metal—.

Blas mira a las niñas y salta contento. Los tres vuelven caminando al pueblo.

Let's suppose that the following list is an exemple of underlined vocabulary:

Vacía

Contento

Un hoyo

Cavar

Arena

Ladrar

Oxidada

Buscar

Encontrar

After we have asked the students for their words and we have written them on the board, we can ask the advanced students for help with the translations We will see that most of the words are quickly translated without our help. Then to reinforce this vocabulary, we might say:

> *¿Van las niñas al pueblo o a la playa?*
>
> *Ellas van a la playa.*
>
> *¿Van ellas al pueblo?*
>
> *No. Ellas van a la playa.*
>
> *¿Está Blas triste?*
>
> *No, él está contento.*
>
> *¿Hace Blas un hoyo o hace una figura?*
>
> *Blas hace un hoyo.*
>
> *¿Dónde hace un hoyo en el pueblo o en la playa?*
>
> *¿Qué hay en la playa…?*

We can then ask the students to form sentences in their practice books from the vocabulary. As the next step, they could share their sentences with their desk partner and we can ask both partners to retell the story without looking at the reading. The homework can then be to write new sentences, or a similar story, or to just read again the story and prepare a retelling without interruptions.

In the following class, we can ask oral questions and recall the story together orally while the sentences referring to the story are written on the board. A homework assignment might be to ask our students to write their own summary in Spanish. Finally, the students should now be able to give an oral recounting of the story in Spanish without looking at their reader.

Reading in Grades 7 and 8

Stories, legends, and literary extracts are vehicles in the language lesson for telling and retelling, which in turn enhance language acquisition. The goal is for the students to be able to retell passages in their own words with some guidance from the teacher. Very often if they are divided in pairs, one student can read a paragraph while the other listens and vice versa. After they have completed a few paragraphs, the teacher can ask the students again in pairs to tell each other what they have read, while helping each other. The class becomes active and loud, but they will be quite engaged in talking and practicing the language. Sometimes the groups for recalling the story can be made of two or four students; the teacher needs to find the most appropriate way to divide them. As a concluding step, we can recall some of the vocabulary words not understood from the reading, just as a repetition, particularly for the students needing a greater level of comfort for understanding and following.

Another way to help a class with new students is to take the legend "Los volcanes," for instance, and on cards create a list of possible vocabulary words from the story. In this case, let's suppose that we chose the following list:

Guerrero joven y fuerte

Triste

Mala noticia

Casarse

Amor verdadero

Mentira

Lucharon

Muerta

Dolor

Lloró.

Terremoto terrible

El valle

Mujer dormida

Montaña humeante

Now we begin the process of retelling after the reading as follows: The teacher holds up the first card, *guerrero joven*, and the class has to find a way to express its relationship to the words in the story. If you hold up the card *guerrero joven*, the students can say:

«*Una princesa azteca amaba a un joven*». Another student will say:

«*El guerrero valeroso fue a la guerra*».

Immediately, the teacher will hold up the next card and say, for example, «*triste*». Again the students need to express in their own words the context of the word on the card.

«*Ahora la princesa está triste porque ella ama al guerrero joven*».

The next card will be «*mala noticia*».

«*Ella recibe una mala noticia: El guerrero joven está muerto*».

«*Otro guerrero, Ollín, dice a la princesa que Popoca ha muerto*».

The next card could say «*Casarse*», and someone can add:

«Ella quiere casarse con el guerrero valeroso».

«Pero ella se casa con otro guerrero, con Ollín». «Ella se casa con Ollín».

The next card can be *«mentira»*.

«Un día el guerrero joven y valeroso vuelve de la guerra».

«Ella vio a Popoca. Ollín, su esposo dijo una mentira».

The next card might be "Lucharon».

«Ollín y Popoca lucharon». (etc.)

Although this way of recounting the story does not cultivate complete free rendering, it can be particularly helpful with a class that has new students and students who need an auditory and visual sequence of directions at the same time. If the class is more advanced, the teacher can allow them to take initiative while guiding the process with oral questions. The complete story can be found in the "Narrative Paragraphs and Stories for Upper Grades."

In grade 8, if we are introducing, for instance, the story of don Quijote, it is quite important to provide again the historical context of the story by explaining to the students when the novel takes place (around the seventeenth century) and what don Quijote believes. Once the teacher has given a synopsis of the situation, the students begin to understand the personality of don Quijote and how his excessive taste for reading books about knighthood leads him to forget time by embarking a mission to save the world from evil—dressed as a medieval knight and accompany by a lame horse and a weighty squire, in what he believes is a different epoch of time.

As Steiner indicates, it is important to give the students an image of the reading at hand. Therefore we can explain how don Quijote, now dressed as a knight, has decided to go wearing ridiculous armor into the world with his crippled horse Rocinante, accompanied by his squire Sancho Panza, a country man of limited wits, short height, and a big belly in search of adventures to serve humanity and to liberate the world from evil.

After describing of them, one can move into describing the geography around Los Molinos de Viento by explaining that La Mancha is a windy and dry region in Spain and that many windmills stand in the fields where the adventure takes place. We can tell the students that don Quijote decides to enter into battle with the windmills because he sees them as evil giants and, in his delirium, he charges them alone.

Now that the students have been presented with the background material, they can begin the reading (see "Narrative Paragraphs and Stories for Upper Grades.)" After the reading from *Los Molinos de Viento* is finished, we begin to analyze the contrasting personalities of don Quijote and Sancho Panza, which Cervantes emphasizes throughout the book. With the help of the students, we might write two contrasting columns on the board; one for words that characterize the ideals and describe the figure of don Quijote, and the other, words that represent the reality and characterization of Sancho Panza. After analyzing the two characters, the listing of the appropriate descriptive words will help us recall the story. Although the students should came up with their own descriptions, here are examples of the comments a class might make. On side of don Quijote, we could write:

    Idealismo
    Alto
    Delgado
    Enamorado de un ideal
    Altruismo
    Irrealidad
    Visionario
    Loco
    Valeroso
    Justicia
    Preocupación por los demás, etc.
    Soltero
    Hidalgo/ señor
    Estudioso
    Altruista
    Lucha por salvar al mundo de la maldad
    Caballero

In the columm of Sancho we could write:

    Realismo
    Bajo
    Gordo
    Hombre de famila
    Verdad
    Actualidad. El momento
    Autenticidad
    Cabal, cuerdo
    Juicioso
    Tranquilo

Honesto (etc.)

Hombre de campo

Simple

Leal

Escudero

Casado

Preocupado por su señor

In addition, at the end of the oral retelling, we can ask the students to write a summary of the reading for homework. We can also ask them to illustrate the famous event «*Los molinos de viento*».

4.4 Creating their own stories in Grades 6 to 8

The student's creation of their own stories always comes after the teacher has worked extensively with a reading, and given then enough tools for acquiring vocabulary and fluency for their creation. At this age, students can manage the regular simple past tense well and although they make mistakes, many students have the impulse to express themselves. One way to help them with their writing, is to first allow the class to completely live into the content and the meaning of a topic as it has been explained before for presentations of stories. Then we ask the students for a summary, a dialog or a composition in writing, in their practice book. This will be a free rendering in their own words of the story's events. After the work is corrected, the students will rewrite the paragraphs in their Spanish book.

The next reading emphasizes the topic of food while introducing the plot of a young girl visiting the city of Segovia in Spain. This topic can be enhanced by the presentation of food in the following chapter.

En el Río

Los muchachos montaron en sus bicis y llegaron al río.

Maribel: *Hola chicos. Esta es Kira, una amiga de los Estados Unidos.*

Todos: *Mucho gusto. ¿Hablas español?*

Kira: *Sí, aprendo español en la escuela.*

Luis: *Mira te presento a nuestros amigos: Juan, Luis, Ana, Tomás, Carmen, y Juan. Miguel está allí.*

Ana: *¿Kira, tienes una bicicleta?*

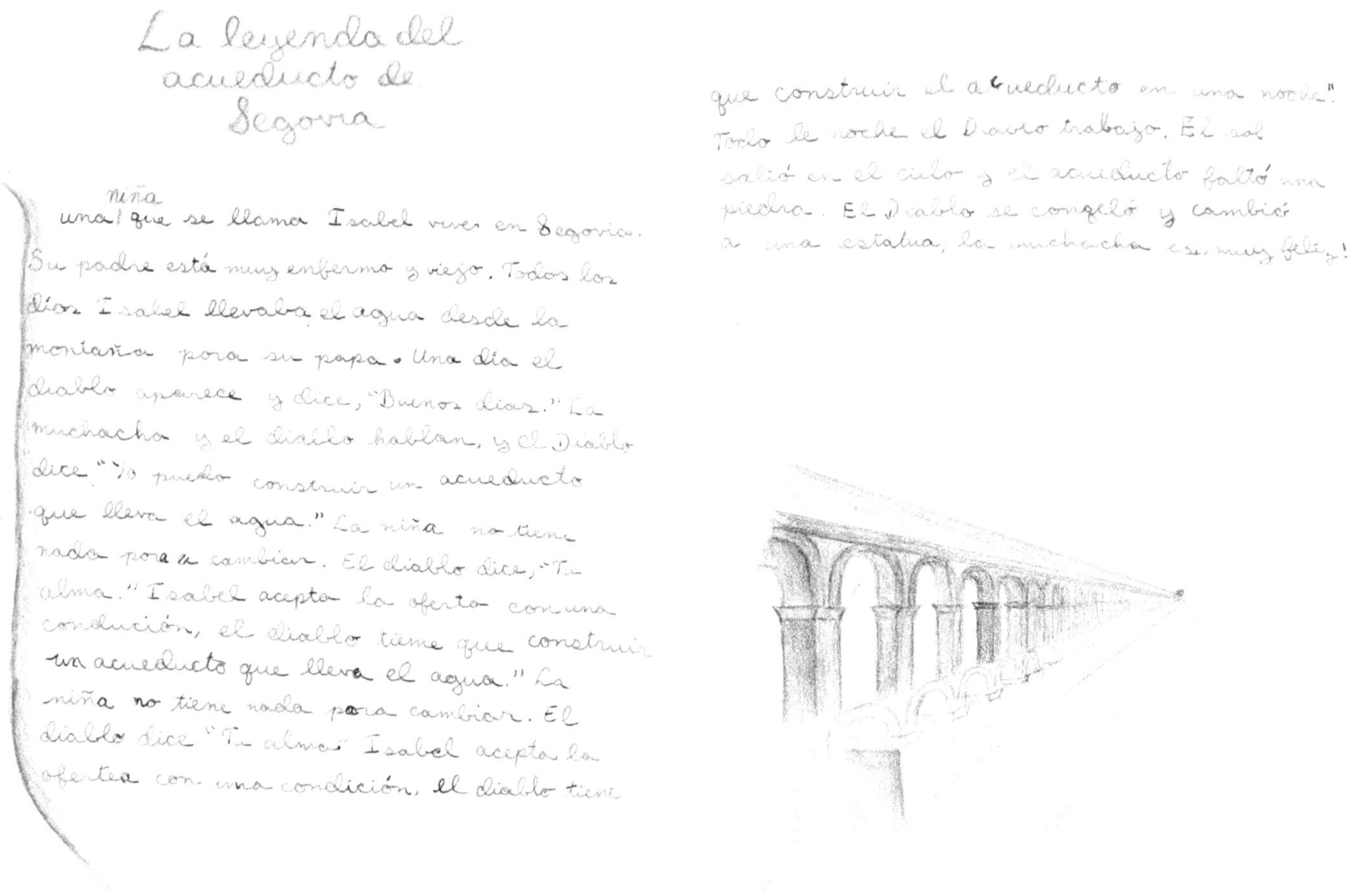

La leyenda del acueducto de Segovia

[Handwritten student text:]

Una niña que se llama Isabel vive en Segovia. Su padre está muy enfermo y viejo. Todos los días Isabel llevaba el agua desde la montaña para su papá. Una día el diablo aparece y dice, "Buenos días." La muchacha y el diablo hablan, y el Diablo dice, "Yo puedo construir un acueducto que lleva el agua." La niña no tiene nada para cambiar. El diablo dice, "Tu alma." Isabel acepta la oferta con una condición, el diablo tiene que construir un acueducto que lleva el agua." La niña no tiene nada para cambiar. El diablo dice "Tu alma." Isabel acepta la oferta con una condición, el diablo tiene que construir el acueducto en una noche." Toda la noche el Diablo trabajo. El sol salió en el cielo y el acueducto faltó una piedra. El Diablo se congeló y cambió a una estatua, la muchacha es muy feliz!

An example from a student in grade 6 at the beginning of the school year, after reading and working with the story La leyenda del acueducto de Segovia
(see "Narrative Paragraphs and Stories for Upper Grades")

KIRA: *Si, esta es mi bicicleta. Todos montaron en sus bicis y llegaron junto al molino. Ellos bajaron de sus bicis y llevaron sus mochilas con la merienda a la hierba.*

ANA: *Yo tengo uvas y sandía. No tengo bocadillos.*

JUAN: *Yo tengo dos bocadillos: uno de chorizo y el otro de queso. ¿Cuál quieres?*

ANA: *El bocadillo de queso, gracias.*

JUAN: *De nada.*

LUÍS: *Yo tengo limonada y galletas.*

ANA: *¿Kira, te gusta la comida española?*

KIRA: *Me gusta mucho. Me gusta comer paella, pollo y verduras pero no me gusta el pescado.*

From Storytelling to Reading, Speaking, and Writing

En el Río

Una niña se llama Kira, visita Segovia. Ella llega a ser amiga de Luis. Kira, Luis y los amigos de Luis van al río en las bicicletas. Ana (una amiga de Luis) tiene uvas y sandía, Juan tiene dos bocadillos, Luis tiene limonada y galletas. Kira siempre le gusta paella, pollo y verduras, no gusta pescado. Ellos van al molino, Tomás ve un señor, se llama Lute. Señor Lute tiene una barba, y fuma en pipa. Todos los muchachos parecían asustados. Los muchachos van a las bicicletas.

A summary from the reading from a student in grade 6

MIGUEL: *En España comemos mucho pescado.*

TOMÁS: *¡Mirad, el señor Lute está en el molino! El señor Lute era un hombre extraño. Tenía barba y fumaba en pipa. Todos los muchachos parecían asustados.*

CARMEN: *¡Él nos ha visto! Rápido, a las bicis. Todos montaron sus bicis y salieron rápidamente del molino. Kira estaba sorprendida y dijo:*

KIRA: *¿Qué pasa, quién es el señor Lute?*

MARIBEL: *Todos tenemos miedo del señor Lute porque él es un hombre extraño. A veces tira piedras o lleva un palo en la mano para asustarnos. Él vive solo en el viejo molino. Después, todos los amigos se despidieron y fueron a sus casas. Kira y Tom también caminaron hacia su casa.*

Although often their drafts (the work is corrected in a draft and rewritten again in their Spanish lesson books) present a number of mistakes, I do not look for perfect correction but rather, how they express themselves. Below you can find a good example of a story written by non-native student, Charlotte Markle, in grade 8. This story was preceded by reading the reading «Juan Gómez Detective» from the book *Realidad y fantasía*. The students created their stories with dialogues. In multiple chapters (illustrations below and opposite).

Capítulo 3

Las chicas ven una ventana que tiene una luz dentro. Ellas miran dentro. La víctima se sienta con su espalda a ellas. Él está solo en el cuarto. La ventana es pequeña abierta. Tabeetha saca una cápsula de su cinturón y tira la cápsula dentro. El cuarto se llena con gas y el hombre se desmaya.

Las muchachas entran y caminan hacia el hombre. Tabeetha saca una cápsula de veneno e inyecta en el brazo de el hombre.

"¿Está muerto?" pregunta Charlotte.

"Sí, sí" dice Tabeetha. Las chicas preparan a salir pero oyen un ruido. Tabeetha sale rápidamente, pero Charlotte se para y mira a la puerta. Entonces la puerta se abre rápidamente y el guardia entra y deja a Charlotte sin conocimiento. Él corre a la ventana pero Tabeetha ha desaparecido.

El mira a la niña inconsciente y al hombre muerto y niega con la cabeza.

Tabeetha pega el volante. Ella está enfadada y preocupada porque su amiga está una cautiva.

Capítulo 4

El guardo se llama Dave. Él mira a Charlotte. Charlotte está encadenada a la silla. Ella abre sus ojos y mira a Dave.

"Mi amiga me puede salvar." Dice Charlotte. Dave no responde.

"¿Hola, Eres sordo?" continúa ella.

"¿Quién te contrato a tí?" pregunta Dave.

"Yo no sé." dice Charlotte. "La persona se anónima. Y si yo puedo informar yo no sigo aún." Ella dice furiosamente.

"Yo no pienso que sí."

Andando Caminos: Teaching Spanish in Waldorf Schools

Oraciones Sobre La Historia

Juan y Maria son hermanos.
Ellos viven en Santillana, cerca del mar.
La casa de Juan y Maria está blanca con muchas flores y una puerta muy grande.
Ellos tienen un perro, Blas.
Blas le gusta jugar en la playa y cavar hoyos.
En la mañana cuando la campana toca, Maria se levanta para pasear Blas.
Maria y Teresa son buenas amigas.
La playa está vacia en la mañana.
Blas está muy contento y salta, corre y cava hoyos.
Maria y Teresa hablan y rien. Blas empieza a ladrar.

Hola,
Me llamo Marissa. Yo vivo en San Francisco y yo tengo once años. Yo soy morena. Yo tengo los ojos de color café. Yo tengo un perro negro que se llama Henry. Henry es muy pequeño. Yo no tengo hermanos. Yo soy alta. Yo estoy en sexto grado en la escuela de Waldorf. Yo vivo cerca de la escuela. Mi color favorito es morado.

*More examples from students, including summaries
as free renderings after the readings in grades 6 and 7*

From Storytelling to Reading, Speaking, and Writing

The images opposite show another approach to writing stories with students in grades 7 or 8. The students were divided into groups of two, three, or four. This activity facilitates speaking as they create their story. First the students were given the following paragraphs:

Ana sale de su casa y camina por la calle. Ella lleva una maleta con documentos importantes para su trabajo. Ella es detective privado. Ana mira su reloj y espera en el parque a otra persona. Un hombre llega corriendo. Ellos hablan atentamente. El hombre da a Ana un documento. Ella pone el documento en su maleta. En ese momento llega un coche. El coche se estaciona en la calle cerca de Ana y del hombre. Otro coche llega. Es un coche de policía.

Then, the students were asked to complete the story with the following (see chapter 6, "Teaching Grammar" for a list of adverbs and prepositions):

1. The date, season of the year, weather, and time.
2. Physical description of Ana—age, nationality, clothes, and favorite activities.
3. Briefcase; describe what is inside.
4. Explain the documents she carries.
5. Explain what she is doing now.
6. Why is she looking at her watch? What time does she needs to be back in her office and why?
7. Who is the man? Name, age, nationality, personal description, his clothes, profession, etc. Is he single or married?
8. Write the conversation between the man and Ana and their relationship.
9. Description of the document. Describe how people are in the car. Describe the people inside the car (appearance, professions, etc.).
10. Describe where Ana's office is, the street name and number.
11. Describe what happens and why the man wants the document. Tell the story of the document. What it is needed for, etc.?
12. Describe what Ana does. Did she call the police?
13. End this part of the story.

Ejemplo de la historia

Es martes, cuatro de enero. Es primavera y hace templado. Hay mucho viento pero no llueve. Son las diez de la mañana y Ana camina hacia el parque antes de ir a la oficina. Ana es una mujer muy bonita, ella es de México. Ella es morena y tiene los ojos negros. Ella es alta y delgada y muy inteligente. Lleva una falda elegante con una camisa de color azul. Lleva una chaqueta en la mano y zapatos de tacón. No lleva un abrigo y bufanda, pero lleva guantes. Ana camina segura y mira la hora en su reloj de oro. Su cartera es grande y de color marrón. Hay muchos documentos importantes dentro de la cartera.

Ana es detective privado y trabaja en un caso importante: un robo de un collar de diamantes.

Ana mira su reloj de oro y espera en el parque cerca de un árbol. Ella tiene que llegar a la oficina a las dos y media para una reunión.

Un hombre llega corriendo. El es joven y lleva un traje de color azul oscuro y una corbata roja. Tiene el pelo castaño y lleva una cartera pequeña. Se llama Juan. Juan es el dueño de una tienda de joyas. Juan busca a los ladrones que robaron un valioso collar de diamantes....

The story can be as long as the students decide they should be. Usually their stories tend to be interesting, with many details, and funny plots. Working in groups facilitates their dialogue, choice of vocabulary, and their enthusiasm for sharing their reading with the rest of the class. This is a good dynamic activity, but it is important to balance the groups: good students, medium, and weak, or new students in the same group, so there is participation and help from everyone.

4.5 Stories for the Lower Grades

El burro, el mantel y el palo

This play can be performed in the lower grades. The class should follow a choral recitation and gestures during the lesson in the weeks before the first rehearsal. When the students have learned some of the verses, the teacher may assign parts.

CAST OF CHARACTERS: Pedrito, la madre, el genio del río, el burro fantástico, el burro del posadero, el posadero, el mantel prodigioso, el mantel del posadero, el palo, y el río.

(Mother and Pedrito in front of the semicircle.)

CHORUS: *Pedrito, Pedrito ve al río a pescar,*
pues no hay comidita para cenar.

(Pedrito takes his fishing pole and walks toward the river; two children move a blue cloth. El Genio appears between the "water.")

Pedrito en el río un pez de oro pescó,
y el pez dorado de esta forma habló:

GENIE: *«El poderoso genio del río soy. Si tú me liberas un premio te doy».*

CHORUS: *Pedrito en el río al pez liberó,*
y una poción mágica, de él recibió.
Unas gotas de esencia el pez derramó.
Un burro fantástico apareció.

(El genio dijo: a child with a mask or costume of a donkey appears.)

GENIE: *«Burro burrito, dame el dinero que necesito».*

CHORUS: *«Oro y monedas el burro escupió,*
y Pedrito contento con el burro se marchó».

En el camino de vuelta a su casa y cuando por una posada pasa, al burro le dice:

(Posadero, hidden, observes Pedrito.)

PEDRITO: *«Burro, burrito dame el dinero que necesito».*
Monedas de oro el burro escupió,
y el posadero ambicioso todo lo vio.

(Posadero changes donkeys.)

CHORUS: *Y mientras Pedrito un pan comía*
el cambio de burro el dueño hacía.
De vuelta a su casa, sin cambio notar,
a su madre el burro quería mostrar;
y al burro dijo:

PEDRITO: «*Burro burrito dame el dinero que necesito*».

CHORUS: *El burro cambiado un rebuzno dio,* (burro brays: I ho, Iho)
y su madre enfadada, a él repitió:

MADRE: *Pedrito, Pedrito ve al río a pescar,*
pues no hay comidita para cenar.

(Pedrito takes his fishing pole and walks toward the river. Two children move a blue cloth, the Genio appears in the "water.")

Pedrito en el río un pez de oro pescó,
y el pez dorado de esta forma habló:

GENIE: «*El poderoso genio del río soy, si tú me liberas un premio te doy*».

CHORUS: *Pedrito en el río al pez liberó,*
y una poción mágica, de él recibió.
Unas gotas de esencia el pez derramó,
y un mantel prodigioso apareció.

El genio dijo:

GENIE: «*Mantel mantelito, dame la comida que necesito*».

CHORUS: *Un banquete opulento se transform*
y el chico contento a su casa marchó.
En el camino de vuelta a casa,
y cuando por una posada pasa,
dice al mantel:

(Pedrito sits on a table to eat and takes out the tablecloth. Posadero looks through the doorway.)

PEDRITO: «*Mantel mantelito dame la comida que necesito*».

CHORUS: *En un banquete opulento se transformó.*
Y el posadero ambicioso todo lo vio.
Y mientras Pedrito una siesta dormía,
el cambio del mantel el dueño hacía.
De vuelta a su casa, sin cambio notar,
a su madre el mantel quería mostrar;

Y al mantel dijo:

PEDRITO: «*Mantel, mantelito dame la comida que yo necesito*».
CHORUS: *El mantel ordinario nada ofreció, y su madre enfadada a él repitió:*
MADRE: *Pedrito, Pedrito ve al río a pescar, pues no hay comidita para cenar.*

(Pedrito takes his fishing pole and walks toward the river. Two children move a blue cloth, the Genio appears in the "water.")

Pedrito en el río un pez de oro pescó,
y el pez dorado de esta forma habló:
GENIE: «*El poderoso genio del río soy,*
si tú me liberas un premio te doy».
CHORUS: *Pedrito en el río al pez liberó,*
y un palo mágico de él recibió.
En el camino de vuelta
a su casa por una posada pasa, (Pedrito sleeps)
El posadero ambicioso
cambia el palo curioso y dice:

POSADERO: «*Palo, palito dame los palos que necesito*».
CHORUS: *Palos y palos el palo le dió,*
y el posadero gritando a todos llamó.
Primero devolvió el burro prodigioso.
Después, el fantástico mantel.
Y el palo curioso, dejó de dar palos,
al posadero ambicioso.

(traditional Spanish; adapted by Elena Forrer)

La lechera (The Milkmaid with a Pail)

This poem is appropriate for grade 3. It can be acted out or presented to the class with the illustrations. Piano or recorder music may be played as the various animals enter the stage.

CAST OF CHARACTERS: La lechera, varios pollitos, dos lechones, una vaca, several market vendors or farmers.

(The milkmaid takes a cántaro as the class sings «Tengo tres cabritillas».)

CHORUS: *Camino al mercado a vender,*
una lechera temprano,
con el cántaro en la mano,
soñaba en dinero obtener.

(The milkmaid stops and begins to dream of the eggs and the chicks. Some children will appear carrying a basket with eggs, and then some chicks will enter the stage. Piano or flute music.)

CHORUS: *Ocho docenas de huevos,*
que luego pollitos se harán,
y en nueva venta darán,
para dos lechones buenos.

(The chicks are traded for pigs carried by a farmer.)

CHORUS: *Comiendo de mis castañas.*
pronto gordos los veré
y una vaca compraré
que corra entre las cabañas.

(The pigs carried by the milkmaid are traded to another farmer for a cow.)

CHORUS: *Contenta la chica saltó,*
brincando de tal manera,
que el cántaro por la ladera,
la leche rodando perdió.

(The animals run from one side to the other, while music is being played.)

From Storytelling to Reading, Speaking, and Writing

CHORUS: No hay ya leche, no hay dinero,
no hay pollitos ni lechones,
ni la vaca entre algodones,
cuidada con tanto esmero.

¡Ay! lechera, tu ambición,
muchas ideas te ha dado,
sin haberte percatado,
que era todo una ilusión.

—SANTIAGO MUELAS MEDRADO, España, 1943

La gallina Marcelina

Storytelling for Grade 3 and Reading for Grade 4

(Characters: Narrador, Marcelina, don perro, don gato, pollitos.)

Narración

NARRADOR: *La gallina Marcelina vivía en una granja. Un día encontró unos granos de trigo en el campo y dijo:*

MARCELINA: *Plantaré los granos de trigo y cuando crezcan, cocinaré un delicioso pan.*

NARRADOR: *Por el camino la gallinita Marcelina se encontró con don Perro.*

MARCELINA: *Buenos días don Perro. ¿Quiere usted ayudarme a plantar estos granos de trigo?*

DON PERRO: *¿Quién yo? Pues no. Estoy muy ocupado. Adiós Marcelina.*

MARCELINA: *Adiós, don Perro.*

NARRADOR: *Después la gallina Marcelina se encontró con don Gato.*

MARCELINA: *Buenos días don Gato. ¿Quiere usted ayudarme a plantar estos granos de trigo?*

DON GATO: *(Bostezando) Aaaaaah, estoy muy cansado. No gracias.*

MARCELINA: *Está bien, está bien. Los plantaré yo sola.*

NARRADOR: *Marcelina fue al campo y plantó los granos de trigo. El trigo creció y la gallinita decidió cortar las espigas. De camino, se encontró a don Perro.*

MARCELINA: *Buenos días don Perro.*

DON PERRO: *Buenos días Marcelina.*

MARCELINA: *¿Quieres ayudarme a cortar las espigas?*

DON PERRO: *¿Quién yo? Pues no. Estoy muy ocupado gallinita.*

NARRADOR: *Poco después se encontró con don Gato.*

MARCELINA: *Hola don Gato. ¿Quieres ayudarme a cortar las espigas?*

DON GATO: *(Bostezando) Aaaaaaah, estoy muy cansado. No gracias.*

MARCELINA: *Está bien, está bien. Las cortaré yo sola.*

NARRADOR: *Y las cortó. Después preguntó a sus amigos:*

MARCELINA: *¿Quieren ayudarme a moler el grano?*

DON PERRO: *No, No. Estoy muy ocupado.*

DON GATO: *No, pues claro que no. Estoy muy cansado (bosteza).*

MARCELINA: *Está bien. Moleré yo sola los granos de trigo.*

NARRADOR: *La gallina Marcelina llevó la harina para preparar un buen pan y de camino a su casa se encontró con don Perro y don Gato y dijo:*

MARCELINA: *¿Quieren ayudarme a preparar un buen pan?*
DON PERRO: *Estoy muy ocupado.*
DON GATO: *Estoy muy cansado (bosteza).*
GALLINITA: *Está bien, está bien, prepararé el pan yo sola.*
NARRADOR: *Y la gallinita cocinó un pan delicioso. Cuando estuvo listo, la gallina Marcelina dijo:*
GALLINITA: *¿Quieren ayudarme a comer este pan delicioso?*
DON PERRO: *¡Guau, guau, claro qué sí!*
DON GATO: *¡Miau, miau, sí, sí, sí!*
GALLINITA: *¡Pues **NO, NO y NO**. Me comeré el pan yo sola con mis pollitos!*
NARRADOR: *Y la gallinita Marcelina y sus pollitos se comieron el delicioso pan.*

(oral tradidition; adapted by Elena Forrer)

CANCIÓN

Clo, clo, clo, cantemos a la vida,
clo, clo, clo, cantemos a la aurora,
clo, clo, clo, yo soy una gallina,
clo, clo, clo, con pico de oradora.
Clo, clo, clo, clo, clo, clo.
Cantemos hijos míos,
pío, pío, pío.
No le temáis al frío,
pío, pío, pío.
Yo soy una gallina,
de mucha tradición,
pues era de mi abuela,
el huevo de Colón.
Chimpón.

(popular)[7]

---

7 From www.weblitoral.com/archivo%20de%20textos/palabras-mayores/cuentos-de-animales/copy42_of_la-que-no-sabia-remedar.

El lobo y las cabritas

Recommended for Grade 1

(Choral recitation with props and small costumes for the different parts. The rest of the class stands in a semicircle.)

CHORUS: *En una casita del bosque*
siete cabritas vivían.
Cerca de los prados saltaban,
cerca de los prados corrían.

Una mañana temprano
mamá cabra les decía:

MAMÁ: *Tengo que salir para el mercado,*
a comprar la comidita.
No abráis la puerta a nadie,
pues el lobo entraría.

CABRITAS: *Sí madre —dijeron todas—*
haremos como tú digas.

(Lobo appears.)

CHORUS: *El lobo llamó a la puerta.*

LOBO: *Tan, tan… ¡Abrid la puerta cabritas!*
Soy vuestra mamá que vuelve,
de regreso a casita.

CABRITAS: *¡No, no! Sabemos que eres el lobo.*
La voz de nuestra madre,
es suave como un vellón de nuestro lomo.

CHORUS: *El lobo se fue saltando,*
gritaba con rabia e ira:

LOBO: *«Comprar huevos yo quiero*
para hacer mi voz más fina».

(Lobo eats some eggs, returns, and speaks with voz fina.)

LOBO:	*«Abrid cabritas, soy vuestra mamá* *que vuelve, de regreso a casita».*
CABRITAS:	*¡No, no. Sabemos que eres el lobo!* *Las garras de nuestra madre,* *son blancas como la harina de don Manolo.*
CHORUS:	*El lobo se fue saltando* *gritaba con rabia e ira,* *«Comprar harina yo quiero* *para hacer mis patas finas».*

(Lobo puts some flour on his paws.)

LOBO:	*Tan, tan… ¡Abrid la puerta cabritas,* *soy vuestra mamá que llega* *de vuelta a casita!*

(Cabritas opens the door.)

CHORUS:	*Entró de un salto el lobo* *adentro de la casita* *y fue comiéndose a todas las cabras,* *menos a la pequeñita.*
CHORUS:	*Mamá cabra ha vuelto a casa* *y sólo está la más pequeñita,* *junto al pozo duerme el lobo* *y en su tripa las cabritas.*
CHORUS:	*Mamá cabra toma un cuchillo* *y saca a todas las cabritas,* *mete piedras en su estómago* *y cose con cinta su tripa.*
CHORUS:	*El lobo se ha despertado* *y del pozo quiere agua beber,* *pero con el peso de las piedras* *se ha caído, y ya nunca podrá volver.*

(oral tradition; verses by Elena Forrer)

Canción del lobo

Aunque esta canción es para un juego, se puede incluir para finalizar la obra de Las cabritas. Todos los niños terminan juntos en círculo y el lobo en el centro. Cada vez que los niños preguntan: ¿Lobo estás listo? El corro cambia de sentido dos veces y terminamos con la primera estrofa.

Jugando al escondite en el monte, amaneció.
El cuco cantando, el miedo nos quitó.
El cuco cantando, el miedo nos quitó.
Cucú, cucú, cucú, cucú.

¿Lobo estás listo?

No, estoy comiendo huevos frescos…
Jugando al escondite en el monte, amaneció.
El cuco cantando, el miedo nos quitó.
El cuco cantando, el miedo nos quitó.
Cucú, cucú, cucú, cucú.

¿Lobo estás listo?

«No. Me estoy comiendo la harina fina».

Jugando al escondite en el monte, amaneció.
El cuco cantando, el miedo nos quitó.
El cuco cantando, el miedo nos quitó.
Cucú, cucú, cucú, cucú.

(tradicional)[8]

---

[8] From ceipacapulcomusical.blogspot.com/2010/03/jugando-al-escondite-en-el-bosque.html.

El Muchachito de Dulce de Mazapán

NARRADOR: *En una casa pequeña vivían un abuelo, una abuela y un chico. Ellos vivían en el campo. Un día la abuela cocinó un delicioso dulce de mazapán y antes de salir a trabajar, dijo al chico:*

ABUELA: *El abuelo y yo vamos a ir al campo a trabajar. Dejo en el horno un dulce de mazapán; pero aunque el dulce huela muy bien, no abras la puerta del horno.*

CHICO: *Si madre. No abriré la puerta del horno.*

NARRADOR: *Respondió el chico.*

(Pasado un tiempo, un olor delicioso salió de la cocina. El chico curioso caminó hacia la cocina. Cuando vio el horno el muchacho no lo pudo resistir, y abrió despacio la puerta del horno. De pronto, saltó fuera una figura de dulce de mazapán y comenzó a correr deprisa por la cocina. El chico asustado gritó.)

CHICO: *¡No corras, ven aquí!*

MUCHACHITO: *¡Ja, ja, ja! ¡No me vas a alcanzar, pues soy el muchachito de mazapán!*

NARRADOR: *Rió el muchachito.*

(El chico corrió detrás de él, pero no le pudo alcanzar. El abuelo y la abuela cuando vieron al muchachito de mazapán, también corrieron detrás de él, pero tampoco le pudieron alcanzar. Y el muchachito de dulce de mazapán siguió corriendo mientras gritaba.)

MUCHACHITO: *¡Ja, ja, ja! ¡No me vais a alcanzar, pues soy el muchachito de dulce de mazapán!*

NARRADOR: *Poco después tres granjeros que vieron lo que pasaba preguntaron al muchachito:*

Granjeros: *¿Quién eres tú y a dónde vas?*

Muchachito: *¡Ja, ja, ja! Soy el muchachito de dulce de mazapán y nadie me puede alcanzar. Me he escapado de un abuelo, una abuela y de un chico. Y ahora, también me escaparé de vosotros porque corro más rápido. ¡Ja, ja, ja! ¡Nadie me puede alcanzar, pues soy el muchachito de mazapán!*

Narrador: *Y los granjeros le persiguieron pero no le pudieron alcanzar y se sentaron a descansar.*

(Poco después el muchachito de dulce de mazapán se encontró con una vaca que le preguntó.)

Vaca: *¿Quién eres tú y dónde piensas que vas?*

Muchachito: *¡Ja, ja, ja! Soy el muchachito de dulce de mazapán y nadie me puede alcanzar. Me he escapado de un abuelo, una abuela y de un chico… y ahora, también me escaparé, porque corro más rápido… ¡Ja, ja, ja! ¡No me vais a alcanzar, pues soy el muchachito de mazapán!*

Narrador: *Y la vaca le persiguió pero no le pudo alcanzar.*

(Poco después el muchachito de dulce de mazapán llegó cerca de un árbol donde estaba una zorra. Y ella dijo.)

Zorra: *¡Un momento! ¿Quién eres tú y dónde piensas que vas?*

Muchachito: *¡Ja, ja, ja! Soy el muchachito de dulce de mazapán y nadie me puede alcanzar. Me he escapado de un abuelo, una abuela y de un chico… y ahora, también me escaparé, porque corro más rápido que tú… ¡Ja, ja, ja! ¡No me vas a alcanzar, pues soy el muchachito de dulce de mazapán!*

Zorra: *Perdón, amigo. No oigo bien tus palabras. Acércate a mi oreja y repite todo otra vez.*

From Storytelling to Reading, Speaking, and Writing

NARRADOR: *Dijo la astuta zorra.*

MUCHACHITO: *¡Ja, ja, ja! Soy el muchachito de dulce de mazapán y nadie me puede alcanzar. Me he escapado de un abuelo, una abuela y de un chico, de tres granjeros y de una vaca... y ahora, también me escaparé de ti, porque corro más rápido. ¡Ja, ja, ja! ¡No me vais a alcanzar, pues soy el muchachito de Mazapán!*

(El muchachito de dulce de mazapán se acercó tanto a la astuta zorra, que abrió la boca y se lo comió. Y este es el fin de historia del muchachito de dulce de mazapán.)

(oral tradition; adapted by Elena Forrer)

Una Señora y Su Sombrero

Mini-play recommended for grades 1 or 2. The class stands in front of the audience in a semicircle. In the middle, a child dressed with funny "old fashioned women's clothes" and an old-fashioned streetlight held by another student at the other side of the semicircle.

CHORUS: *Estaba una señora,*
dando un paseo
y ha roto una farola,
con su sombrero.
Al ruido de los cristales
salió el gobernador.

(Another child, dressed with a tall black hat and a cape as the *gobernador*, enters the scene.)

GOBERNADOR: *¿Quién ha sido la señora*
que ha roto el farol?

SEÑORA: *Señor gobernador*
que yo no he sido,
que ha sido mi sombrero
por atrevido.
Si ha sido su sombrero
una multa pagará,
para que su sombrero
sepa por donde va.

(The major charges the lady a fine; she happily touches her «sombrero» and nods to the major.)

(popular; adapted by Elena Forrer)

Las tres cabritas (Teatro)

Música: «Tengo tres cabritillas». Un día las tres cabritas decidieron subir a la montaña para comer hierba fresca y verde. Para subir a la montaña, tenían que cruzar un puente donde vivía un ogro enorme y feo. Como tenían mucha hambre, primero pasó la cabrita más joven.

CABRA PEQUEÑA:	*Trin, trin, trin, trin*
NARRADOR:	*(Pateaba con sus pezuñas).*
OGRO:	*¿Quién patea sus pezuñas y cruza mi puente?*
CABRITA:	*Soy yo, la cabrita pequeñita.*
OGRO:	*Pues yo soy el ogro cruel y te quiero comer.*
CABRITA PEQUEÑA:	*No, no me comas. Cabra mediana está más gorda y está mejor que yo.*
NARRADOR:	*El ogro pensando en la cabra mediana dijo:*
OGRO:	*Está bien, te puedes marchar.*

(Música)

NARRADOR:	*Más tarde llegó cabra mediana, haciendo ruido con sus pezuñas.*
CABRA MEDIANA:	*Tran, tran, Tran, tran*
OGRO:	*¿Quién patea sus pezuñas y cruza mi puente?*
CABRA MEDIANA:	*Soy yo, la mediana de las cabritas.*
OGRO:	*Pues yo soy el ogro cruel y te quiero comer.*
CABRA MEDIANA:	*No, no me comas. Cabra grande está más gorda y está mejor.*
NARRADOR:	*El ogro pensando en una cabra más grande y gorda dijo:*
OGRO:	*Está bien, te puedes marchar.*

From Storytelling to Reading, Speaking, and Writing

NARRADOR:	*Poco después llegó cabra grande, haciendo un ruido muy fuerte con sus pezuñas.*
CABRA GRANDE:	*Tron, tron, tron, tron.*
OGRO:	*¿Quién patea sus pezuñas y cruza mi puente?*
CABRA GRANDE:	*Soy yo, la más grande de las cabritas.*
OGRO:	*Pues yo soy el ogro cruel y te quiero comer.*
CABRA GRANDE:	*¡No me comerás! Tengo dos cuernos como lanzas y con ellos te empujaré.*
NARRADOR:	*Cabra grande empujó al ogro con sus largos cuernos y el ogro se cayó al río rodando.*

(Efectos de sonido)

Después, Cabra Grande cruzó el puente y subió a la montaña con el resto de las cabritas a comer la hierba fresca y verde del campo.

(Música)

(oral tradition [9]; adapted by Elena Forrer)

---

9 From www.cancioneros.com/nc/1174/0/remende-o-paloma-del-palomar-popular-espanola.

4.6 Stories for the Middle Grades

Francisco y la Misión

Francisco vive cerca de la misión. Él vive con su padre en un rancho. Francisco corre por el rancho con su perro. El perro se llama Pinto. Francisco y su padre cazan animales. Ellos venden las pieles y la carne a los frailes de la misión. Los frailes preparan pan y medicinas para curar el dolor. La Misión es muy bonita. Es blanca y es alta. A Francisco le gusta la misión porque la torre tiene una campana. La puerta de la misión es muy grande y sólida. En el jardín de la misión hay un patio con una fuente y un pozo. Los frailes tienen un huerto para plantar verduras y flores.

From Storytelling to Reading, Speaking, and Writing

Un día Francisco camina con su perro Pinto hacia la misión. La puerta de la torre está abierta y Pinto sube las escaleras. Francisco llama a Pinto:

—¡Pinto, Pinto!

Pinto persigue a un tejón y no escucha a Francisco.

De pronto toca la campana:

—Ding, dong, ding, dong.

—¡Pinto, Pinto! —*llama Francisco.*

Francisco sube las escaleras deprisa y los frailes sorprendidos salen al jardín.

Francisco agarra a Pinto y le dice en la oreja:

—Pinto, eres un perro malo. ¡Sssssshhhh!, silencio.

—¿Quién está ahí? —*preguntan los frailes.*

Francisco y Pinto no responden.

—¡Qué extraño, parece que hay un fantasma en la torre! —*responden los frailes.*

—Elena Forrer

La ratita presumida

Una vez una ratita barría con su escoba la puerta de su casa y cantaba:
«Tralará, lariatá…barro mi casita. Tralará, larató…con mi escoba barro».

De pronto, vio una moneda en el suelo.

—¡Qué suerte tengo! –dijo la ratita- ¿qué me compraré?…¿un libro?…¿caramelos?…¡ya sé! Me compraré un lacito para mi cola.

La ratita fue a la tienda y compró un lazo rosa y se lo ató en su cola. Después se sentó enfrente de la puerta de su casa. Y se puso a cantar:

«Tralará, lariatá…barro mi casita. Tralará, larató…con mi escoba barro».

Poco tiempo después, pasó un perro. Cuando el perro vio a la ratita dijo:

—Ratita, ratita…que bonita estás.

—Hago muy bien porque tú no me lo das.

—¿Te quieres casar conmigo?

—¿Y qué voz tienes al hablar? —preguntó la ratita.

—¡Guau, guau, guau! —dijo el perro.

—¡Ay no, no, no…que me asustarás!

Y el perro se fue triste y la ratita siguió cantando:

«Tralará, lariata…barro mi casita. Tralará, larató…con mi escoba barro».

Unos minutos más tarde, pasó un gallo muy elegante por la casa de la ratita. Cuando vio a la ratita dijo:

—Ratita, ratita…que bonita estás.

—Hago muy bien porque tú no me lo das.

—¿Te quieres casar conmigo?

—¿Y qué voz tienes al hablar? —preguntó la ratita.

—¡Kikirikí, Kikirikí! —dijo el gallo.

—¡Ay no, no, no... que me asustarás!

Y el gallo se fue triste y la ratita siguió cantando:

«Tralará, lariata... barro mi casita. Tralará, larató... con mi escoba barro».

Después pasó un gato y al ver a la ratita le dijo:

—Ratita, ratita que bonita estás.

—Hago muy bien porque tú no me lo das.

—¿Te quieres casar conmigo?

—¿Y qué voz tienes al hablar? —preguntó la ratita.

—¡Miau, miau! —dijo el gato.

—¡Sí, si! ¡contigo me casaré!

Y la ratita y el gato se casaron. A la hora de comer, el gato preguntó:

—¿Ratita, qué tenemos para comer?

—Verduras y queso —dijo la ratita.

—¿Verduras y queso? A mí no me gustan las verduras y el queso, a mí me gusta comer carne de ratón.

Y el gato abrió la boca y se comió a la ratita.

Y este es el final de la Ratita Presumida.

(oral tradition; adapted by Elena Forrer)

Leyenda del pájaro Chogüi

En la selva guaraní hay un pajarito muy lindo que se llama Chogüi. A este pájaro le gusta cantar y volar entre los árboles y picotear las naranjas.

Cuenta la leyenda, que un niño guaraní vivía con su mamá. Al niño guaraní le gustaba subirse a los árboles y comer las deliciosas naranjas. Todos los días, su madre salía a trabajar lejos de su casa. La mamá del niño no quería que él saliese solo al bosque porque habían muchos animales peligrosos. El niño no obedecía a su madre porque le gustaba mucho el bosque.

Un día, su madre salió temprano al campo a trabajar. El niño fue otra vez al bosque de naranjos y se subió a un árbol. El árbol estaba lleno de deliciosas naranjas. Como era tarde, el niño se subió a la rama más alta para ver llegar a su madre y comer una deliciosa naranja.

Mientras esperaba a su madre, la mamá del niño llegó a casa. Ella le llamó:

— ¿Hijo, dónde estás?

El niño bajó muy deprisa del árbol, pero se resbaló y cayó al suelo. Su madre llegó corriendo. En el momento, su mamá le tomó en sus brazos y el niño cerró los ojos. Cuando cerró los ojos, el niño sufrió una trasformación: se convirtió en un pájaro precioso, el pájaro Chogüi. El pajarito Chogüi empezó a volar cerca de su madre entre las hojas. Desde entonces, el pájaro Chogüi vuelve a visitar a su madre y vuela entre las naranjas de los árboles cantando: Chogüi, Chogüi, Chogüi…

Cuando las personas oyen su canto, saben que el niño guaraní llama a su madre.

(Leyenda de Paraguay; tradición oral)

El pájaro Chogüi (canción)

Cuenta la leyenda,
que en un árbol se encontraba,
encaramado un indiecito Guaraní,
que sobresaltado por un grito de su madre,
perdió apoyo y que cayendo se murió.

Y que entre los brazos maternales,
por extraño sortilegio, en Chogüi se convirtió:

Chogüi, Chogüi, Chogüi, Chogüi,
cantando está, volando va,
perdiéndose en el cielo azul turquí.

Chogüi, Chogüi, Chogüi, Chogüi,
que lindo está, volando va,
perdiéndose en el cielo guaraní.

Y desde aquel día, se recuerda al indiecito,
cuando se oye como un eco, aquel Chogüi;
es el canto alegre y bullanguero,
del precioso naranjero, que repite su cantar;
salta y picotea las naranjas, que es su fruta
preferida repitiendo sin cesar...

Chogüi, Chogüi, Chogüi...
　　　　—Guillermo Breer, Argentina 1916[10]

---

10 Esta canción popular, se puede encontrar en www.youtube.com/watch?v=OoxsSjYrx2M.

El gallo Kiriko

Play recommended for grade 4. The class could follow a choral recitation for the "narrator" and different students could speak the characters. The character of "Kiriko" should be fanny and exaggerated. Piano music should be played before "Gallo Kiriko" meets each one of the characters. He should walk in front of the audience, before he meets each one of them.

CAST OF CHARACTERS: Narrador, Kiriko, gusanito, hierba, cabra, Palo, fuego, agua, vaca y muchacha.

(Narrador a un lado del escenario. Todos los personajes en diferentes puntos del escenario.)

NARRADOR: *Un día un gallo muy elegante y presumido iba a la boda de su tío Perico. Por el camino, vió a un gusanito en el barro y dijo:*

(Kiriko paseándose ve al gusanito.)

KIRIKO: *Pico o no pico. Si pico me mancho el pico y no podré ir a la boda de mi tío Perico.*

(Música: Gusanito desaparece detrás de la cortina.)

NARRADOR: *Y el gallo se comió al gusanito y se manchó el pico. Poco después llegó a un campo de hierba fresca y dijo:*

KIRIKO: *Hierba, límpiame el pico, que voy a la boda de mi tío Perico.*

HIERBA *(cruzándose de brazos)*: *Te limpiaré el pico si me dices dónde está Gusanito.*

KIRIKO: *¡Gusano, Gusanito! ¿Dónde estás que no te he visto?*

GUSANITO: *¡En la tripa del gallo Kiriko!*

HIERBA: *Pues... ¡no te limpiaré el pico!*

(Música: Kiriko sigue hacia el otro lado del escenario).

NARRADOR: *Por el camino, Kiriko se encontró con una cabra.*

KIRIKO *(señalando)*: *Cabra, cómete a la hierba, que no quiere limpiarme el pico para ir a la boda de mi tío Perico.*

CABRA: *Me comeré a la hierba si me dices dónde está Gusanito.*

KIRIKO: *¡Gusano, Gusanito! ¿Dónde estás que no te he visto?*

GUSANITO: *¡En la tripa del gallo Kiriko!*

CABRA: *¡Pues no me la comeré!*

NARRADOR: *Por el camino, Kiriko se encontró con un palo.*

KIRIKO (señalando): *Palo, pégale a la cabra, que no quiere comerse a la hierba y que no quiere limpiarme el pico para ir a la boda de mi tío Perico.*

PALO (cruzándose de brazos): *Pegaré a la hierba si me dices dónde está Gusanito.*

KIRIKO: *¡Gusano, Gusanito! ¿Dónde estás que no te he visto?*

GUSANITO: *¡En la tripa del gallo Kiriko!*

PALO: *¡Pues no le pegaré!*

(*Música*)

NARRADOR: *Por el camino, Kiriko se encontró con un fuego y le pidió:*

KIRIKO: *Fuego, quema al palo que no quiere pegar a la cabra, que no quiere comer la hierba y que no quiere limpiarme el pico para ir a la boda de mi tío Perico.*

FUEGO: *Lo quemaré si me dices dónde está Gusanito.*

KIRIKO: *¡Gusano, Gusanito! ¿Dónde estás que no te he visto?*

GUSANITO: *¡En la tripa del gallo Kiriko!*

FUEGO (cruzándose de brazos): *Pues no lo quemaré.*

(*Música*)

NARRADOR: *Por el camino se encontró con un río lleno de agua y dijo:*

KIRIKO: *Agua, apaga el fuego que no quiere quemar el palo, que no quiere pegar a la cabra, que no quiere comer la hierba y que no quiere limpiarme el pico para ir a la boda de mi tío Perico.*

AGUA: *Lo apagaré si me dices dónde está Gusanito.*

KIRIKO: *¡Gusano, Gusanito! ¿Dónde estás que no te he visto?*

GUSANITO: *¡En la tripa del gallo Kiriko!*

AGUA: *¡Pues no lo apagaré!*

NARRADOR: *Por el camino se encontró a una vaca y le dijo:*

KIRIKO: *Vaca, bébete el agua que no quiere apagar el fuego, que no quiere quemar el palo, que no quiere pegar a la cabra, que no quiere comer la hierba y que no quiere limpiarme el pico para ir a la boda de mi tío Perico.*

VACA (*con un mugido*): *La beberé, si me dices dónde está Gusanito.*

KIRIKO: *¡Gusano, Gusanito! ¿Dónde estás que no te he visto?*

GUSANITO: *¡En la tripa del gallo Kiriko!*

VACA: *¡Pues no la beberé!*

NARRADOR: *Por el camino se encontró con una muchacha.*

(*Kiriko, muy triste llora*).

MUCHACHA: *¿Qué te pasa gallo Kiriko?*

KIRIKO: *Yo me comí a Gusanito, me manché el pico y la hierba, la cabra, el palo, el fuego, el agua y la vaca no han querido limpiarme el pico. Y no puedo ir a la boda de mi tío Perico.*

MUCHACHA: *Yo te limpiaré el pico. Pero antes, tienes que sacar a Gusanito de tu tripa.*

KIRIKO: *Si, le sacaré.*

(*Kiriko tose y tose y Gusanito finalmente sale*).

MUCHACHA: *Yo te limpiaré el pico.*

(*La muchacha le limpia el pico. Kiriko se pone contento*).

KIRIKO: *¡Kikirikí!...*

NARRADOR: *Y Kiriko fue a la boda de su tío Perico.*

(*Piano music*)

FIN

(popular Hispanic tale from the oral tradition; adapted by Elena Forrer)

From Storytelling to Reading, Speaking, and Writing

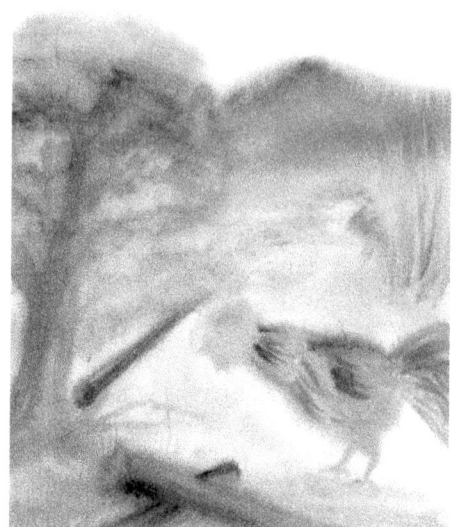
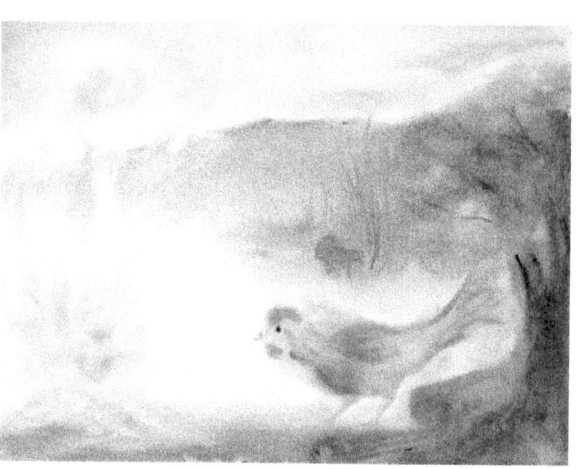
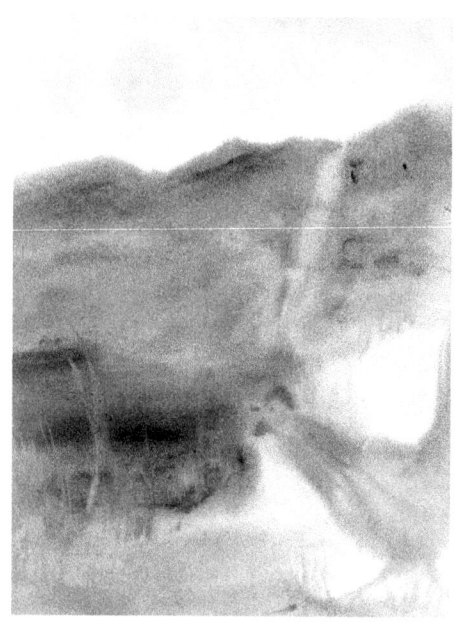
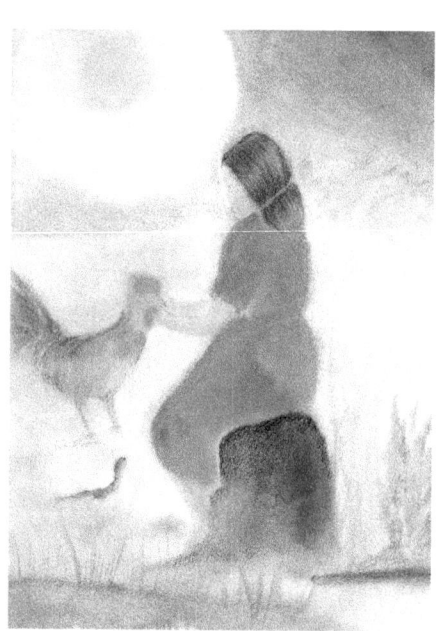

Platero y yo

Platero es pequeño, peludo, suave; tan blando por fuera, que se diría todo de algodón, que no lleva huesos. Sólo los espejos de azabache de sus ojos son duros cual dos escarabajos de cristal negro.

Lo dejo suelto y se va al prado, y acaricia tibiamente con su hocico, rozándolas apenas, las florecillas rosas, celestes y gualdas… Lo llamo dulcemente: «¿Platero?», y viene a mí con un trotecillo alegre que parece que se ríe, en no sé qué cascabeleo ideal…

Come cuanto le doy. Le gustan las naranjas mandarinas, las uvas moscateles, todas de ámbar; los higos morados, con su cristalina gotita de miel…

Es tierno y mimoso igual que un niño, que una niña…; pero fuerte y seco por dentro, como de piedra… Cuando paso sobre él, los domingos, por las últimas callejas del pueblo, los hombres del campo, vestidos de limpio y despaciosos, se quedan mirándolo:

— Tiene acero…

Tiene acero. Acero y plata de luna, al mismo tiempo.

(«Platero y yo»; fragmento Juan Ramón Jiménez)

4.7 Narrative Paragraphs and Stories for the Upper Grades

La Mendiguilla

I give this tender passage to my students in grade 6. Although it seems rather difficult, it is surprising to see how much they enjoy reading it with some help. After we are finished, I have them do a picture in their lesson books, according to the reading and as a dictation.

From Storytelling to Reading, Speaking, and Writing

Es invierno, y Mercedita Saro está siempre con su mantoncillo de pico, cuarta parte, cortado, de uno de mujer, tapándose con él la boca. Graciosísima la niña. Su cabecilla redonda, peinada lisa (cierto esmero ¿de quién?), y su tieso rabito trenzado con una cinta blanca al fin, me recuerdan la luna llena con una estrella cerca.

Ya me conoce, y sus ojitos nuevos y alegremente tristes me ven venir, y me sonríen, desde todos los lejos de estas calles. Yo, en vez de darle dinero que va al bolsillo colilloso del hombre borracho de la esquina, la llevo a una panadería o a una confitería y le compro algo que le guste; y ella se viene conmigo paseando y contándome cosas, hasta que se come del todo lo que sea.

Creo que se siente defendida por mí. Sin duda, se figura, confusamente, que su padre de la esquina es hombre de no sabe qué derechos. Y si le anda de cerca, la niña me dice, disimulando contra mi abrigo: «Señorito, tenga usté mucho cuidao, que está ahí mi pare, y no quiere que yo coma dulses».

—Juan Ramón Jiménez

La nota misteriosa

Tom y Kira son hermanos. Ellos visitan unos amigos en la ciudad de Segovia en España. Es verano y la familia decide ir al teatro por la tarde. El teatro está al aire libre cerca del acueducto romano de la ciudad. En el descanso, ellos deciden comprar un helado, porque hace calor.

Tom: *¡Kira, Kira!*

Kira: *¿Qué pasa Tom?*

Tom: *Mira, alguien me dio esta nota para ti.*

Kira: *¿Qué es eso?*

Tom: *Una nota.*

Kira tomó el papel rápidamente y empezó a leer:

¡Hola!

Yo sé que tu nombre es Kira. Tú eres de California. Tú eres rubia y tus ojos son azules. Tu hermano se llama Tom y es más pequeño. Él es moreno y es muy simpático. Tú y tu familia están en la casa de unos amigos en Segovia. ¿Quieres ser mi amiga?... Yo soy de Segovia.

Yo soy alto, soy moreno y soy un poco tímido. Estoy en sexto grado en la escuela local. Tengo muchos amigos españoles pero no tengo amigos de otros paises. Yo hablo un poco de inglés y tengo un perro negro que se llama Chispa. Chispa es muy gracioso y muy pequeño.

Yo vivo cerca de la casa de tus amigos. Si quieres conocerme, mañana estaré delante de la puerta de la catedral, a las doce del medio día.

Un amigo misterioso...

Kira miró alrededor, pero no vio a nadie. Miró otra vez y vio a un muchacho moreno. Kira tomó la nota en su mano y miró al muchacho. El muchacho miró a Kira y Kira volvió la cabeza. Después de unos minutos, Kira volvió a mirar pero el muchacho ya no estaba.

(«*Historias de ayer y de hoy*», Elena Forrer)

La cuesta de las bodegas

Al día siguiente la pandilla se reunió en la plaza con sus bicis.

Miguel: *¿Dónde vamos?*

Carmen: *Vamos a la cuesta de las Bodegas.*

Kira: *¿Qué es eso?*

Luís: *Son unas cuevas en una cuesta. Antiguamente la gente guardaba el vino en las cuevas. Ahora están abandonadas.*

Ana: *Vamos.*

La pandilla salió en las bicis hacia «la cuesta de las bodegas». Ellos Bajaron por varios caminos, doblaron a la derecha del río y tomaron un camino abandonado hacia las cuevas. Después de dos millas, ellos llegaron a «la cuesta». Kira vio muchas cuevas en la montaña.

Tomás: *¿En qué cueva entramos?*

Maribel: *Vamos a la cueva de allí arriba.*

Dejaron sus bicis y empezaron a subir la cuesta a pié. Kira vio muchas cuevas a la izquierda y a la derecha. Subieron a lo alto y ellos entraron en una cueva estrecha. No había luz. Luís sacó una linterna y los muchachos bajaron las escaleras de piedra. Había muchas telas de araña y un olor fuerte a vino, a vinagre y a moho.

Ana: *¡Mirad las cubas, son enormes!*

Tomás: Yo no sigo más. Este lugar me da miedo.

Maribel: *Vamos Tomás.*
  Los muchachos entraron dentro de la cueva. La cueva era larga y estrecha.

De pronto Juan dijo:

Juan: *¡Escuchad los ruidos! —Todos escucharon unos ruidos.*

Maribel: *¿Quién está ahí? —Pregunto Maribel,*

Voz: *Grraaaa…muchachos* —Respondió una voz misteriosa y profunda.

Luis: *¡Pronto salid, deprisa!*

> *Todos salieron rápidamente. Kira era la última. Kira escuchó la voz misteriosa muy cerca y ella empezó a correr entre las cubas viejas de vino. Todo estaba oscuro. Todos los chicos salieron de la cueva con la linterna. De pronto, Kira tropezó y se lastimó la pierna.*

Kira: *¡Ay, mi pierna! No puedo mover mi pierna.*

Voz: *Muchacha, ¿te has hecho daño?*

Kira: *¿Quién es usted?*

Voz: *Soy el señor Lute.*

Kira: *¡Oh, no!*

Señor Lute: *No te asustes. Yo puedo ayudarte a salir.*

El señor Lute ayudó a Kira a salir de la cueva. Kira miró fuera de la cueva y no vio a nadie. ¡Los chicos no estaban!

From Storytelling to Reading, Speaking, and Writing

La cuesta de las bodegas

Al día siguiente la pandilla se reunió en la plaza con sus bicis.

Miguel: *¿Dónde vamos?*

Carmen: *Vamos a la cuesta de las Bodegas.*

Kira: *¿Qué es eso?*

Luís: *Son unas cuevas en una cuesta. Antiguamente la gente guardaba el vino en las cuevas. Ahora están abandonadas.*

Ana: *Vamos.*

(La pandilla salió en las bicis hacia «la cuesta de las bodegas». Ellos Bajaron por varios caminos, doblaron a la derecha del río y tomaron un camino abandonado hacia las cuevas. Después de dos millas, ellos llegaron a «la cuesta». Kira vio muchas cuevas en la montaña.)

Tomás: *¿En qué cueva entramos?*

Maribel: *Vamos a la cueva de allí arriba.*

(Dejaron sus bicis y empezaron a subir la cuesta a pié. Kira vio muchas cuevas a la izquierda y a la derecha. Subieron a lo alto y ellos entraron en una cueva estrecha. No había luz. Luís sacó una linterna y los muchachos bajaron las escaleras de piedra. Había muchas telas de araña y un olor fuerte a vino y a vinagre y a moho.)

Ana: *¡Mirad las cubas, son enormes!*

Tomás: *Yo no sigo más. Este lugar me da miedo.*

Maribel: *Vamos Tomás.*

Los muchachos entraron dentro de la cueva. La cueva era larga y estrecha.
—De pronto Juan dijo:

Juan: *¡Escuchad los ruidos! —Todos escucharon unos ruidos.*

Maribel: *¿Quién está ahí? —Pregunto Maribel,*

Voz: *Grraaaa...muchachos —Respondió una voz misteriosa y profunda.*

Luis: *¡Pronto, salid deprisa!*

(Todos salieron rápidamente. Kira era la última. Kira escuchó la voz misteriosa muy cerca y ella empezó a correr entre las cubas viejas de vino. Todo estaba oscuro. Todos los chicos salieron de la cueva con la linterna. De pronto, Kira tropezó y se lastimó la pierna.)

KIRA: *¡Ay, mi pierna! No puedo mover mi pierna.*

VOZ: *Muchacha, ¿te has hecho daño?*

KIRA: *¿Quién es usted?*

VOZ: *Soy el señor Lute.*

KIRA: *¡Oh, no!*

SEÑOR LUTE: *No te asustes. Yo puedo ayudarte a salir.*

El señor Lute ayudó a Kira a salir de la cueva. Kira miró fuera de la cueva y no vio a nadie. ¡Los chicos no estaban!

«La cuesta de las bodegas» *(a short summary from a student and a rendering of the reading)*

From Storytelling to Reading, Speaking, and Writing

NUMANCIA

The class can begin with the poem «*Numancia*» by Gerardo Diego, or the poem «*El Enemigo*».[11] This offers an opportunity to speak of the land of the Iberian Peninsula and its geography. We can bring a map of Spain and Portugal to guide the students, showing all the regions, mountains, seas and the Atlantic Ocean. If the students are learning about Rome, we can conquer of the land and talk about the strategic situation for the Roman Empire.

Breve historia de Numancia

Numancia fue la última ciudad que luchó contra la invasión de El imperio romano. Los habitantes de Numancia eran celtíberos.

La conquista romana de las costas de Hispania (España) fue corta y sencilla; duró veinticinco años y la conquista del centro tomó más de sesenta años.

Al fin los celtíberos (habitantes de Hispania) tenían una ciudad grande y fuerte : la ciudad de Numancia. Esta ciudad era muy valiente y sus guerreros siempre vencían al ejército de Roma. Después de ocho años de intensas guerras, Roma envió a Hispania su mejor general: Escipión Emiliano para vencer a Numancia. Él decidió rodear la ciudad con una muralla de piedra. Los numantinos, no podían adquirir comida. Así duraron ocho meses de asedio. Cuando el hambre y la sed llegó a su límite, los numantinos prefirieron la muerte a la esclavitud de Roma. Entonces decidieron incendiar la ciudad diciendo: «Sacrificio, muerte y la espada antes que cualquier rendición».

Los numantinos prendieron fuego a su ciudad y murieron bajo el fuego de las llamas. Cuando los romanos entraron en la ciudad, solo había cenizas y no pudieron conquistarla. Desde entonces se recuerda el carácter indómito de los numantinos y su amada ciudad: Numancia.

(Oral tradition; compiled by Diamela Wetzl)

ACTIVITIES SUGGESTED WITH THIS READING:
1. The students read in parts the reading.
2. They identify the cognates.
3. What words do you recognize?
4. What verbs do you remember?
5. What adjectives do you see?
6. Then, we read it all together.

---

11 Selection of poems for the upper grades from chapter 7, "Poetry and Recitation through the Grades."

La leyenda del acueducto de Segovia

This legend presents a good opportunity for the teacher to speak about Spain, its main cities, its geographical location (before it is presented the students can draw a map of Spain in their books), and its main characteristics. It also serves as a good opportunity for the students to enhance their knowledge of Roman architecture by talking about the aqueducts and by drawing this particular aqueduct in their lesson books as well as a map of the Iberian Peninsula. A short summary of the story can follow the oral recapitulation, completing the lessons.

NARRADOR: *Hace muchos años vivía una muchacha en Segovia, que se llamaba Isabel. Era una muchacha joven y bonita que cuidaba a su padre viejo y enfermo. Todos los días Isabel llevaba el agua desde la montaña a su casa con gran esfuerzo. Un día el diablo quiso apoderarse de su alma y le dijo:*

DIABLO: *Buenos días muchacha. ¿Qué haces?*

ISABEL: *Llevo el agua del río a mi casa en este cántaro.*

DIABLO: *¿Dónde está tu casa?*

ISABEL: *Allí lejos, en la ciudad.*

DIABLO: *¡Qué esfuerzo! ¡Qué trabajo! Tu casa está muy lejos. ¡Cómo pesa tu cántaro!*

ISABEL: *Sí señor. Mi padre está enfermo y yo tengo que trabajar para ayudar a mi familia.*

DIABLO: *Qué pena, niña. Tu cántaro pesa mucho y el camino hasta tu casa es muy largo… creo que te puedo ayudar.*

ISABEL: *¿Quiere usted llevar mi cántaro?*

DIABLO: *Oh no, niña. Yo no necesito usar mis manos. Yo soy muy poderoso y con mi magia puedo construir un acueducto que lleve el agua del río hasta tu casa.*

ISABEL: *¿Puede usted construir un acueducto?*

DIABLO: *Claro que sí; pero a cambio de algo.*

ISABEL: *¿Cambiar algo? Yo no tengo nada para cambiar. Mi padre y yo somos pobres.*

DIABLO: *Hay algo que tú tienes y que yo quiero.*

ISABEL: *¿Y qué es?*

DIABLO: *Tu alma niña, tu alma.*

ISABEL: *¿Mi alma?*

DIABLO: *Sí…piensa que si el agua pasa por tu casa, no tienes que trabajar más.*

ISABEL: *Acepto tu oferta con una condición.*

DIABLO: *¿Qué condición?*

«Leyenda del acueducto de Segovia»

ISABEL: *Tienes que construir el acueducto en una sola noche.*

DIABLO: *Está bien. Es difícil, pero mañana aquí tendrás el acueducto y tú me darás tu alma.*

NARRADOR: *Toda la noche el diablo trabajó y trabajó mucho. Las personas que vivían en la ciudad miraron nerviosas y atentas el trabajo del diablo, disfrazado de gran constructor, moviéndose rápidamente. Pero cuando solo faltaba una piedra, el sol salió entre las montañas.*

TODOS: *¡Mirad, solo falta una piedra! ¡Amanece, sale el sol!*

NARRADOR: *El diablo mira al cielo y ve el sol brillante. Furioso grita y el eco llega a todas las ciudades de la tierra. Ahora todos ven que es el diablo y no un gran constructor. Finalmente, en una nube gris, el diablo desapareció.*

La muchacha, ganó el trato y al acueducto le faltó una piedra para estar completo. Desde entonces una estatua del diablo se puede ver en lo alto del acueducto, como prueba de la leyenda…

(oral tradition; adapted by Elena Forrer)

El Cid Campeador

El Cid, caballero leal del rey Sancho, vuelve a Castilla después de una de las guerras a que había sido mandado y recibe la noticia de que el rey Sancho ha muerto asesinado.

JUGLAR: *Muerto el rey Sancho, su caballero, el Cid, sospecha que el hermano de Sancho y nuevo rey, Alfonso, participó en su muerte. Reuniendo a todos los nobles en la iglesia de Santa Gadea de Burgos, el Cid hace jurar al rey Alfonso que es inocente de la muerte de Sancho. Así lo hace Alfonso pero no perdona al Cid su duro juramento.*

CID: *Señor, ¿juráis señor, no haber tomado parte en la muerte de vuestro hermano?*

REY: *No tomé parte. Soy inocente. ¡Lo juro!*

(Silencio)

REY: *Duras son tus palabras con tu rey. Cid, estás desterrado de Castilla. Si alguien os da de comer o de beber será penado con la muerte.*

CID: *Siempre seré leal a mi rey como caballero que soy. Lucharé contra los infieles, defenderé a los pobres, protegeré a los débiles, por mi honor y en el nombre de Castilla y de su rey. Volveré pronto a Burgos victorioso.*

REY: *Toma a tu fuerte caballo Babieca y a doce de tus caballeros y sal de Castilla en el plazo de nueve días y para siempre.*

(El Cid hace una reverencia y sale de la corte del rey Alfonso.)

REY: *Maldigo el nombre del Cid por suponerme traidor.*

JUGLAR: *El Cid desterrado de Castilla, cabalga con doce caballeros hasta el reino de Valencia. Conquista muchas tierras y lucha contra las tropas musulmanas invasoras. También se hace amigo de otros reyes árabes amistosos.*

Cuentan que en su última batalla, su amigo moro, el rey Qadir, le pidió que luchara contra numerosas tribus de almorávides que eran sus enemigas. Durante la batalla, hirieron al Cid de gravedad. Cuando vinieron a ayudarle, él dijo:

«El Cid Campeador»

CID: *Atadme a mi caballo Babieca y sujetadme la espalda con un palo.*

QADIR: *Morirás. Tu herida es grave y sangra mucho.*

CID: *Hacedlo así. Todos creerán que estoy vivo si me ven en mi caballo.*

JUGLAR: *El Cid murió y después de muerto le ataron a su caballo Babieca como él dijo.*

Cuando las tropas enemigas vieron al Cid, pensaron que era un caballero invencible y tuvieron miedo. Todos abandonaron el campo y las tropas del Cid ganaron la batalla. Desde entonces la gente dijo: «El Cid ganó batallas después de muerto».

(oral tradition; adapted by Elena Forrer)

La Leyenda de las Flores Blancas

El joven Cosijoeza, es el rey de los zapotecas. Él es bondadoso, sabio y valiente. Es un gran guerrero. Le gusta la naturaleza. El jardín del palacio está lleno de árboles de flores blancas. Los árboles solo crecen en Juchitán, Oaxaca. El rey Ahuizolt, su enemigo, quiere obtener los árboles de las flores blancas para sembrar en Tenochtitlán.

«Leyenda de las flores blancas»

El rey Ahuizolt envía sus guerreros, pero pierden la batalla. El rey Ahuizolt está furioso y crea un plan. Él habla con su hija Coyolicatzin y pide su ayuda. La princesa ayuda a su padre, el rey Ahuizolt. Ella sale en secreto del reino y va al bosque cerca del palacio del rey Cosijoeza. El rey Cosijoeza ve a la princesa y se enamora de ella. El rey Cosijoeza pregunta a la princesa:
—¿*Quieres ser mi esposa?*

La princesa responde: «Mi padre es el rey Ahuizolt y ustedes son enemigos».

Coyolicatzin vuelve a su casa triste. Cuatro días más tarde el rey y la princesa reciben muchos regalos del rey Cosijoeza. El rey Cosijoeza y la princesa Coyolicatzin se casan.

El rey Ahuizolt está contento, el plan está resultando. La princesa descubre y aprende los secretos del reino zapoteca: cómo construir y cómo envenenar flechas para las batallas.

Pero la princesa está triste. Ella ama al rey Cosijoeza y le confiesa el plan de ella y de su padre. El rey Cosijoeza perdona a la princesa y envía árboles de flores blancas al rey Ahuizolt. Hoy día la ciudad de los aztecas, se llama Ciudad de México y en la ciudad hay muchos árboles de flores blancas.

(adapted by Elena Forrer and Enid Silvestry)

La leyenda de los volcanes

En un reino lejano, en un valle muy grande, vivía una princesa de belleza extraordinaria. Se llamaba Xóchitl, que en lengua náhuatl, la lengua de los aztecas, significa «flor». Ella amaba a un guerrero joven y fuerte, que se llamaba Popoca. Un día, Popoca fue a la guerra. Ella estaba muy triste, pero prometió esperarlo. Después de varias semanas, otro guerrero, Ollin, le dio a Xóchitl una mala noticia: Popoca estaba muerto. Triste y deprimida, Xóchitl no quería vivir más.

Ollin quería casarse con ella. Su padre consintió, y ella tuvo que aceptar. Una semana más tarde, los guerreros aztecas regresaron a casa. Cuando la princesa vio a los guerreros, reconoció entre ellos a Popoca, su amor verdadero. Ella estaba furiosa con su marido, porque todo había sido una mentira.

Entonces ella corrió hacia el lago, y Ollin corrió detrás de ella. Popoca vio que los dos corrían, y corrió también detrás de ellos. Cuando ella paró, los dos hombres lucharon. Ollin, el esposo de Xóchitl, escapó. Popoca buscó a la princesa, pero era muy tarde: Xóchitl estaba muerta. Ella no pudo soportar el dolor y la vergüenza. El guerrero gritó con toda su fuerza y lloró. Después cubrió a la princesa con flores blancas. Los pájaros cantaron tristes canciones.

Esa noche hubo un gran cataclismo en la tierra. Las nubes cubrieron el cielo. Hubo un terremoto terrible.

Al día siguiente, en donde estaba el valle, había dos montañas blancas enormes: una con forma de mujer dormida, y otra alta y elegante, como un guerrero, junto a ella. Las dos montañas están en las afueras de la Ciudad de México, en el valle del Anáhuac, y se llaman Iztaccíhuatl, «Mujer blanca» o «Mujer dormida», y Popocatépetl, o «Montaña humeante», el guerrero que está por siempre al lado de su amor.

(tradición oral; adapted by Nora Hidalgo)

Note from the author:

Estos textos son un ejemplo para usarse en los grados superiores, en 7o o bien 8o grado. La intención no es que dominen cada palabra del texto, sino que se familiaricen con el uso de la lengua mediante la lectura de textos ligeramente por encima de su nivel.

Concepto de la muerte en el mundo azteca prehispánico

La antigua creencia mexicana sobre la muerte, es que no es la vida, sino la manera de morir, lo que determina donde descansa el alma después de la vida.

El paraíso del dios sol, sólo está reservado para los soldados que mueren en combate o son sacrificados. Los que mueren de enfermedad, van al paraíso del dios de la lluvia Tlaloc.

Los demás, tienen que pasar por nueve pruebas mágicas antes de alcanzar Mictlán, otro paraíso. Mictlán es un paraíso en forma de casa sin puertas y sin ventanas.

No es fácil llegar allí. El alma tiene que superar varias pruebas que duran cuatro años. Para ello, un perro acompaña al alma en su camino.

1 *En la primera prueba, el alma tiene que cruzar un río. El perro que acompaña al alma, ayuda al alma a cruzar el río.*

2 *Más tarde el viajero llega a unas montañas juntas. El alma tiene que pasar entre estas montañas.*

3 *En esta región, el alma tiene que subir unas montañas con cuchillos de obsidiana.*

4   *El alma tiene que pasar por una tierra dónde el «viento de obsidiana» corta su cuerpo.*

5   *El alma pasa por un «lugar donde las almas flotan como banderas».*

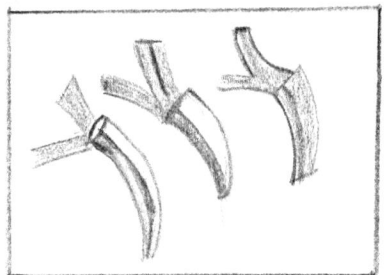

6   *El alma tiene que superar las flechas que se dirigen contra ella.*

7   *En la siguiente región, el alma pasa por un lugar donde las bestias se comen el corazón humano.*

From Storytelling to Reading, Speaking, and Writing

8 *El alma tiene que pasar por una región dónde hay una niebla que ciega los ojos.*

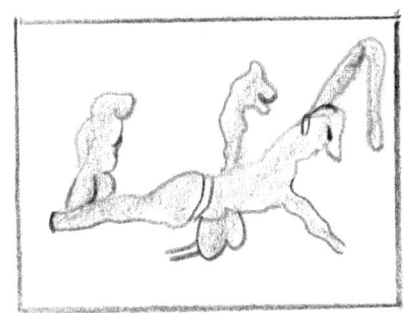

(Illustrations from Codex Vaticanus A, Nahua [12])

9 *Las almas encuentran el camino hacia los nueve ríos y tienen que atravesar esos ríos montados encima del perro que les acompaña (Xoloitzcuintle). Finalmente, el alma llega a Mictlán. Las almas que no llegan a Mictlán, se pierden en otras regiones.*

En Mictlán, el señor de los muertos Mictlantecuhtli, recibe el alma.

(adapted by Elena Forrer [13])

---

12 See http://en.wikipedia.org/wiki/Aztec_codices.
13 Poesía, "Semilla." Atahualpa Yupanqui; www.youtube.com/watch?v=U6U9N8Ntc4g&feature=related.

Los Aztecas

Según la leyenda el pueblo Azteca llegó de Aztlán, un lugar mitológico al noroeste de México. Alrededor de del siglo XIII, los aztecas buscaban un lugar para establecerse y finalmente llegaron al valle de México. Ellos encontraron que la mejor tierra estaba ocupada por otras tribus.

Un día mientras caminaban por el lago de Texcoco su dios Huitzilopochtl, envió una señal: ellos vieron como un águila se posaba sobre un cactus que crecía cerca del lago. Los aztecas vieron que el águila tenía una serpiente en su pico.

«Esta es la nuestra señal»— pensaron ellos. —«Aquí construiremos nuestra ciudad».

National Emblem of Mexico

Poco a poco los aztecas comenzaron a construir casas con juncos y barro. Ellos eran la tribu más pobre del lugar, pues ocupaban las tierras húmedas junto al lago Texcoco. Al principio no tenían madera para comerciar con otras tribus y tenían que pagar tributo a las tribu dominante, los Tepanecs, que controlaban la tierra firme. Ellos hablaban la lengua Nahuatl. En poco tiempo, los aztecas construyen en el centro del lago Texcoco una isla flotante con cañas y con maderas y conectan la ciudad-isla, a la tierra firme por medio de puentes. Estos puentes se podían izar (levantar) en caso de guerra con otras tribus. Los aztecas también construyen unos jardines flotantes en su ciudad: la ciudad de Tenochtitlán. Dentro de la ciudad edificaron templos, casas, escuelas y un lugar para el mercado.

Los aztecas eran feroces guerreros y, con el tiempo, las tribus vecinas pagaban tributo a los aztecas. Su dios Tonatiuh da vida a la tierra y al cielo; pero Tonatiuh necesita sangre humana para su alimento. Para alimentar a su dios, los aztecas sacrificaban a sus prisioneros.

Cuando llegaron los españoles a Tenochtitlán y vieron la belleza de los jardines colgantes (chinampas) y los enormes templos de piedra en medio del agua, ellos pensaron que era un sueño, que era una visión y no la realidad.

(from *The Aztecs*, by Tim Wood)

Los Incas

El imperio inca se extiende de costa a costa por la cordillera de los Andes, principalmente en Perú. Ellos viven en lo alto de las montañas, donde construyen sus casas de piedra. Las dos grandes ciudades incas son Machu Picchu y Cuzco. Estas ciudades están construidas en los altos de las montañas. Los incas principalmente cultivan papa y maíz. Para poder cultivar, ellos construyen un sistema de terrazas en lo alto de la montaña. También hacen objetos de barro y tejen telas con bellos dibujos en su ropa. Los incas no conocen la escritura, pero tienen un sistema para contar los hechos y para comunicarse. Este sistema consiste en un orden de cuerdas anudadas que se llaman «quipus». Los quipus son de diferentes colores. Cada cuerda, cada color, cada nudo, tiene un significado diferente. Los quipus se transportaban por medio de corredores de relevos. Cada corredor corría durante varias millas y entregaba el quipu al siguiente corredor. De esta forma, las noticias llegaban rápidamente de un lugar a otro.

The Incas

Para controlar un reino tan largo (desde el norte de Suramérica hasta el sur de la misma), para los incas es necesario poder comunicarse rápidamente. Ellos construyen en las montañas de los Andes, dos caminos principales con puentes suspendidos con cuerdas. Estos caminos conectaban con todas las ciudades del imperio inca.

Los incas creen que su jefe inca es hijo del sol. Los sacerdotes, los guerreros y los funcionarios, también son parte de la nobleza inca y tienen mucho poder. Ellos hacen ceremonias religiosas. La cultura inca duró poco tiempo, menos de cien años. Francisco Pizarro y sus hombres llegaron en una época de guerra civil, y conquistaron fácilmente todo el imperio.

Los mayas

Entre los siglos 200 y 1200 AD, *muchas tribus migraron en el continente americano. Una de estas tribus fueron los mayas. Ellos principalmente se establecieron en los bosques y las junglas de la península de Yucatán, además de en Guatemala. En el siglo VIII, los mayas fueron una civilización avanzada, culta, productiva y con grandes conocimientos astronómicos. Allí construyeron enigmáticas pirámides, ciudades, centros religiosos y plazas para el juego de pelota. Las más famosas son las de Tikal, Chichén Itzá, Palenque y Copán. Los mayas tenían una escritura por medio de jeroglíficos y seguían un calendario religioso que predecía los eclipses y los eventos futuros. La sociedad maya tenía varias clases: un rey, los nobles, y los sacerdotes. Estas clases sociales vivían en palacios. La clase común cultivaba el campo y construía los templos.*

El juego de pelota tuvo un papel ritual, político y posiblemente económico. Este juego simboliza la lucha de las fuerzas opuestas del universo, entre el bien y el mal, entre la luz y la oscuridad. La pelota en constante movimiento representa al movimiento de los astros.

Los mayas tenían un sistema numérico basado del cero al veinte. Los jeroglíficos narraban historias en los códices y en las paredes de los centros. La obra principal de los mayas es el Popol Vuh. El Popol Vuh relata el mito de la creación.

Los mayas hablaban la lengua maya, esta lengua todavía se habla en algunos lugares de México y Guatemala. En el siglo IX, los mayas abandonaron sus ciudades misteriosamente.

Teotihuacan: La ciudad de los dioses

Teotihuacan fue la primera civilización urbana en el valle de México. Los historiadores conocen muy poco de la gente que vivió en Teotihuacan, solo que vivieron entre el siglo IV y el siglo VIII. Después, la civilización desapareció. Los habitantes de Teotihuacan dejaron unas impresionantes y misteriosas ruinas de pirámides, además de largas calles.

Siglos después, el pueblo azteca ocupó el valle. Los aztecas tuvieron tanto respeto a estas ruinas, que las llamaron «La ciudad de los dioses».

Teotihuacan tiene un diseño geométrico de gran precisión de acuerdo con cálculos astronómicos. Los teotihuacanos conocían las estrellas y su movimiento en el cielo. La calle principal de la ciudad es una larga calle que se llama «La calle de los muertos».

Hay tres enormes construcciones en la calle de los muertos: La pirámide del Sol, la pirámide de la Luna y el templo a Quetzalcoatl. La pirámide del Sol mide 65 metros y es la tercera pirámide antigua más grande del mundo. Esta pirámide se construyó sobre una cueva. Las cuevas, en la mitología antigua de Mesoamérica, significan la entrada secreta al submundo. Expertos piensan que la pirámide del Sol simboliza el mito de la creación de la humanidad. En la pirámide del Sol se practicaban ritos de fertilidad y prosperidad.

La pirámide de la Luna se encuentra en un punto estratégico, ya que es donde se inicia la ciudad. En esta pirámide se ofrecían celebraciones públicas.

El templo al dios Quetzalcoatl significa «La serpiente emplumada». Es un dios que está relacionado con la fertilidad. En toda la mitología de Mesoamérica es el dios principal.

La ciudad llegó a tener entre ciento cincuenta y doscientos mil habitantes. Estos habitantes desaparecieron misteriosamente en el siglo VIII. Los aztecas llegaron posteriormente al valle, en el siglo XIII. Cuando los aztecas vieron las construcciones de Teotihuacan, ellos pensaron que era imposible que manos humanas hiciesen esas construcciones. Tuvieron tanto respeto a estas ruinas, que las llamaron la ciudad de los dioses por considerarlas sagradas.

La historia de la Virgen de Guadalupe

Hace mucho tiempo, en 1531, en una mañana fría de diciembre, Juan Diego, un indio nativo de México, caminaba hacia la iglesia para escuchar la misa. De pronto, en una colina, vio una luz muy brillante y escuchó música de ángeles. En el centro de la luz, vio a una mujer joven y hermosa, con piel morena. La señora le habló:

Juanito, Juan Diego, el más pequeño de mis hijos. —¡La señora sabía su nombre!— Ella dijo: Yo soy la Virgen María de Guadalupe. Habla con el obispo y dile que quiero una iglesia en este lugar para que la gente pueda visitarme y rezar. Yo siempre te voy a proteger, a ti y a tu pueblo.

Juan Diego fue a visitar al obispo. El obispo no podía creer la historia de Juan Diego y no lo escuchó. Él dijo que quería ver una prueba.

Al día siguiente Juan Diego pasó otra vez por la colina de Tepeyac y otra vez vio a la Señora. Ella dijo:

Our Lady of Guadalupe *(ca.1800)*
by Pedro Antonio Fresquís (1780–1880)
(Smithsonian American Art Museum)

—¿Adónde vas, Juan Diego?

—Yo voy a buscar a un médico porque mi tío está muy enfermo.

— Tu tío ahora está bien. —respondió la señora. —Toma estas flores y dáselas al obispo.

Juan fue a casa del obispo y le contó otra vez de su encuentro con la Virgen de Guadalupe. Le dio las rosas al obispo. El obispo se quedó admirado.

—¡Rosas en invierno, muchacho! Imposible. ¿De dónde las has sacado?

—La señora me dio las rosas.

El obispo estaba confundido. Quería otra señal. Entonces Juan Diego abrió su manto y hubo un milagro: el manto tenía pintada la hermosa imagen de la Virgen morena.

El obispo construyó una pequeña iglesia en la colina de Tepeyac donde Juan Diego encontró las rosas el 12 de diciembre de 1531. Hoy en día, hay una basílica enorme en el norte de la Ciudad de México. Es la basílica de la Virgen de Guadalupe. La visitan miles de personas cada año. Hasta hoy, la imagen de la Virgen está intacta en el manto de Juan Diego.

(oral tradition; adapted by Nora Heredia)

El legado del moro

Primera parte

La ciudad de Granada es famosa por el maravilloso palacio de La Alhambra, que fue la casa del último rey árabe Boabdil. La singular belleza de La Alhambra y de sus jardines ha dado lugar a leyendas de tesoros escondidos, lugares encantados y cuentos árabes. Esta es una de ellas.

Hace muchos años, vivía en Granada un hombre bueno y honrado que se llamaba Perejil. Vivía solo con su esposa y un burro para el trabajo. Era aguador, oficio muy común allí por estar la ciudad en lo alto. Los aguadores iban con sus cántaros para recoger el agua de las fuentes del río y venderla.

Una noche, cuando Perejil vuelve a su casa, se encuentra en el camino con un pobre enfermo, que le dice:

—¡Ayúdame! Estoy enfermo, pero te pagaré mucho si me das agua.

Perejil le da agua, pero el pobre hombre, un árabe extranjero, no puede beber y le suplica:

—¡No me abandones aquí, por favor!

Perejil lleva a casa al infiel. Nadie le ve excepto su vecino, el hombre más chismoso de la ciudad.

Su esposa, al verlos entrar, protesta diciendo: —¡No tenemos comida para todos y tú traes un vagabundo! ¿Cómo crees tú que él puede pagar?

Mujer... —dice Perejil—, no importa. Está enfermo y necesita ayuda.

A pesar de los gritos y protestas, Perejil lleva en silencio al pobre moro a su cuarto y le da un poco de agua. El hombre no puede comer ni beber y con una voz muy débil le dice a Perejil:

—Este es mi pago por tu bondad. Alá será generoso contigo.

Y le entregó una caja de madera de sándalo. Poco después, muere sin dolor.

Segunda Parte

Perejil llama a su mujer, quien inmediatamente abre la caja. Ambos ven que en su interior solo contiene una vela y un pergamino escrito en árabe.

—*¡Oh estúpido esposo! ¡Aquí no hay nada de valor! ¡Vamos! Tienes que deshacerte de ese hombre muerto.*

Perejil, en silencio, coloca el cadáver del moro en su burro y sale para enterrarlo.

El vecino chismoso le ve salir y piensa que Perejil ha robado el dinero del moro. Decide ir a hablar con su amigo, el alguacil. El vecino relata lo que ha visto y los dos, ambiciosos, se dirigen de inmediato a casa de Perejil para cogerle el dinero.

Perejil les abre la puerta.

El alguacil le pregunta por el moro y él les cuenta toda la historia.

—*¡A ver, dame esa caja! —dice el alguacil— y cuando Perejil se la da, la abre y no ve nada de dinero.*

—*¡Bah!, está vacía... aquí no hay nada, ¡vámonos! —y el alguacil, cogiendo del brazo al vecino muy enojados, se marchan.*

Al día siguiente, Perejil coge la caja con el pergamino y se la lleva a un amigo suyo, que es un comerciante africano de Tánger que vive en Granada y conoce el árabe. Después de leer el pergamino cuidadosamente, dice:

—*Amigo Perejil, este pergamino habla de un encantamiento dentro de las paredes de La Alhambra.*

—*¿Un encantamiento? —repite asombrado Perejil.*

—*Sí. Aquí dice que dentro de los muros de La Alhambra se encuentra un tesoro magnífico escondido. También dice que repitiendo estas palabras mágicas a la luz de una vela especial, se abrirán las paredes y se podrá llegar a ese tesoro maravilloso.*

—*Pues... aquí también hay una vela... ¡aquí está.! —dice Perejil temblando de emoción y sacando de la caja de sándalo la vela.*

Un olor de esencias y especias exóticas llena la habitación. El comerciante la toma con su mano y la acerca a su nariz.

—¡Es asombroso!, —dice— estas esencias son muy difíciles de encontrar.

Tercera parte

Los dos amigos deciden ir en busca del tesoro. Por la noche, con la caja de madera de sándalo y el burro de Perejil se dirigen hacia La Alhambra. Siguiendo las instrucciones del pergamino, bajan cinco pisos de escaleras hasta llegar a un lugar siniestro y oscuro. Perejil empieza a temblar lleno de miedo. Un murciélago le roza el cuello. Su amigo le tranquiliza, enciende la vela y lee las palabras mágicas escritas en árabe.

Con horrísono estruendo, el muro de la pared se parte en dos y se abre por la mitad. De pronto, un raudal de luz les ilumina. Los dos se quedan sin aliento. Delante de ellos aparece un tesoro increíble que brilla con propia luz: cofres de oro con piedras preciosas de todos los colores, estatuas de oro macizo y bloques de plata.

Cuando se recuperan de contemplar tal maravilla, llenan varios sacos y los suben fuera del muro de La Alhambra.

—¡Volvamos a por más! —dice Perejil.

—Amigo Perejil, el fuego de la vela puede extinguirse. No debemos ambicionar más.

Perejil comprende que su amigo tiene razón. Hacen dos partes iguales con lo que han sacado y los dos se prometen no decir nada a nadie.

Cuando Perejil llega a su casa, su mujer, muy enojada grita y protesta porque les falta el dinero.

Sin decir nada, Perejil saca del paquete una pulsera de oro y se la entrega. La mujer, ambiciosa, pregunta y pregunta a Perejil para averiguar de dónde ha sacado la joya. Al final, el pobre hombre se lo cuenta todo.

Al día siguiente, la esposa de Perejil, vanidosa y chismosa, cuenta a sus vecinas que ahora es muy rica.

El vecino sospecha otra vez de Perejil y convence al alguacil para volver a visitarle. Perejil, que es un hombre bueno y simple, les dice todo sobre el tesoro. Los otros dos quieren que les acompañe a casa del comerciante, a lo que Perejil accede. Una vez allí, le preguntan al comerciante, que les responde:

—Es verdad. En la Alhambra hay un tesoro inmenso suficiente para todos.

Aquella misma noche, los cuatro acuerdan ir al palacio de La Alhambra. El comerciante repite el encantamiento después de encender la vela. En seguida se escucha un gran ruido. El alguacil y el vecino, asombrados y llenos de ambición, bajan las escaleras. Perejil y su amigo salen fuera después de llenar sus bolsillos. Observan al alguacil y al vecino tratando de subir un cofre muy pesado. Como no pueden con él, les piden ayuda:

—Este cofre es muy pesado. Está lleno de tesoros, necesitamos ayuda.

El comerciante les grita desde arriba:

—Ya tenemos suficiente. No queremos más. La vela puede apagarse en cualquier momento y el muro se cerrará para siempre.

—La mitad del cofre es tuyo si nos ayudas.

—No amigos. No quiero más.

El alguacil y el vecino tratan de subir las escaleras con el cofre.

Perejil grita: —¡Subid ya!, dejad el cofre!

A lo que el comerciante dijo: —Se está apagando la vela!, ya no la puedo sujetar!

Los otros dos no quieren soltar el cofre, y de pronto la vela se les apaga.

Suena un ruido profundo y espantoso al tiempo que tiembla la tierra y el muro se cierra de golpe, dejando dentro al alguacil y al vecino, por ambiciosos.

El comerciante murmura con tristeza:

—Es la voluntad de Alá.

Los dos amigos se despiden para siempre con un abrazo fraternal.

Nota: El comerciante árabe se volvió a África y Perejil con su mujer, se fueron a vivir a Portugal. Pasados los años, Perejil se hizo famoso y todos le llamaron Don Pedro Gil, famoso por sus riquezas y por su bondad.

(adapted by Elena Forrer from Washington Irving's *Tales of the Alhambra*)

Don Quijote y Los Molinos de Viento

NARRADORES: *Don Quijote y Sancho iban caminando por el campo de Montiel cuando descubrieron treinta o cuarenta molinos de viento en el campo. Cuando don Quijote los vio dijo a su escudero Sancho:*

DON QUIJOTE: —*La fortuna está guiando nuestras cosas mejor de lo que podemos desear; porque ves allí, amigo Sancho, treinta o pocos más enormes gigantes, con quienes pienso entablar batalla y quitarles a todos la vida. Es buen servicio a Dios eliminar la maldad de la faz de la tierra.*

SANCHO PANZA: —*¿Qué gigantes?*

DON QUIJOTE: —*Aquellos que allí ves, de los brazos largos, que los tienen algunos de casi dos leguas(*).*

SANCHO PANZA: —*Mire vuestra merced, que aquellos que allí parecen ser gigantes son molinos de viento, y lo que en ellos parecen brazos son aspas, que cuando el viento las mueve, hacen andar la piedra del Molino.*

DON QUIJOTE: —*Es fácil ver que no estás versado en aventuras: aquellos que ves allí son gigantes, y si tienes miedo, sal de mi camino que yo entraré en desigual combate.*

NARRADORES: *Y arrodillándose en el suelo dijo:*

DON QUIJOTE: —*Oh! Señora Dulcinea del Toboso, dame valor para la lucha contra estas malvadas criaturas.¡No huyáis cobardes y viles seres, pues es un solo caballero el que os ataca!*

NARRADORES: *Y diciendo esto se lanzó con su caballo Rocinante a todo galope con la lanza en la mano.*

Sancho desde lejos gritaba:

SANCHO PANZA: —*¡Señor !, ¡señor Don Quijote!, ¡que no son gigantes, que son molinos de viento!*

NARRADORES: *Don Quijote se lanzó contra los molinos. En ese momento el viento comenzó a mover las aspas del Molino, golpeando al caballo y al caballero, que cayeron rodando por el campo. Sancho Panza salió corriendo para ayudar a su amo:*

SANCHO PANZA: —¡Válgame Dios!— no advertí a vuestra merced que eran molinos y no gigantes.

DON QUIJOTE: —Calla amigo Sancho, que las cosas de la guerra, más que otras, están sujetas a frecuentes cambios. Por eso yo pienso que el encantador Fristón ha transformado esos gigantes en molinos de viento para quitarme la gloria de su derrota; tal es la enemistad que me tiene. Pero al fin, poco podrán hacer sus malas artes contra la bondad de mi espada.

SANCHO PANZA: —Amén.

NARRADORES: *Respondió Sancho Panza, y ayudó a Don Quijote a levantarse y a subir a su caballo Rocinante. Así, siguieron su camino.*

(adapted by Santiago Muelas from Miguel de Cervantes, *El Ingenioso Hidalgo Don Quijote de la Mancha*)

Los Molinos de Viento

5

INTEGRATING A VOCABULARY TOPIC INTO A STORY OR CONTEXT

5.1 Introduction to Vocabulary through the Grades

Whether we, as teachers, present new or old material, we need to do so in an imaginative way. The children in Waldorf schools live into the images we create for them, and it is important when teaching vocabulary to remember to bring it to the class by weaving together new and old topics. The language teacher has the opportunity to bring inherently imagistic material full of originality and cultural beauty into the classroom and to work in an imaginative way, which enables the children to experience the whole language. It is through mental images that we create a living reality that allows the children to form and express thoughts in the language being studied. The formative qualities of any language enrich children in their own being, cultivating their speech and nourishing their souls.

When we teach a topic, we begin with a story that allows the children to experience the wholeness of the language. During this process it is important to review what has been introduced in the past, and never assume that the children know the topic, particularly when we are teaching vocabulary. When planning the lesson, we need to incorporate the new vocabulary whenever it is possible, first at the beginning of the lesson, through movement and repetition in a rhythmic way, and then through the story. The lesson is created out of the whole topic and then proceeds to the parts, and should not be separated into disparate, unrelated activities, such as by the use of flash cards. When we bring a new topic we try to incorporate it in context, through a story, rather than through dissection and analysis. The children need to experience vocabulary in images and these images will flow when integrated into a story.

The following is an exploration of vocabulary teaching through the grades, beginning with the theme of clothing.

5.2 Grades One and Two

In the earliest grades, children still immerse themselves deeply into the images we create for them imaginatively and they learn through imitation of what they see and hear. When receiving a theme, children enter into the soul of the culture, even without understanding the meaning of

Integrating a Vocabulary Topic into a Story or Context

what they are repeating. Therefore, instead of displaying separate items pulled from a box when building vocabulary, the teacher might weave them into a scene or short story. For instance, when teaching clothing, rather than taking different items out of a suitcase and naming them, teachers can use their imagination and tell a story that includes an adventure involving articles of clothing; by doing so, they will give the students a sense for the wholeness of the language and help to engage their feeling.

Consider the following example for teaching clothing: The teacher brings to class a gnome, a large autumn leaf, small felt cutouts in the shape of clothing, a sack, and a silk cloth for making the rain and the river. The story is told in the foreign language and acted out with the props according to the following narrative in Spanish:

> *El gnomo Martín navegaba en una hoja con su ropita en un atillo. Llovía mucho y su casita estaba inundada de agua. Él sólo tuvo tiempo de meter en su atillo alguna ropita. Tenía frío y su ropa estaba mojada y solo quería tener ropa calentita, una bufanda y una manta.*
>
> *Una hoja grande navegaba por el río y Martín saltó encima de la hoja porque todo estaba inundado de agua. Él navegaba en el río y lloraba porque estaba solo y se había olvidado su paraguas chiquitito.*

"The gnome Martín was sailing on a leaf with his little clothes all bundled up in a cloth. The rain had been pouring down and had flooded his little house. He only had time to pack a sack with some clothes. It was cold, his clothes were wet, and he wished to have warm clothes, a scarf, and a blanket.

A big leaf had landed on one side of the river and Martín had to jump in because everything was flooded with rain. He was navigating the stream, and he was crying because he was alone and had forgotten his little umbrella."

Here the teacher stops and says: "Now let's see what the gnome Martín needs to feel warm."
"What clothes does Martín need to feel warm?"

The teacher will take out the appropriate felt cutouts from the sack after the children respond in Spanish,

> Yes, he needs boots.
> Yes, he needs socks.
> Yes he needs a scarf, a hat, and coat.
> No, he does not have a blanket today, but we can give him a sweater.
> Now that he is feeling better, we will see what Martín has managed to pack in his sack.

Now the teacher uses the felt board or simply shows the students the different clothing cutouts that the gnome Martín carries in his sack, such as pants, boots, scarf, sweaters, socks, shirts, hats, and coat. The students repeat the name of each item as the teacher displays it. Then we may ask the students to repeat again all the clothes and practice the vocabulary asking,

> *¿De qué color son los pantalones? ¿De qué color es el sombrero?, etc. She can then ask the students: ¿Qué es esto? She can also ask a volunteer to put together an outfit for Martín or just ask what he needs because he is cold. At the end, she can play an observation game: the students close their eyes and one takes an item off the felt board. Then they open their eyes and she ask, ¿Qué falta?* (What is missing?)

The story can continue in the next class meeting by telling the class the following in Spanish:

> One day the king of gnomes Martinón was very angry and he decided to send a storm to the kingdom of the duendecillos. Martín, one of the youngest gnomes, jumped on a leaf and he sailed all day and all night on it until the rain stopped. He managed to jump off the leaf when he saw a house, and found a hole under the door to slip under. The house was warm and comfortable and Martín quietly entered a room and laid his head on a pillow. No one was in the room and after a nice nap, Martín got up and looked in his sack for dry clothes.

Here the teacher can repeat the names of the clothing in different ways. Perhaps today the we even bring a small paper umbrella for Martín and a blanket. We can ask a student to pack some of the clothes in the sack and have the class guess what is inside, continuing this several times, and ending with the game "Simon Says."

Another activity to support learning the articles of clothing in the lower grades is to call one student to the front to describe what she or he is wearing. The teacher can call on two or three different students for a few weeks. By doing so, the strong speakers model while the students who need more repetition can repeat the new vocabulary inwardly.

On the third day, after telling the two stories, we repeat a summary of the events in Spanish, but now we tell the children that Martín's clothes are all wet. Martín rests and we begin to hang the "clothes" with a clothesline and small clips. We then ask different children to come to the front and hang his clothes after naming each one: *Una camisa, los pantalones, las botas de fieltro, los calcetines, un suéter y un abrigo, un sombrero*, etc.

This story could be brought to the class one more time by adding more to the story, or just by reenacting and calling students to the front. Guessing games tend to be a favorite for this age. The class could think of someone in class wearing blue pants. Who is this? Another favorite game is to bring a chart with illustrations made by hand. The chart may contain illustrations of a shirt, a sweater, a scarf, a skirt, a dress, a jacket, a coat, shoes, boots, socks, hat, gloves, etc. A child comes to the front and thinks of a piece of clothing from the chart and whispers it to the teacher. The class will have five chances to guess what item it is. The student who correctly guesses the item then comes to the front and choose a new item, and the game continues.

The story of Martín can continue throughout the year, as the teacher stresses different topics and adventures.

5.3 GRADE 3

During the third grade, though the children have been acquainted with the vocabulary of clothing presented the year before, the reality is that some children will be new to the class and many will have forgotten the vocabulary and need to review it. Because it is very important always to review with a lot of repetition at the beginning of the lesson, the teacher could include in her opening "repertoire" (see 3.2 " Beginning Steps: Forming a Repertoire"), movements, and actions that have to do with clothing in the following manner to reacquaint the children and also add new vocabulary: The children, standing, repeat each instruction after the teacher, acting it out together in a group.

> *Por la mañana me levanto, me lavo la cara, me lavo los dientes y me visto. Me pongo los calcetines, me pongo la camisa, me pongo un pantalón y los zapatos. Hace frío y me pongo un sombrero, los guantes, la bufanda y un abrigo. Entro en la clase y saludo a mi maestro. Me quito el abrigo, me quito la bufanda, me quito los guantes, me quito el sombrero y me siento.*

The instructions can be repeated or acted out, since we are just reviewing what the students have learned before: "This is the sweater. This is the scarf. This is the shirt. These are the pants. That is a skirt, etc."

After the teacher has finished a rhythmic oral repertoire and the students are seated, a student is asked to describe what another child is wearing. The class repeats each item's name. After two more students have been called to the front, the teacher asks another student to describe his or her own clothes. The next step could be to ask questions of the class such as:

> "Is Mary wearing a scarf?"
> "Is John wearing gray pants?"
> "What is Elizabeth wearing?"
> "Is Claire wearing a dress?"

By asking questions we encourage alertness and the students pay greater attention to the specifics of the question. The students should answer in complete sentences, adding the color of the clothing. The activity can be finished by saying, "I am thinking of a student wearing blue pants and a shirt. This student is not wearing a scarf. Who is this?"

Integrating a Vocabulary Topic into a Story or Context

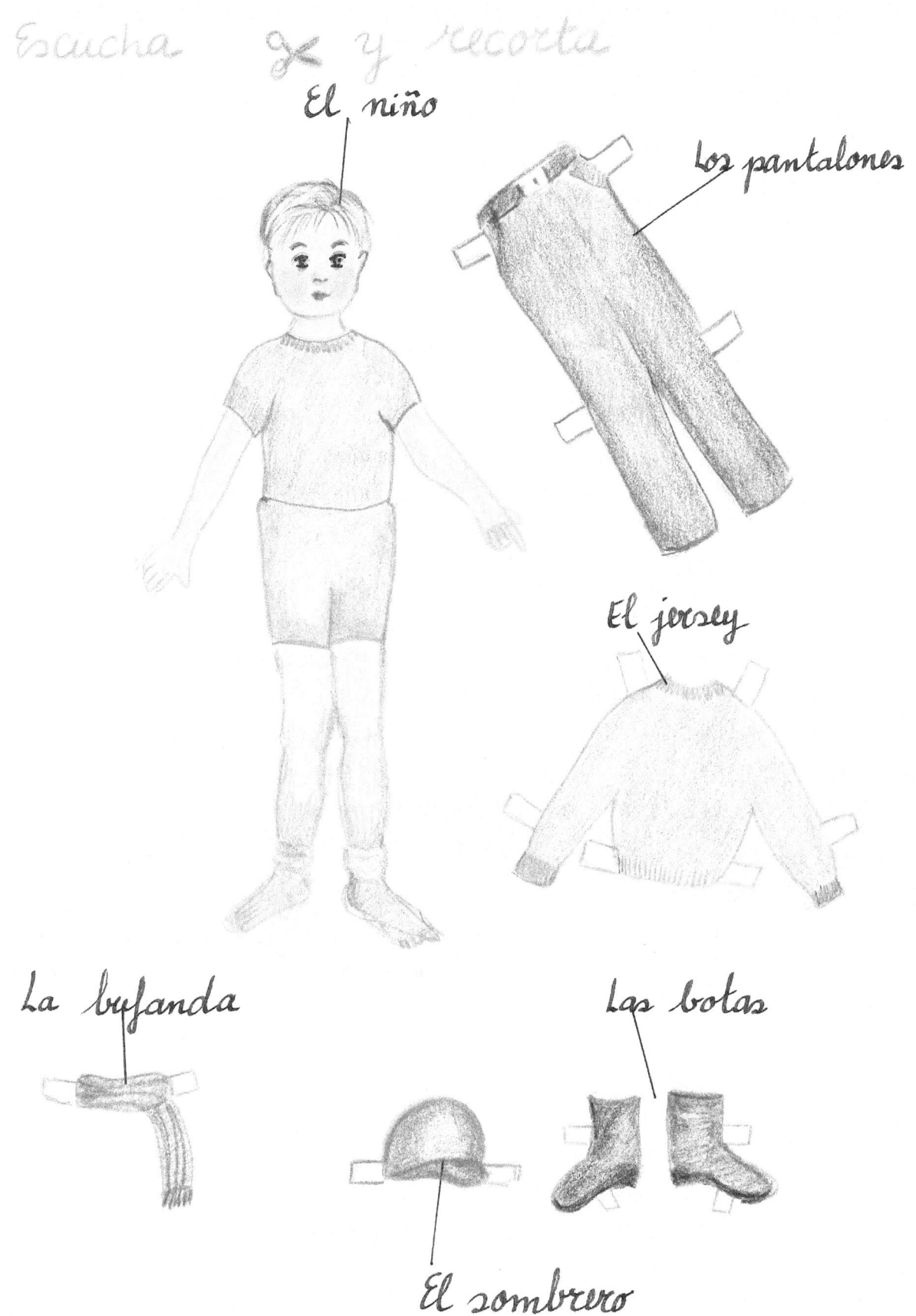

When the students are well acquainted with the names of the clothing they wear, it is helpful to show a chart containing handmade drawings of all the most common clothing, adding new clothes to those learned the year before. At this age it is very important to include an element of challenge as the children learn new things. In the third grade, students will follow less by imitation alone. For instance, we can say, "I would like to know if someone can tell me at least six items of clothing from the chart." Someone steps to the front, and the teacher allows the child to point to or state all the garments he or she knows. After several volunteers have gone to the front, the teacher asks the class, «¿De qué color es el chaleco? ¿De qué color son los calcetines?», etc. After a few questions, the topic can rest until the next lesson.

In the following lesson, we again bring the chart with color illustrations of clothes for a girl and a boy and then repeat all the items; then we say, "I am thinking of something on this chart and will give you five guesses to figure out what it is." If the class is large we can say, for instance, "I see someone wearing something long. What is it?"

In another activity, once we have finished "the repertoire," we can say, "I need a volunteer who can act out everything I say. I will begin from the moment you get up." Once the volunteer has approached the front, the teacher can say,

Hoy me levanto pronto, camino hacia la ventana y miro por la ventana. Hace mucho frío y hace viento. Me visto, me pongo los pantalones, la camisa, los guantes, el sombrero, los calcetines y las botas; bajo las escaleras. Me pongo el abrigo y digo adiós a mi padre. Abro la puerta y salgo a la calle. Camino hacia la escuela, entro en la escuela, subo las escaleras y abro la puerta de mi clase. Entro y saludo a mi maestra. Me quito el abrigo, me quito la bufanda, los guantes y el sombrero y me preparo para la clase.

Another game I often play involves packing a small suitcase with real clothing. I always find it helpful to make drawings of the items if I cannot find real clothing to use. After the whole class is able to recall all the clothing, I like to close this topic by bringing some paper dolls to do a final review. First I distribute an envelope to each student, and then I allow the children to color the clothing by giving them a dictation such as:

Colorea la falda de color verde.
Colorea la camisa de color azul.
Colorea los guantes amarillos. (etc.)

When finished, I give the students a pair of scissors and ask them to cut out the clothing and display all the items on their desk. While I speak, they can dress their paper doll according to my instruction: «Juan lleva botas, pantalones, un jersey marrón y un abrigo azul. No lleva guantes, pero lleva un sombrero».

Then, I ask a student to describe what the paper doll is wearing, using complete sentences. I sometimes also ask the students to dress their paper dolls and then to describe what they are wearing. When this activity is ended the students collect all the pieces in their envelopes.

If the teacher has a spacious classroom, another way to end the block is to play the traditional Hispanic game "El lobo" (see 8.3, "Games").

5.4 Clothing, Grade 4

In the grade 4, the children are well acquainted with vocabulary related to clothing. However, it is always helpful to review by playing "Simon Says" or naming clothing at the start of a lesson. When all recitations or songs are completed, the teacher can recall the vocabulary through a "picture dictation," asking the children to draw two figures—say, David and María—in their Spanish lesson books. The characters of David and María can be familiar characters introduced into the class previously in a paragraph, a story, or a picture dictation.

> *María vive en Madrid. Ella va a la escuela Waldorf. En invierno ella lleva un vestido verde y una bufanda azul. Lleva calcetines verdes, zapatos negros y guantes, María lleva un abrigo azul. Ella no lleva una falda.*
>
> *David es el hermano de María. Él lleva pantalones azules, una camisa roja y una chaqueta negra. David lleva un sombrero no lleva zapatos pero lleva unas botas para la lluvia. Él lleva un impermeable amarillo y un paraguas.*

After they finish their picture dictation, the children can describe orally what they have done and the teacher can write on the board as they give the descriptions.

Another activity is to draw a closet with hangers. Have the children draw the clothes according to the teacher's instructions. (The teacher always needs to explain to the students that the picture-dictation is not for them to complete freely, but rather to listen and draw based on what they hear.) When finished, the students can form sentences such as:

> *En el armario de María hay un vestido, una falda y una bufanda. Ella tiene una camisa y una chaqueta verde.* (etc.)

After they have recalled orally, they can write the title in their books: «El armario de María y el armario de David».

As explained earlier, the new vocabulary should always be introduced in the context of a story. As the students grow older, more content is added to the topic, as it has been illustrated above. The theme of clothing can be reviewed and enhanced in the fourth and fifth grades, particularly when teaching the seasons. Since third grade the students have begun the lesson with questions about the weather, the seasons of the year, and the date. By the fourth grade the students are comfortable forming sentences when answering such questions as:

¿Qué tiempo hace hoy? ¿Hace viento? ¿Cuál es la fecha? ¿En qué estación estamos hoy? ¿Qué ropa llevas tú hoy?

Hoy hace frío y llueve. Hoy no hace viento. Hoy es martes 16 de enero. Hoy es invierno. Hoy llevo…

After the students write in their lesson books, a little paragraph about each season, I usually have them illustrate a wheel with the four seasons.

Many students in the class will be able to write some sentences while others will need help. Therefore you can have the class recall what happens in every season, and what type of clothing one must wear based upon the season and write the sentences on the board, leading the students with questions and writing answers as you begin to collect their thoughts and weave the vocabulary about clothing into work with vocabulary related to the seasons.

5.5 Beginning Compositions

In grade 4, the children attempt to write their first little paragraphs. When they begin their compositions, the children need a lot of direction (see 4.2 "Reading and Writing in the Middle Grades") The teacher needs to plan the writing exercise with plenty of oral practice first through dialogues and activities, as previously described. It can be helpful to guide them with the writing through questions such as:

¿Qué tiempo hace en invierno? ¿Qué hacen los niños en invierno? ¿Qué te pones tú en invierno? (etc.)

If the class is able, they should all write their sentences in their practice books, and then the sentences should be corrected. If there are new students and the class needs extra help, it is always useful to collect their answers on the board and form a little paragraph all together. Here is an example of such a paragraph completed in different seasons and lessons:

En invierno hace frío y nieva. Los árboles no tienen hojas. Los niños juegan con la nieve. Yo me pongo un abrigo, los guantes, un sombrero (gorro), unas botas, un suéter de lana, una bufanda y salgo a jugar. En invierno los días son cortos y las noches son largas.

En primavera hace templado y llueve. Hay nubes y a veces hace sol. Los árboles tienen hojas y las flores florecen. Los pájaros hacen nidos y las mariposas vuelan por el campo. En primavera yo me pongo un impermeable, unas botas, unos pantalones, un suéter y llevo un paraguas.

En verano hace calor. Hace sol y no hace viento. Los niños no van a la escuela y nadan en el mar. En verano yo me pongo un sombrero, una camiseta, unos pantalones cortos y sandalias. Cuando voy a la playa yo me pongo un bañador.

En otoño hace viento y las hojas de los árboles se caen al suelo. Hay nubes en el cielo, hace viento y llueve. En otoño los niños van a la escuela y las ardillas recogen las nueces de los árboles. En otoño yo me pongo unos pantalones, una camisa, un jersey, unos zapatos y una chaqueta.

5.6 Grades grades 5 through 8

Students from grades 5 and up have already become well acquainted with all the clothing. In grades 5 and 6, I usually review clothes at the beginning of the lessons with a picture dictation or individual questions as has been described before. "Simon Says" is always an excellent game for reviewing clothing and can be included in the beginning repertoire. (We can use commands such as "touch or point to some pants"; "point to shirt"; "touch your socks"; "touch or point to some boots"; etc.) It is always helpful to review with questions related to the weather or the seasons and of course, also clothing. Once the students have written short paragraphs about the seasons and the weather, these can also be incorporated into the review.

As the students move into the upper grades, there are specific topics that the teacher needs to reinforce with the class. Vocabulary topics such as food, family members, landscape descriptions, directions, city, hospital, personal descriptions, and so on can be incorporated into dialogues and class practices. Some topics are easy to present, but for some, we need to create a situation where the students can communicate about them, for instance, when talking about health or traveling.

As they also move into the upper grades, certain mastery of verb conjugation is also necessary in their expression. Often the teacher asks for practice with sentences independently from the summaries of the stories. I found it very helpful during the recall to ask the students to write sentences in their practice books dictated in their mother tongue. For instance, in grade 5 if we are reviewing clothes, I can say to them, "In your practice books translate the following sentences into Spanish":

1. She wears a scarf.
2. They wear coats.
3. My grandmother carries a handbag.
4. We wear swimsuits.
5. You (formal) wear a hat.
6. You carry a bag.

7. You (group) wear sandals.
8. He wears gloves.
9. You (addressing a group) wear glasses.

The students need to be paying attention to the conjugation of the verbs and of course, use newer vocabulary. They usually love this recall and become very quiet. When the sentences are finished, they correct them on the board.

When all the sentences are corrected, I ask the students to formulate questions, and usually they do this without writing. When we are finished, I ask them to give me the sentences in interrogative or in negative form: «¿Lleva ella una bufanda?», «Ella no lleva una bufanda». This activity does not take very long, and then we can move to a new grammatical topic or a story.

5.7 WORKING IN PAIRS

In grade 5 and grade 6 it is quite helpful to have the students work in pairs when learning vocabulary in conversation. Often we receive transfer students and notice that the students' ability levels begin to vary more widely. The children have more desire to communicate and we should be able to provide them with these opportunities in the classroom. Often, the students are seated in pairs, and without much commotion, we can ask the students to work with their desk partner in planned dialogues and activities promoting speaking and communication with each other rather than just listening. Rudolf Steiner says quite often in the *Conferences with Teachers*: "You will find that [the children] take tremendous delight in conversing together in a foreign language, while the teacher does nothing except make corrections or at most guide the conversation."[1]

Now we are going to focus on a specific drill, rather than encourage more free rendering. For instance, if we want the class to practice the verbs *llevar* and *ir* and review family, personal pronouns, clothes, and places, the following example can provide the opportunity.

First we give the class a list with three columns. In one column we write all the personal pronouns (we can also include family members or people), in a second column, clothes, and in the third, we write places. When forming the sentences they need to be aware of the verb conjugation of *llevar* and *ir*. The objective is to form sentences individually and to take turns practicing with their desk partners.

---

[1] Steiner, *Practical Advice to Teachers*, p. 135.

Integrating a Vocabulary Topic into a Story or Context

	(LLEVAR)	(IR)
Mi madre	unos pantalones	a la playa
Mi padre	un abrigo	a la escuela
Mis amigos	una falda	a las montañas
Nosotros	una bufanda	a la ciudad
Usted	un jersey (suéter)	al jardín
Mi primo	una corbata	al banco
Tú	unas botas	a la oficina
Mi abuelo	unos zapatos	al campo
Mi familia	un vestido	al parque
Mi amigo	un chaleco	a mi casa
Mi amiga	una camisa	a la iglesia
Ustedes	unas sandalias	a la tienda
Él	un sombrero	al lago
Yo	una falda	al mercado
Ellas	una corbata	a la biblioteca

For instance, the first student might say: «*Mi abuelo lleva una corbata y va a la oficina*».

The second student might say: «*Mi madre lleva una falda y va al banco*», etc.

As you can see, these sentences should become more complex than those given in the earlier grades since the students need to be aware of the verb conjugations of *llevar* and *ir*.

Throughout this activity, the students correct one another's mistakes and translate one another's sentences. At the end, as homework, we can challenge the students to write several sentences in their practice books without the help of the list.

5.8 INTEGRATING VOCABULARY AND GRAMMAR USING CLOTHING VOCABULARY

In grade 7, the students are quite comfortable with simple vocabulary, therefore grammatical objectives, such as teaching the reflexive verb *ponerse*, become more important when teaching this topic. One might choose to give the class (after always reviewing it orally) a list of vocabulary that they have learned in the past, adding less common vocabulary words such as *medias, una pulsera, zapatos de tacón, un collar, una corbata*, etc. The objective is to teach them how a reflexive verb acts in Spanish, and the vocabulary will help the students understand the verbs *ponerse or quitarse*. Since grade 3, the students have practiced many reflexive verbs and they understand well if they are given instructions such as this: «*Me levanto, me visto, me peino. Me lavo la cara, me cepillo los dientes y me pongo los pantalones. Me pongo la camisa, me pongo los calcetines, los zapatos y voy a la escuela».* (etc.)

By grade 5, the students will have moved a step forward in their reflexive activities. For instance, we can formulate these questions:

1. *¿Qué haces tú por la mañana?, ¿Qué haces tú por la tarde?, ¿Qué haces tú por la noche?*

    me levanto /me visto / /me lavo la cara / me lavo los dientes / / desayuno / me peino / voy a la escuela / estoy en la clase y estudio/ salgo al recreo/ como mi almuerzo/ salgo de la escuela/ leo un libro en mi casa / juego con mis amigos/ completo la tarea/ ceno /me duermo.

When they are finished, we can also present the students with a story. They will have to change to the third person singular in the flexible verb, as well as practicing the tense:

¿Qué hace Pablo por la mañana?¿Qué hace por la tarde?¿Qué hace por la noche?

Es temprano por la mañana y Pablo se despierta porque el sol entra por la ventana.

¿Qué hora es? Él mira el reloj. Son las seis y media de la mañana. «El libro» —Piensa Pablo. Él se levanta rápidamente, camina hacia el baño, se lava la cara y se cepilla los dientes, se viste y sale del cuarto muy despacio. Pablo no ve a nadie. Él baja con cuidado y llega al sótano. Pablo busca el libro y no está. Él mira y ve una puerta muy pequeña al final del cuarto. Camina lentamente hacia la puerta y abre la puerta. Pablo entra con dificultad, es muy pequeña.

2. *Dibuja cada reloj marcando la hora de las actividades de Pablo.*

    Cuando son <u>las seis</u> de la mañana se levanta:
    Cuando son <u>las siete</u> de la mañana, él desayuna:
    Cuando son <u>las ocho y media</u> de la mañana, él entra a su clase:
    Cuando son <u>las nueve y cuarto</u> de la mañana, él está en su clase y estudia:
    Cuando son <u>las diez y media</u> de la mañana, él sale al recreo:
    Cuando son <u>las doce del medio día</u>, él come su almuerzo:
    Cuando son <u>las tres y media</u> de la tarde, él sale de la escuela:
    Cuando son <u>las cinco menos cuarto</u> de la tarde, él juega en su casa:
    Cuando son las <u>seis menos veinte</u> de la tarde, él prepara la cena:
    Cuando son <u>las siete</u> de la noche, él come su cena
    Cuando son las <u>ocho menos cuarto</u>, él lee un libro en su cama:
    Cuando son las <u>nueve de la noche</u>, él se duerme:

Integrating a Vocabulary Topic into a Story or Context

However, the students are not conscious of precisely how the reflexive verb is used. They are also not aware of the completed conjugation. Given the complexity of these verbs, teaching students in the context of a situation makes it far easier for them to grasp their use.

After such a review has been completed and the students, now seated, have completed their recall, I show the class a few items such as a mirror, a hat, a scarf, or gloves and say:

Yo me lavo la cara, pero yo lavo la mesa. (I act it out)

Yo miro a John, pero yo me miro al espejo. (Using the mirror)

Yo me pongo un sombrero, pero yo pongo un sombrero en la mesa. (I put on a hat).

Yo me pongo una bufanda, pero yo pongo una bufanda a John. (someone in class).

John se pone los guantes, pero yo pongo un guante sobre la mesa.

Ella se lava la cara, pero ella lava la mesa.

Nosotros nos ponemos los zapatos. (etc.)

Then I ask in English, "What happens in this situation in Spanish?"

I lead the class to the following formulation: "When the action falls upon the same subject, then you use *se, te, nos,* or *me,* depending on the conjugation."

It is important that the students form a real image for the nature of a reflexive action in Spanish by experiencing the situations. These images stay with them and will help them to memorize the conjugation of the reflexive tenses. The students come up with the answer. Then we conclude with a review of most common verbs in the infinitive and the complete conjugation of *ponerse,* conjugated with the pronouns *me, te se, nos, os,* and *se.* We can now write the rule in our books, along with the list of the most common reflexive verbs.

YO	INFINITIVES	(AR/ER/IR ENDINGS +SE)
Me levanto	levantarse	
Me ducho	ducharse	
Me baño	bañarse	
Me lavo	lavarse	
Me visto	vestirse	
Me cepillo	cepillarse	
Me pongo	ponerse	
Me quito	quitarse	
Me peino	peinarse	
Me miro	mirarse	
Me divierto	divertirse	

In the next class we conjugate the verbs *ponerse* and *quirarse* in the present tense and have the students practice the conjugation of *lavarse* and *mirarse*.

PONERSE	QUITARSE
yo me pongo	me quito
tú te pones	te quitas
él, ella, usted se pone	se quita
nosotros nos ponemos	nos quitamos
vosotros os ponéis	os quitáis
ellos, ellas, ustedes se ponen	se quitan

Conjugación en el presente (AR/ER/IR endings + SE)

lavarse   *ponerse*   *mirarse*

When the class has grasped the use of the reflexive verb *ponerse*, we can add more vocabulary words related to clothes to those already known:

This is an example of a longer vocabulary list of clothing that can be added to their review:

los pantalones:	la camisa/ blusa
los calcetines:	las medias
los zapatos:	las botas
las zapatillas de deporte:	el suéter (jersey)
la chaqueta:	el vestido
la falda	el abrigo
la impermeable	el anorak
el traje	la corbata
los zapatos de tacón	los guantes
la bufanda	el chaleco
el bañador	los pantalones cortos
el bolso/a	las gafas
el sombrero	la gorra
las sandalias	el chal (el pañuelo)
el impermeable	la camiseta
la sudadera	la mochila
la ropa interior	el collar
la pulsera	el anillo
el pañuelo	los pendientes/los aretes

Again, we should provide questions that incorporate this vocabulary into real situations. Some examples:

>*¿Qué te pones cuando vas a la escuela?*
>*¿Qué se ponen las muchachas en el día de su graduación?*
>*¿Qué se ponen los muchachos en el día de su graduación?*
>*¿Qué se ponen ustedes cuando hace frío?*
>*¿Qué te pones cuando vas a la playa?*
>*¿Qué te pones tú cuando vas a una fiesta?*
>*¿Qué se pone tu madre cuando va a una boda?*
>*¿Qué se ponen los hombres cuando van a la oficina?*
>*¿Qué se ponen ustedes cuando van a la nieve?*

First, I like to ask some students a few oral questions, to which they can respond individually or in pairs. At the end, I ask a pair of students to ask and answer these questions without reading them first. It is also helpful to have each one report what his or her partner has answered.

5.9 Teaching Vocabulary for Food through the Grades

Third grade is an excellent time to introduce vocabulary for food through the gardening activities in the curriculum. Vegetables and fruits are introduced first and then one can add vocabulary for different grains while preparing food with the class that they can enjoy together, such as salads and soups.

Although cooking projects are very well received by the students, often the vocabulary itself needs to be reinforced with more formal practice in class. For this practice, many days before the activities will take place, I usually prepare a big box containing food items such as jars with different grains, beans, sugar, a small empty box of eggs, sacks with rice and flour, a little box for butter, a small milk container without the label, etc. I also bring a number of fruits and vegetables made out of beeswax, papier-mache, or good quality plastic, and several children's toys of market food such as canned goods or pasta, etc. Whatever is missing, such as meats, I draw on little cards.

The first step is for the students to become acquainted with all the vocabulary for these foods. We start by asking the students several questions and "challenge" them to name as many foods as they can remember. For instance:

>"Let's see how many items you can remember that are green."
>"How many are long?"
>"How many are red?" Orange? Yellow?

"How many are round?"

"What do I need to make a green salad?"

"What do I need to make a fruit salad?" (etc.)

When the children are able to name most of the items in the box in Spanish, then we can display all the items in an improvised "marketplace" and we can play "Going to the market." This is a guided activity with a child coming to the front as the shopkeeper and three others as clients with a basket and some pretend money. Such a little mini-play presents a good opportunity for the children to follow a dialogue: "Converse in the foreign language from the beginning on. Provide many opportunities for the children to speak. Always connect the word to the object"[2]

The rest of the class observes the interaction between the shoppers and the shopkeeper. We usually play going to the market at the end of the lesson during "active work." At the end of the lesson we can present the class with a story such as «La Gallina Marcelina»,[3] and in the following days we can add all the activities of the story as part of our "repertoire." For instance:

Con la semilla siembro, con la regadera riego, con la hoz corto, con el molinillo muelo, con la harina preparo el pan, en el horno horneo el delicioso pan.

The following is an activity for Grade 3, contributed by Marcela Mejía Ronan.

THE MEXICAN FEAST

During the third grade, working with their peers toward a common goal such as a feast lessens somehow the feeling of isolation that children this age experience, and allows them to practice new abilities. The Mexican Feast is a great way to combine and celebrate the experiences and vocabulary covered during practical units such as professions; fruits, vegetables, and grains; market and money; time; measuring; cooking; and of course work on the land.

The goal is to cook a Mexican feast with the children after they have heard stories, represented or acted out the farmer's work in the fields, created a little book with different occupations or foods, learned and played with food vocabulary, played the roles of buyer and seller in the market using basic dialogues, weighing and counting foods, and of course, paying and giving change. It is a challenge to create many opportunities for the children to work hard and all at the same time, so one can divide the jobs by stations. There are various books referenced in the bibliography for this section that you can review for inspiration and to support your work around the ideas of gratitude for our food, the rhythms of the seasons and the Earth, and working together.

---

2 Steiner, *Conversations with Teachers*, June 22, 1919 (CW 192).

3 See "Stories for Lower Grades," page 66.

Integrating a Vocabulary Topic into a Story or Context

Poems, and games for the Mexican feast

The following is a poem to recite while working, by Marcela Mejía, based on a folk game she learned in 1988 from Gloria Valencia Mendoza.

Molinito de Maíz

Muele molinito de maíz
muele los granitos para mí
muele... muele...

Muele molinito de maíz
presiono con mis dedos
el maíz
muele muele

Muele molinito de maíz
gira ya mi brazo mas que un tris
trabajo con ahínco
muele molinito de maíz
con mis compañeros muy feliz
muele muele...

This is a rhyme for little hands from Colombian follore that is great for opening the topic. Change the way you make the *arepitas* so it is not so childlike. You can substitute the names with your students' names, and the final name in the last verse with the main lesson teacher's last name:

Arepitas de Maíz Tostado

Arepitas de maíz tostado
para el papá que está sentado.

Arepitas de maíz dorado
para Ruddy que se ha parado.
Arepitas de maíz trillado
para Andrew que esta cansado
Arepitas de maíz cocido
para el Sr. Loyd que ya se ha ido.

Tortillitas

Tortillitas de maíz
para el niño que está feliz
tortillitas de maíz
las más bonitas para mamá
las quemaditas para el papá.

   (From the Latin-American folklore)

Con mi cuerpo trabajo yo

Con mis brazos aro la tierra
con mis brazos aro yo.
Con mis manitos muelo los granos
con mis manitos muelo yo.
En un tazón amaso la masa
en un tazón amaso yo.
Con mis manitos formo una bola
una bolita formo yo.
Con una prensa formo las tortillas
presiono la prensa, presiono yo.
En el buen fuego cocino las tortillas
en el buen fuego cocino yo.
Con mis amigos celebro contento
nuestro trabajo celebro yo.

   (adapted by Marcela Mejía)

The following is a traditional game adapted and compiled by Marcela Mejía.

Juego: Las cuatro esquinas

Choose four ingredients, tools, or objects that you will be using during the Mexican feast. You may change them every time you play with the children; in this way, they can practice more vocabulary. Use pretend ingredients or cards with pictures to help those who have not yet learned the vocabulary or those who are more visual to understand which words are going to be used. Designate four corners. Divide the class into four small groups and ask the children to choose a corner for each group. Choose one child who is going to be the initial "buyer" from any group.

Remind the children that the group is going to have a smaller number now. In other words, if you have a group of 28 children, you form four groups of seven, but by choosing one "buyer" from one of the groups, that corner is always going to have only six members regardless of who forms that group, while the other three groups will always have seven members each.

Secretly tell each group one ingredient, object, or tool from the four that you presented initially. Make sure that all the children identify which ingredient or tool has been given to them and that they know exactly how many children can be standing in each corner. Ask the more alert students to tell the secret to those in their group who may not have understood.

The child who is the "buyer" has to go to one of the corners and ask, «¿*Tienen cilantro?*» or «¿*Tienen un exprimidor para exprimir limones?*» or whatever the child chooses from the four objects initially presented. If possible, you may want to display the pictures of the four ingredients or objects to help the student remember the possibilities.

If the group doesn't have that object, everyone in the group answers, «*No, no tenemos cilantro, ¡en la otra esquina!*» while pointing the buyer to another corner. At this point, players from each group can make facial expressions of agreement to players of another group, and exchange places quickly while the "buyer" is moving to another corner. If the "buyer" sees them, the "buyer" can try to take one of these two places, and the "buyer" now is the one who has lost his or her space. If the "buyer" does not see the exchange or decides to ignore it, she or he just keeps going to another corner and tries to "purchase" something again.

If the "buyer" asks for the ingredient or object that was designated to that group, the children have to say loud and clear, «*Sí, si tenemos rallador para rallar el queso...*» or whatever it is that they have, and everyone from all the groups has to run and change corners. The "buyer" gets to take someone's spot, each group counts how many participants are standing in that corner, and a new "buyer" goes to the center. The teacher or a designated student gives new ingredients or objects to each group, and the game starts again.

Make sure that when using tools you include information about what each tool is for. For example, instead of just saying, «*el cuchillo*» say «*el cuchillo para cortar*» or instead of saying «*el molino*» say «*el molino para moler*». Start playing with a small group inside of the classroom with only five children, then expand to ten, and then play outside with the whole class. Have fun «*en la otra esquina*».

The Mexican Feast

As the day of the feast approaches, I give the children paper money and set up a marketplace. Carrying some baskets, we pretend to go to the market to buy and trade everything that we will need for our cooking. You may use felted, wood, decorative plastic, and/or real produce. I also use cards with pictures.

You may want to start with an activity that consists of only handmade corn tortillas with salsa and/or butter, sugar, and cinnamon. For this basic approach, you would need only three cooking-working stations. One for grinding previously cooked corn, another one for mixing the ground corn with previously made masa and for pressing the tortillas, and a third one for cooking the tortillas either at the stove or with fire on a grill. When the tortillas are cooked, wrap them in a clean kitchen towel and save them for the end. Since this approach allows only a certain number of children to work, you need to plan something for the rest of the children to do while waiting their turn, you should recruit at least two volunteers. One volunteer can supervise or play with the children who are not with you, and the other one can assist you with the cooking. Some ideas for things children can to do while waiting their turn can be:

> Drawing, making thank-you cards, sweeping and setting the space for eating, visiting younger grades and singing a song, or playing "courtesy cards."[4] Courtesy cards is a game whose goal is to form pairs like "Go Fishing." It provides good practice in asking and answering simple questions in Spanish.

When the first group has completed the work at the three stations, you have exchanged groups with your volunteer, and both groups have had the chance to work, form the children in a circle. Together, everyone speaks a blessing in Spanish, holding hands, and then we break the circle into two lines: one for fixing the tortillas with salsa and one for cinnamon-and-sugar butter. After trying one kind, the children are welcome to join the other line to try the other flavor. This is a good opportunity for the children to express their preferences in Spanish.

After eating, we can include traditional games from «*Las Cuatro Esquinas*» and hear a story from the main lesson teacher.

Don't forget to designate a "Fire Master," who will start the fire in advance, supervise the children when placing and flipping the tortillas on the grill, and put the fire out afterward. It is also important to designate a timekeeper, who will ring a bell at certain intervals to announce that the children must move to another workstation.

Consider talking with the main lesson teacher to make sure that you arrange a longer period. You must consider space, weather, and other classes when planning this activity. You may also

---

4 Refer to chapter of games, "Alto!: Vocabulary Game," page 294.

Integrating a Vocabulary Topic into a Story or Context

want to plan a visit to a parent evening to explain to the families what is it that you intend to do, why, and how they can support the project

Tasks and Foods

1. Handmade blue, white, and yellow corn tortillas (Grinding/Pressing the corn inside the grinder/Emptying the ground corn into big bowls).
2. Making the dough or *masa* (Mixing ground corn with a little bit of previously made dough/Kneading the mix/Forming small balls of dough).
3. Fresh produce station: avocados, tomatoes, green onions, onions, cilantro, chilies without the seeds, and garlic. Making guacamole, *salsa picante y salsa no picante* and chopping ingredients for other dishes (washing produce/shaking/patting/ drying/peeling/taking seeds out/chopping/pressing/separating/mixing/adding/testing/serving)
4. Lettuce with lemon (wash/dry/chop/squeeze/mix).
5. Beans with onions, tomatoes, and garlic sauce (sort/clean/rinse/drain/cook/bring to fresh-produce station/measure/pour/sauté/add/mix/taste). In olive oil, sauté onions, green onions, tomatoes, garlic, salt, and pepper; add this to beans and let simmer, mixing frequently.
6. Red rice. Have rice ready. Separate rice with forks in a big bowl, add some tomatoes and onions from fresh produce station, measure a little bit of water and oil, and warm up (take out/separate/pick up/mix/warm up/serve).
7. Grated *Cotija* cheese and sour cream. Serve in two different bowls. For the sour cream, mix plain yogurt with sour cream to reduce fat and create more jobs. Instruct the children to mix a spoonful of yogurt with a spoonful of sour cream, one at a time (remove cheese from package/cut/grate/serve/mix).
8. Drinks station. Lemonade and Jamaica water (hibiscus) with ice. Have the Jamaica concentrate already made (squeeze/strain/add/mix/taste/serve in pitchers/dry pitchers).
9. Grated coconut and pineapple over ice cream. Have the coconut and pineapple already peeled and cut in big pieces. The children will cut and grate the fruit, place it in two small bowls, each with a serving spoon, and serve ice cream in tiny paper cups (cut/grate/serve/place/save).

These are the tools you will need: Two grinders, two tortilla presses, one big grill, three big bowls, four medium bowls, four small bowls, two graters, six chopping boards and six knifes, four lemon squeezers, one pan to sauté the ingredients for seasoning the beans, and many serving spoons.

Other Activities

- In the language books, have the students either reflect on the experience by drawing the activities, their favorite jobs, foods, a memory of the event or even a recipe.
- Make a recipe book.

Grade 4

In grade 4, I bring to class a large chart with the most common foods. My goal is that the whole class learns all the items and most common foods including vegetables and fruits. Many of these items will be a review from the year before, but now a few more items will be added to the chart. Then the students can begin to record in their books what they have learned in class. In grade 4 as they study the Missions of California, I usually take the students to a Mexican *taquería*. Since the students know that they need to express themselves in Spanish, they take pride in learning all the foods from the chart before we go to the restaurant. I make arrangements beforehand with the restaurant to gain their cooperation in expecting the students to ask and respond in Spanish when interacting with the restaurant staff. The preparation of the trip also includes the practice of a dialogue for ordering and paying in Spanish. The following is one student's chart for vegetables and fruits in the market.

En el mercado

Integrating a Vocabulary Topic into a Story or Context

In grades 5 through 7 this topic will be also enhanced by first allowing the students to identify the food from a poster-size chart which contains handmade drawings of foods. Then we can ask the class to identify the food combinations from Spanish to English as follows:

«*Yo quiero un plato de arroz con carne asada y espárragos*».
«*Para desayunar yo quiero huevos fritos con jamón y salchichas. Para beber, yo quiero jugo de naranja y un vaso de leche*».
«*Para cenar, yo quiero pescado con arroz y ensalada de espárragos con aceite y vinagre*».
«*Pollo frito y espinacas con crema*».

As the students learn to name more foods, they also learn to express how they want these foods cooked. For instance, we add to our vocabulary new verbs such as: fried, grilled, steamed roasted, etc. The chart below can serve as a reference for the students to converse in pairs about some foods. (I chose to teach vegetables and fruits with props in order to leave more room for other foods on the chart.) This chart will also help their visual memory when forming sentences.

Chart for foods

Now that the students are confident with the review of all the foods, we reverse the exercise and I ask them to translate from English to Spanish. For instance:

"For breakfast I would like cereal with milk, orange juice and bread and butter, and a cup of hot coffee with sugar and without cream."

This is a very well-liked practice that can be easily arranged in pairs to practice orally with one another or for the teacher to recall during class.

Our second step is to review and add new vocabulary from less well-known vegetables and fruits. The students can also draw a picture of most common fruits and vegetables found in the market:

lechuga	fresas
brócoli	plátanos/bananas
tomate	piña
pepinos	sandía
cebolla	melón
espinacas	melocotones/duraznos
patatas/papas	manzana
pimientos	peras
ajos	limones
espárragos	frambuesas
setas/hongos	naranjas
zanahorias	mandarinas
maíz	ciruelas
calabazas	cerezas
repollo/col	coco
coliflor	mangos
aguacates	uvas
apio	(etc.)
guisantes etc.	

"You and your partner need to tell each other what you like or what you do not like, use the following model and take turns."

Model

«Me gusta la lechuga pero no me gusta el ajo».
«No me gustan los tomates pero me gustan las peras».

Integrating a Vocabulary Topic into a Story or Context

In grade 6 we review all the "old vocabulary" from our chart and props and add many new words to our repertoire. By grouping the words into a practical context, the students connect immediately the vocabulary to their surroundings by association. However, they still need to place the word in a meaningful sentence or story to remember it. The following is a vivid example of items found in the pantry and in the refrigerator. In this way we enhance their "old" vocabulary with new words such as: cans, bottles, frozen food, pastries, etc.

En el refrigerador/ nevera	*En la despensa*
mermelada	harina
mantequilla	arroz
leche	fríjoles
crema	latas
queso	galletas
mostaza	bote de tomate
salsa	azúcar
frutas	aceite
verduras	pan
congelados	pasteles
carne	cereal
pescado	caramelos
pollo	chocolate
yogurt	latas
huevos	cerveza
salchichas	vino
jamón	dulces
mostaza	vinagre
bebidas/ refrescos	aceite
café / té	miel
helado	sal y pimienta

By grade 6, the students have learned most of the vocabulary, so we should also review the past tense of the verbs *comer, desayunar almorzar,* and *cenar.*

Conjugación en el Presente de Indicativo y en Pretérito indefinido:

	Presente	Pretérito
yo	_____	_____
tú	_____	_____
él, ella, usted	_____	_____
nosotros, nosotras	_____	_____
vosotros, vosotras	_____	_____
ellos, ellas, ustedes	_____	_____

Now the students are ready for a different type of practice, such as a dialogue like this:

¿Qué comiste ayer en la cena? (¿Qué cenaste?)

¿Qué comes tú en el desayuno?

¿Qué almorzaste ayer?, Etc.

After they are finished with their speaking practice, the students are ready for different activities such as these:

- Creating a menu for a restaurant. The menu will have different sections: *El desayuno, El almuerzo o La comida, y La cena*. The menu will have: *Bebidas frías. Bebidas calientes; Entradas, Aperitivos, Sopas y Ensaladas. Plato principal con verduras, ensaladas, acompañamientos y postres.*
- Describing the foods inside the refrigerator and in the pantry in their home.
- Creating a menu for a party with salads, appetizers, other dishes and drinks.
- Creating a dialogue that takes place in a restaurant with two guests and a waiter/waitress. The students create a skit and a menu.

During the lesson we can also plan to give the students a reading related to the vocabulary topic. The example *En el río* presented in chapter 4, "From Storytelling to Reading and Writing," illustrates how a vocabulary topic can be introduced into the context of a story. After telling or reading, the students will be asked to recall the story. This strategy will force the students to remember and sequence the information of the language according to the sound, thus creating a mental picture of this particular situation.

Integrating a Vocabulary Topic into a Story or Context

The following are two quotations by Rudolf Steiner on the absorption of language through the years, and the importance of offering images to the children when acquiring language:

> Thus from the seventh to the ninth year we should not attach importance to translation—that is to say, rendering a word in one language by a word in another—but the children simply learn to speak in the language, connecting the words with the external objects, so that they do not need to know, or rather do not need to think of the fact that, when they say "table" in English, it is called *Tisch* in German.[5]

> If you bring the analytical perspective into a picture, that is good. You should always work toward developing a picture, and analysis is part of that picture.... No hour should pass without the child experiencing something pictorially.

> You should not begin teaching them grammar before the age of nine or ten. Develop your language teaching during the earlier stages purely from speaking and from the feeling for what is spoken, so that the child learns to speak from feeling. At that age, which is, of course, not completely fixed but lies between the age of nine and ten, you should begin with grammar. Working with the grammar of a language is connected with the development of the "I."[6]

Children learn best through stories because they are able to form a mental picture of a situation. Even though the teacher needs to review particular topics, such as clothing, food, or housing, the above activities complement the storytelling work. The activities are prepared and given in a manner similar to that which we use to tell a story. The teacher must connect deeply and consciously with the vocabulary, be able to visualize it clearly and weave it into games, dialogues, and exercises and review it in a lively and imaginative way. As the students grow older, there are always ways to incorporate new and expand old vocabulary.

---

5 Stockmeyer, *Rudolf Steiner's Curriculum for Waldorf Schools*, p. 63 (trans. revised).
6 Steiner, *Faculty Meetings with Rudolf Steiner*, pp. 371–372 and 764.

5.10 Outline of Contents and Vocabulary by Grades for Spanish

	1st	2nd	3rd	4th	5th	6th	7th	8th
Greetings	→							
Body Geography	→							
Family	→							
Classroom Objects	→							
Seasons and Weather	→		→					
Activities During the Seasons	→				→			
Numbers	→							
Days of the Week			→					
Months			→					
Colors	→							
Clothes	→							
Daily Activities (action verbs)	→							
Fairytales	→							
Animals/ Fables	→	→						
Vocabulary with a seasonal content	→							
The House			→					
The Garden			→					
The Farm			→					
Food			→					
Occupations/Professions			→					
The Clock/Telling Time			→					
Routine of the day				→				
The date					→			
Sports						→		
Retelling Stories	→							
Transportation (The city and neighborhood)				→	→			
Giving Directions				→				
Places: the mountains, church, store, etc.					→			
Traveling							→	
Geography of region				→				
Geography of Spanish-speaking countries					→			
Personal tastes and preferences					→			
Description of Emotional States and Moods						→		
Health							→	
Topics from History of Spanish-speaking countries					→			
Biographies (Artists, Poets, Musicians, historical personalities)							→	

6

TEACHING GRAMMAR:
FROM THE PICTURE TO THE CONCEPT

Children up to the age of nine must be grounded in the human, that is, they need to be in contact with nature, not with what emanates from media imagery. It is later, between ages nine and ten, when children acquire in their movements an element of purpose motivated by an awareness of "I," or one's self. As a result of this awareness, children begin to feel separate from their surroundings. From this point forward, insights into the elements of language have to be *awakened* rather than taught, so that the children can come to understand the grammatical aspects and rules of the language. However, careful consideration has to be given to how to bring these aspects into the lesson; it is the task of the teacher to evoke these capacities in the children and to awaken them to the particularities of the language.

When talking about grammar, Rudolf Steiner explained that the first step for teachers is to acquire a feeling for the genius of language and an understanding of how *wise* language is. For Steiner, language is a smarter and wiser creation than even we are. By consciously penetrating the structures of its genius, we can feel the active power (the "language genius") of the spirit of language. As teachers, we can stimulate the will impulse in children by allowing a "flow of the language" in ourselves, which arises when we fully feel its sound and beauty, especially in poetry, and by understanding the structures of the language we speak. Steiner also explained the danger of language becoming abstract through our teaching when we lose awareness in our speech—in other words, detaching or abstracting language from its source, its connection to the real world, in the formation of consonant and vowels.[7]

To elevate the structure of language to consciousness we must not become familiar with language from a pedantic point of view, but through awareness of the living reality of the language. For Steiner, language education is not a matter of abstract teaching, but the realization of a *living reality* as a result of observation. His point is that we should educate children to become aware of their surroundings and fellow beings. By bringing awareness to the elements of grammar, we move precisely toward this point. Steiner posed and answered this question:

> What do we do when we raise unconscious speech to the grammatical realm, to the knowledge of grammar? We make a transition with our students: We lift speech from

---

[7] See chapter 7, "Poetry and Recitation through the Grades."

the unconscious into the conscious realm.... Unconsciously or semiconsciously, human beings do indeed use the world as a ladder up which to climb in a manner that corresponds to what we learn in grammar.[8]

Karl Stockmeyer summarizes Steiner's indications:

> Before the ninth year children's relationship to language is a feeling one. Their self-awareness could not develop if we did not introduce them to the greater thinking quality of language. It is therefore important to bring this thinking element to children through grammatical rules taught in an appropriate way.[9]

We prepare our future grammar lesson for the early grades by orally rendering stories and descriptions so students develop a feeling for speech and its musical element. Gradually, the children become acquainted with most of the vocabulary that refers to their surroundings and are able to give brief descriptions, but they are not aware of the elements of the Spanish language, their placement, and their agreement in the sentence. Of course, they are also unaware of verb tenses and conjugation. By grade 4, the language teacher gradually begins to awaken this unconscious element and brings awareness to the students when they form their sentences. For instance, when children up to grade 4 form sentences, they are unaware of the gender of the nouns or the agreement with the adjective. However, after grade 4, we point out these elements, allowing the children to draw conclusions and judgments in their observations so that, even later, they can form concepts. Instead of just learning nouns, verbs, and adjectives, the first step is for students to acquire a feeling for the language and its genius and for the teacher to create a *living* lesson to awaken gradually the children's awareness of the whole language. Here are some thoughts regarding nouns, adjectives, and verbs in relation to the external world and human beings:

> Nouns are names for objects, for objects that in a sense are self-contained in space. It is not without significance for us that we find such objects in life. All things that can be expressed by nouns awaken us to the consciousness of our independence as human beings. By learning to name things with nouns, we distinguish ourselves from the world around us. By calling a thing a table or a chair, we separate ourselves from the table or chair; we are here, and the table or chair is there.[10]

Then Steiner explains that it is another matter when we describe things with adjectives. For instance, "When I say, 'the chair is blue,' I am expressing a quality that unites me with the chair. The

---

8 Steiner, *Practical Advice for Teachers*, p. 55.
9 Stockmeyer, *Rudolf Steiner's Curriculum for Waldorf Schools*, p. 33 (trans. revised).
10 Steiner, *Practical Advice to Teachers*, p. 56.

Teaching Grammar: From the Picture to the Concept

characteristic that I perceive unites me with the chair. By naming an object with a noun, I dissociate myself from it; when I describe it with an adjective I become one with it again."[11]

When talking about verbs Steiner explains their intrinsic quality. If for instance I say, "Sarah is painting," I participate in the action of Sarah's physical body; in a certain way I and my listeners join in the activity inwardly. On some level, the "I" of the speaker has united with the gesture, by evoking the action with speech and movement. A child speaking in this way understands the meaning, but is not grammatically conscious. "If I say a verb—for example, 'a woman writes'—I not only unite with the being in relation to whom I used the verb, I also do with her what she is doing with her physical body. I do what she does—my 'I'-being does what she does.... I unite my 'I' with the physical body of the other when I use a verb."[12]

In the lower grades teachers incorporate a number of actions in their *repertoire*, and the students act them out, connecting themselves with each activity. By doing this, through both speech and movement, the "I" of the child unites with the action. The following is a list of activities that the children could practice in class:

Con mis ojos miro	(With my eyes I see)
Con el lápiz escribo.	(With the pencil I write)
Con mis manos trabajo.	(With my hands I work)
Con el pincel pinto.	(With the brush I paint)
Con los brazos nado.	(With my arms I swim)
Con las orejas escucho.	(With my ears I listen)
Con el corazón siento.	(With my heart I feel)
Con la boca hablo.	(With my mouth I speak)
Con la escoba barro.	(With the broom I sweep)
Con los pies salto.	(With my feet I jump)
Con las piernas corro.	(With my legs I run)
Con las orejas eschucho.	(With my ears I listen)
(etc.)	

By the end of grade 3 we probably have enhanced the repertoire with more activities such as:

Con el molinillo muelo.	(With the grinder I grind)
Con las semillas siembro.	(With the seeds I plant, etc.)
Con la regadera riego	
En la cocina cocino.	

---

11 Ibid.
12 Ibid.

Con la masa amaso.
Con el peine me peino
Con el vaso bebo
En mi cama duermo.
Con la aguja coso
Con el tinte tiño
Con la flauta toco
(etc.)

After the children are seated we can ask the following questions:

¿Qué haces con las manos?
R — Con las manos trabajo.

| *¿Qué haces con el pincel?* | (What do you do with the brush?) |
| *R —Con el pincel pinto.* | (With the brush I paint.) |

| *¿Qué haces con la boca?* | (What do you do with your mouth?) |
| *R —Con la boca hablo.* | (With my mouth I speak.) |

¿Pintas con el pincel o escribes con el pincel?

By presenting the question as a dichotomy we can help the new or the slow child to understand and also participate with a response. At this age children can follow the teacher with a number of questions. It is important to remember that if we continue to use actions relying solely on a rhythmic level as the students get older, without elevating the lessons to awaken the children's conscious responses, we have not completely engaged their will. If in later years the class is conducted in such a way that new vocabulary is only introduced in a rhythmic way, the students will begin to feel "that we are not learning in the Spanish class." We must activate the rhythmic with the conscious awakening.

It is quite possible for the students to arrive at **grade** 4 having already learned more than thirty or forty verbs. Until now they have developed a feeling for the language, and have perceived the whole activity by moving along when repeating actions; the children are still connected to their surroundings. Now is when we can look back at these actions and by finding the infinitives, the children can observe the changes in the verbs. Because at around this age the children begin to become more self-conscious, the language teacher can bring to their awareness all actions they repeated in the previous grades as follows:

«Yo pinto con el pincel».

The action is *pintar. Yo miro con mis ojos,* and we point out that the action is *mirar.* After several infinitives have been brought to the attention of the students, they and the teacher can begin to list them on the blackboard:

Cantar, hablar, tocar, pintar, escribir, beber, correr, leer, vivir, jugar, dormir, saltar, nadar, cocinar, caminar, aprender, trabajar, comer, mirar, comprender, estudiar, comer, escuchar, pensar (etc.)

Then, we could ask them to comment on their observations. Soon they will notice the radical and the three endings for Spanish: *AR, ER, IR.* Then, we can highlight the verbs with three colors according to their endings or place them in three columns. When the students have become aware of these endings, then they are ready for the introduction of conjugation. For instance if we chose the verb *tocar* in the present tense as an example, we can toss a ball to one of the students and say:

TEACHER:	*Yo toco la guitarra. ¿Qué instrumento tocas tú?*
	—*Yo toco el violín.*
TEACHER:	*Tú tocas el violín.*

These answers are repeated by the whole class and then written on the board:

«*Tú tocas el violín*».

TEACHER:	*¿Qué instrumento tocas tú?* (Directing the answer to a boy)
	—*Yo toco la flauta.*
TEACHER:	*Él toca la flauta.*
ALL TOGETHER:	*Él toca la flauta.*
TEACHER:	*¿Qué instrumento toca ella?* (Indicating a girl)
	—*Yo toco el piano.*
ALL TOGETHER:	*Ella toca el piano.*

Now the teacher explains to the class the formal "you" in Spanish by saying:

TEACHER:	What instrument do I play?
CLASS:	*Tú tocas la guitarra.*

Now is the moment when the teacher can say:

TEACHER:	*Tú tocas la guitarra* or *usted toca la guitarra.* What do you think?

CLASS:	*Usted toca la guitarra.*
TEACHER:	Why do you think it is *usted* instead of *tú*?
CLASS:	Because you are talking to a teacher, and this is why we use *usted*.

We then, can talk about the two pronouns *tú* and *usted*.

Until now, we have established all the personal pronouns and the conjugation in the singular of the AR ending for regular verbs. In the following lessons we can continue with the pronouns in the plural and the rest of conjugation. For instance:

TEACHER:	*¿Qué instrumento tocan ustedes?*
CLASS:	*Nosotros tocamos la flauta.*
TEACHER:	*¿Qué instrumento tocan los niños de segundo grado?*
CLASS:	*Ellos tocan la lira.*

We then add on the board *ellos*. Here we can direct the question to the class:

TEACHER:	How many girls play the violin?

Soon we will have a few hands up and then we can say:

TEACHER:	*Ellas tocan el violín.*

Now that we have established *nosotros, ellos* and *ellas*, we move into the form *Ustedes*. Which is far more complicated. The teacher can ask:

TEACHER:	*¿Tocan ustedes la flauta?*
CLASS:	*Sí. Nosotros tocamos la flauta.*
TEACHER:	*Ustedes tocan la flauta.*

It is important to establish all the forms of *you* by again reviewing with the class:

TEACHER:	How many ways do I have in Spanish to say the word *you*?
CLASS:	*Tú, usted, and ustedes.*

We can now ask the class *when* to use each one. At this point most of the personal pronouns and the endings are established when conjugating *tocar* in the present tense, with the exception of *vosotros*. Some teachers do not introduce *vosotros* in order to avoid confusion at this early stage, but everyone should feel free to do so or not according to personal preference.

Once the regular conjugation for the *Ar* verbs in the present tense has been established, we can move on to practice other *AR*-ending regular verbs:

TEACHER:	*Tú trabajas en la escuela.*
	¿Dónde trabaja él?
CLASS:	*Él trabaja en la escuela.*
TEACHER:	*¿Dónde estudian los estudiantes?*
CLASS:	*Ellos estudian en la clase.*
TEACHER:	*¿Pintamos nosotros en el jardín?*
CLASS:	*No, nosotros pintamos en la clase.*
	(etc.)

In following lessons, during the recall, the teacher needs to make sure that what has been taught is living in the child consciously. At this age the children become confused when learning personal pronouns in Spanish, particularly differentiating *tú, usted, ustedes, and ellos.* Careful attention has to be given to this step.

In grade 4 it is also appropriate to introduce the irregular conjugation of *tener*, a verb the students have been well acquainted with orally in the lower grades. Now we can also help the students to become aware of its conjugation by referring to different items or to the students themselves:

TEACHER:	*Yo tengo una bufanda. ¿Qué tienes tú?*
CLASS:	*Yo tengo un sombrero.*
TEACHER:	*Él tiene un sombrero, y él también tiene un sombrero.*
	Ellos, John and Kyle tienen un sombrero.
	(etc.)

From grade 5 on, Spanish teachers will dedicate a great deal of time to verb conjugation by encouraging the students to form sentences. One way to help the students become active and aware of the changes in the verb is for the teacher to give a few examples in their mother tongue, and have the students translate the sentences focusing on the verb endings. Since this activity will leave many children still unaware, it is helpful to have them write the sentences in their practice book and then to correct the grammatical errors together on the board. In this way the students not only grasp the feeling element but also the thought element through recognizing the rules in the verb changes. For instance, if the conjugations in the regular present tense of the *AR, ER, IR* ending of regular verbs have been established, we can begin with a few oral examples such as:

> You (group) study Spanish in the school.
>
> We paint with Miss Smith.
>
> The children write in their lesson book.
>
> We play the flute in the classroom.
>
> He runs to the park.
>
> She lives in Sacramento. (etc.)

Now that some practice has been reviewed orally, we can do the same in writing. In this way the whole class becomes active, not just a few students.

> We clean the classroom
>
> They dance after class.
>
> She writes in her book. (etc.)

When we conjugate these verbs, we should perform the actual activity or use a humorous example to awaken the children's consciousness as much as possible.

It is usually during grade 5 that we can add the rest of the regular verb conjugations, *ER* and *IR*, and also a few irregular verbs, such as *ser, estar, tener, dormir, jugar, volver, venir*, and *ir*, to name a few. In the upper grades we can continue in this fashion with other verb conjugations, more practice, and more irregular conjugations in the present tense. The verb conjugations can also be recited rhythmically at the beginning of the lesson as part of the *repertoire*.

When talking about conjugation, Steiner explains that the child's soul can become more flexible when we, for example, pose a sentence in English and one in Latin, and then direct the child's attention to the sentence in Latin in which the "I" is inside the verb. This evokes the child's feeling capacities in such a way that those capacities can disappear and become assimilated once the child no longer needs them.

Rudolf Steiner indicates that these examples need to be part of a free practice, aimed at illustrating the grammatical rules; rather than copying the teacher's examples from the board, the students should be led to formulate their own:

> You will have to see to it that the children do not write down these sentences illustrating grammatical rules. Instead of being written down in their notebooks, they should be worked on; they come into being, but they are not preserved. This procedure contributes enormously to the economical use of your lessons, particularly foreign language lessons, for in this way the children absorb the rules in their feelings and after a while drop the examples.[13]

---

13   Steiner, *Practical Advice to Teachers*, p. 124.

Teaching Grammar: From the Picture to the Concept

Steiner suggests the use of "subjectless sentences" to engage the students through reference to real life, natural events that they can observe, such as the greening of a meadow after the rain. It is through our observations that we first form *conclusions* in everyday life. Then, conclusions pass on to *judgments,* and from judgments we form *concepts*. This progression can guide our approach to teaching grammar. In *Practical Advice to Teachers*, Steiner gives the following example: "Start by shaping a complete sentence and not more than a sentence. Point to what is going on outside—at this very moment you would have an excellent example."[14] Then, he gives the following examples:

"It is raining." —(conclusion)
"The meadow is green."—(judgment)
"The green meadow."—(concept)

In Spanish:

«*Está lloviendo*».
«*La hierba es verde*».
«*El prado verde*» or «*la pradera verde*».

The first step is to draw attention to something that is happening around us, such as: "It is raining." Steiner explains that we arrive at this sentence as a *conclusion* of what we experience; mainly it is an expression of activity. Then, he adds, we draw the attention of the student to what happens around this activity, *where* it is raining, leading the students to the *judgment:* "The meadow is green" or "The meadow is greening" *(la pradera verde está creciendo)*. From this sentence, we then lead the student to the *concept:* "The green grass" or "The green meadow."

We direct the students' attention toward the expression in the foreign language by using logic and by eliciting their feelings in connection to the sentence. For instance in these sentences from the activity "it is raining," we tell the students to think of what happens when it rains in the meadow, leading the students to say, "the grass is growing green," and then directing the students to the last step, "the green grass" (concept). Steiner reminds us to teach grammar in a practical and economical way as part of what is happening around us, not only through readings or a text book, but as part of a living reality. The examples formed in class are not to be written down and fossilized that way, but just practiced joyfully as ephemera used to illustrate a rule, which is the only thing to be written in a notebook by the students.

In a large classroom when reviewing with the students some grammatical topics, for instance the uses of *ser* and *estar*, I tell the students a situation in English, and I have them express it

---

14 Ibid., p. 121

in Spanish. After we have done several examples I let the students create their own sentences in their practice book. This is not a practice copied from the board, but a practice that allows all the students to take part, instead of calling on just a few. When they have understood the different uses of *ser and estar*, then they write this rule in their books. Let's look now at the introductions of these two verbs through the grades.

In the grade 3, language teachers bring many descriptions to the children. For instance, using illustrations, teachers can ask the students whether the table is long or short; whether climbing a mountain is easy or difficult; whether the door is closed or open; whether a shirt is clean or dirty; whether a cup of coffee is hot or cold; whether the day is light or dark; or whether a road is narrow or wide, small or big.

These practical descriptions begin to foster in children a sense for lasting or temporal description of the state of "being" as we practice *ser* and *estar*. As children enter grade 4, these characteristics are pointed out during class by bringing some awareness to their speech. However, by grade 5, it is important to bring awareness to children of how to use of *ser* and *estar*. This will be a guided process to awaken in students an understanding of the various uses of *to be* in Spanish.

Now let's consider possible steps to take during this process.

In grade 5 we can review some of the descriptions learned in other years by practicing sentences referring to the following topics:

Yo soy:	*Mi casa es:*	*Mi animal es:*
alto – alta	grande	un gato, una gata
mediano – mediana	mediana	un perro, una perra
bajo – baja	pequeña	un pájaro
rubio – rubia	ancha	una tortuga
moreno – morena	estrecha	un ratón
pelirrojo – pelirroja	antigua	un conejo
simpático – simpática	moderna	un caballo
agradable	de color: blanca	un pez…
inteligente	verde, azul…	
listo – lista		
cariñoso – cariñosa…		

In grade 5, the students will be able to form quite a few sentences based on their familiarity and feeling for the meaning of these phrases, but often they will be confused about when to use *ser* or *estar*, because they cannot differentiate the situations logically. A good way to begin is to point out the uses of *estar* when we talk about "location." It is good to present the students

Teaching Grammar: From the Picture to the Concept

with two different situations and then ask them what they notice. For instance in the following sentences we bring *ser* "description" and *estar* "location":

Yo soy baja, yo soy morena y soy la maestra de español.

And then we can say:

Yo estoy en la escuela. La escuela está en California. California está en Norteamérica.

After presenting to the class these two situations, students will notice the two different uses. They might say, "You are using *ser* when you describe yourself and *estar* when you talk about location."

The students will need more examples for *ser* before they fully comprehend its placement in different situations, so we will concentrate on *estar* first. Once the students are able to differentiate this first step in the use of *estar*, then before adding other uses of *estar*, we move on to examples related to the class that use *estar* as location. For instance:

Yo estoy en California
Tú estás en la escuela.
Mi gato está en mi casa.
Mi madre está en la oficina.
Nosotros estamos en la escuela.
Ellos están en la granja.
Yo estoy en la clase de español.
Usted está delante de la clase.
Tú estás detrás.

Another example for practicing "*estar* location" is to present the students with the layout of a house from the reading «*En la casa de los Tíos*» as suggested in the chapter "From Storytelling to Reading, Speaking, and Writing." We incidentally also review the following vocabulary from "the house":

la sala el tejado, el dormitorio, el suelo, el piso, el sótano, el cuarto misterioso, la alberca (piscina), la planta de arriba, el jardín, el patio, la cocina, las escaleras, la planta de abajo, el cuarto de baño (etc.)

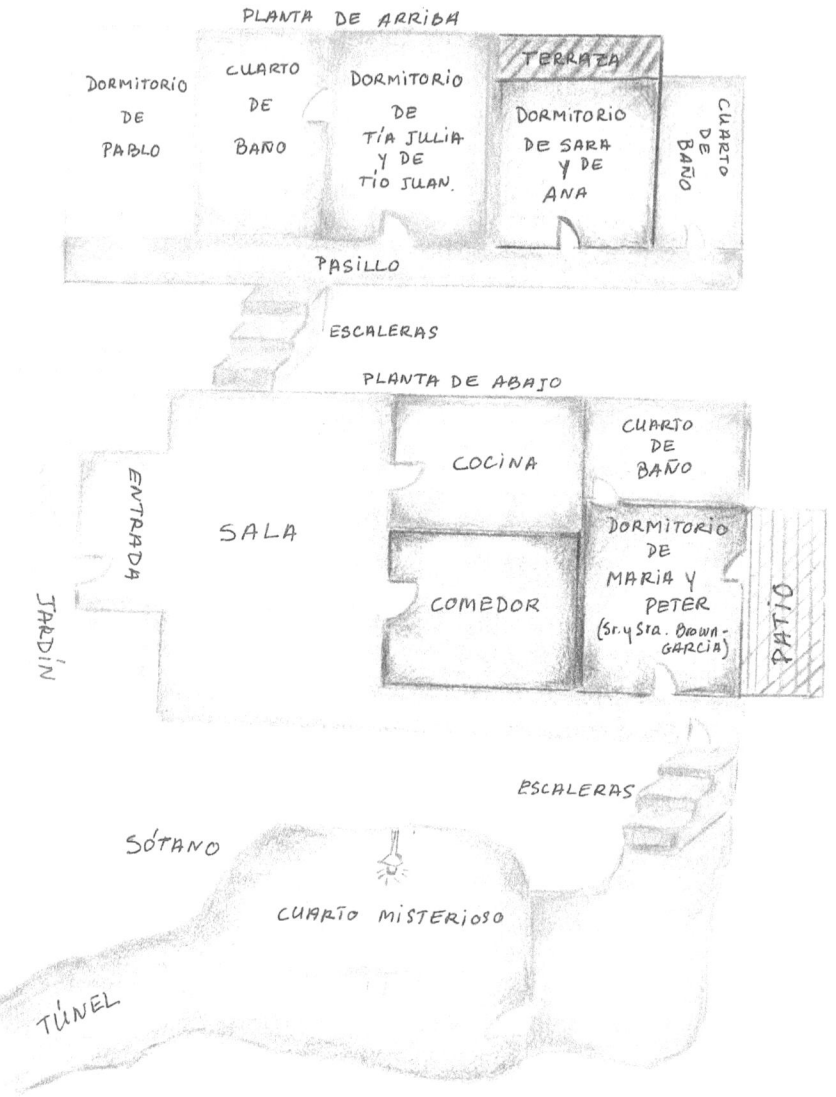

Next, we can ask questions such as: *¿Dónde está la cocina? ¿Dónde están las escaleras? ¿Dónde está el dormitorio de Pablo?* Now the conjugation of *estar* has been established and the students can write in their books. This conjugation has also been added to the *repertoire* at the beginning of the lesson.

In grade 6, students are comfortable with the use of *estar–location*, but are still confused about differentiating the rest of the situations. Again, we can conduct a recall of *ser* by describing ourselves, pets, and so on. Then, we can offer our students a simple reading such as the following fragment presented in the section "Narrative Paragraphs and Stories for Upper Grades" with the title, «*La Nota Misteriosa*».This passage gives us the opportunity to review the verb *ser* in the descriptions of a boy, thus allowing the students to quickly review some adjectives as well as the uses of *ser*. For instance:

Teaching Grammar: From the Picture to the Concept

El muchacho es de Segovia, es moreno, es alto y es tímido.

Yo soy de California, soy rubia y no soy tímida.

Tú eres mi amiga./ Yo soy amigo de Robert./ ¿Quieres ser mi amiga?

Tom es hermano de Kira./ Tom es moreno y es simpático./ Tú familia es de California.

Nosotros no somos de Segovia./ Chispa es gracioso y es pequeño.

Kira es rubia

Usted es de España.

Nosotros somos estudiantes de español.

Kira y Tom son de California.

The following is an example of a composition from a student in grade 6 after practicing *ser*:

¡Hola!

Sé que tu nombre es Zoe. Tu eres de Belgium. Tu eres rubia y tus ojos son cafés. Tu hermano se llama Yann y mas pequeño. Tu hermano es rubio y es muy simpático. Tu y tu familia están en la casa de unos amigos en Ibiza. ¿Quieres ser mi amiga y mi penpal? Me llamo Justine. Yo vivo en San Francisco, California y yo tengo once años. Yo soy rubia y mis ojos son de color cafés. Yo tengo muchas amigas de Japon, Alemania, Francia, pero no tengo amigos de Belgium.

Si quieres conocerme, escríbeme una carta a: 1024 Filbert Street
SFCO, CA 94133
USA

Justine Lippens

¿Vas tu a la escuela?
 Si, yo voy a la escuela Waldorf de S.F.
¿Tienes tu hermanos?
 Yo no tengo hermanos.
¿Cómo te llamas?
 Me llamo Justine
¿Donde vives?
 Yo vivo en San Francisco.
¿Cuántos años tienes tu?
 Yo tengo once años.
¿Tienes tú un perro?
 Yo no tengo un perro

Now we can provide the students with a review from some of the "descriptive adjectives, describing a permanent condition," and we can also incorporate some into their *repertoire*. For instance:

Bonito, bello, simpático, antipático, gracioso, serio, amable, inteligente, vanidoso, divertido, lindo, precioso, tímido, extrovertido, deldado, flaco, gordo, tonto, listo, ancho, estrecho, sincero, mentiroso, normal, mediano tranquilo, nervioso, desagradable, fantástico, largo, corto, rubio moreno, viejo, joven (etc.)

From this review, we can move on to practice the following questions:

¿Cómo es tu animal? ¿Cómo es tu casa? ¿Cómo es tu abuelo? ¿Cómo es el sofá?
¿Cómo es la pizarra? ¿Cómo son los exámenes? ¿Cómo son las clases de música?
¿Cómo eres tú? ¿Cómo es una fiesta? ¿Cómo es tu madre? ¿Cómo son las espinacas? (etc.)

Mi hermano es simpático, mi madre es alta. Mi maestro es amable, nosotros somos inteligentes, ustedes son divertidos (etc.)

The students need to be reminded of the agreement between adjective and noun when forming sentences.

The third step is to reiterate the idea of the uses of *estar* when we talk about the feeling of our state of being, or describe a temporal condition. Very often this is confusing because we are also "describing what we are feeling." Here, again, we guide the students with examples from real life as much as possible, usually pointing to people or things around us with sentences such as:

Nicholas está cansado.
Los estudiantes de la clase de sexto están nerviosos porque tienen un examen.
¡Yo estoy contenta porque los estudiantes hacen la tarea de español!
Emma está aburrida practicando gramática en la clase.
La ventana está sucia.
Los estudiantes están atentos. (etc.)

Again, the students can perceive the uses of *estar* in other situations; however, they now need a list of adjectives to review and to add to their vocabulary in order to be able to describe. In the lower grades, as it has been said before, the children have been acquainted with some adjectives of ser and *estar* but not in a conscious way. Now we will provide the students with a larger list of descriptions including adverbs (*¿Cómo está?*... or... *¿dónde está?*).

Adjectives that Refer to Feeling or a "State of Being"
(changing mood or condition)

cansado/a	*dispuesto/a*
triste	*alegre, contento/a, feliz*
animado/a	*desanimado/a*
dormido/a	*despierto/a*
aburrido/a	*interesado/a*
gordo/a	*delgado/flaco/a*
sucio/a	*limpio/a*
nervioso/a	*tranquilo/a*
enfermo/a	*sano/a*
lleno/a	*vacío/a*
claro/a	*oscuro/a*
caliente	*frío/a*
bueno/a	*malo/a*
blando/a	*duro/a*
roto arreglado/a	*reparado/a*
suave	*áspero/a*
enfermo/a	

Now we practice the two conjugations side by side and also add them to our *repertoire* at the beginning of the lesson. When the students become clear about the different situations and uses, then they can write the conjugation and the rule for the uses of *ser* and *estar* in their books.

In **grade** 7 when we teach the present progressive tense or *gerundio* in Spanish, the students will question why we use *estar* and not *ser* in the formation of this tense in Spanish. Let them answer this issue and discuss the reasons with one another and then talk about situations in which the present progressive is used in Spanish. Here, your imagination, your connection to the language, and your preparation is essential. It is also important to help the students find their own examples within the class.

Sentence Agreement

From middle school on, another grammatical topic we bring to the lesson is the agreement of elements in the Spanish sentence. This simple aspect for native speakers becomes rather challenging because the concept is so unfamiliar to English speakers, particularly when talking about gender in words and articles. During the lower grades, especially in grade three, the children have been thoroughly acquainted with sentences in singular and plural. For instance:

La cortina de la clase es rosa/ las cortinas de la clase son rosas.

One way to bring this to the consciousness of the students around grade 4 is by first asking them to name objects around the classroom, such as:

pizarra, ventana, cortina, libro, puerta, techo, cuaderno, maestra, silla, mesa, mochila, papel, niño, niña, lápiz, sombrero (etc.)

After these items have been named verbally, the teacher can ask the students which article they think is appropriate for each: *el* or *la*?

Out of habit learned by heart from the lower grades, many will right away answer with the correct articles:

la pizarra, la ventana, la cortina, el libro, la puerta, el techo, el suelo, el cuaderno la maestra, la silla, la mesa, la mochila el papel, el niño, la niña, el lápiz, la flauta, el sombrero. (etc.)

Then we can ask the students what they noticed. In no time we will have several hands up by students noticing the ending "o" for the article *el* and *la* for the naming word ending in "a." They also will notice that not all the naming words in Spanish end in a vowel. But certainly the students and the teacher can make this observation. The teacher can then name the two genders in Spanish. The next step could be to add the plural to the first given list of naming words and again ask the students to provide the plural articles for each word. Soon the students will be aware of the changes in the articles for the plural in the masculine and the feminine gender in nouns and definite articles. Afterward, we can practice with objects in the classroom or our clothing, vegetables, fruits, and so on. Then, in the following lessons the teacher can bring adjectives. We can then say:

La puerta es blanca, el libro es rojo, el sombrero es pequeño, la tiza es amarilla.

Soon the students again will notice that the adjective will also change to "o" or to "a" for each gender. Then they realize that in Spanish, the article, the noun, and the adjective will all be in agreement of gender. When the students have arrived at this concept, then we can move to the plural forms, always guiding the students and allowing them to form their own examples:

Las puertas son blancas, los libros son rojos, los sombreros son pequeños, Las tizas son amarillas.

Teaching Grammar: From the Picture to the Concept

After this grammatical point has been sufficiently practiced, then the students write the rule in their books, adding that there are also exceptions to the rule.

Interrogative and Negative Sentences

As the students move to the upper grades, we can bring consciousness to the formation of the negative or interrogative sentence. For instance, utilizing examples given before, we ask the students for a list of sentences, and then we can begin to put them in the negative:

> *La puerta no es blanca.*
> *El libro no es rojo.* (etc.)
> *Los estudiantes no son inteligentes.*
> *Los niños no comen en la clase*

Forming negative sentences in Spanish is usually quite easy for everyone, but interrogative sentences are bit more complicated. First, we need to guide the students toward the change in modulation of the voice. We also point out to the students the opening interrogation point when we write the question in Spanish. Then soon someone will be able to notice the change of the verb and say:

> *¿Es la puerta blanca?*
> *¿Es el libro rojo?*
> *¿Son los estudiantes inteligentes?*
> *¿Comen los niños en la clase?*

In the upper grades, *reflexive verbs* raise another important topic in the Spanish lesson. From mainly grade 3 onward we lead the students with an activity. For instance, in grades 3 and 4 the students are familiarized with some reflexive verbs and have acted out «*me levanto, me visto, me peino, me lavo la cara*» (etc.) as part of their repertoire. In grade 4 or 5, the teacher introduces these actions with more consciousness. For instance, we can bring pictures representing all these activities. Although the students usually repeat the actions in the first person «*yo me levanto, yo me visto*», occasionally we can begin describing the actions of the boy or the girl from the illustration in the third person singular (she): *Ella se lava la cara, ella se peina*. In grade 6, the teacher introduces the students to more reflexive verbs in the infinitive and the first person singular (I). For instance the infinitives: *ducharse, cepillarse, ponerse, quitarse, divertirse*. But it is in grade 7 that the students usually come to the full conjugation of the reflexive verbs. In the section "Integrating Vocabulary through the Grades," there is ample reference to this grammatical topic.

The following page contains an example from a student in grade 8 practicing interrogative and negative sentences.

querer
empezar
preferir

TAREA: 15 sentences, afirmative, interrogative, negative

1. Kira prefiere fresas.
 ¿Prefiere Kira fresas?
 Kira no prefiere fresas. ✓

2. Yo quiero helado.
 ¿Quiero yo helado?
 Yo no quiero helado. ✓

3. Nosotros empezamos a pintar.
 ¿Empezamos nosotros a pintar?
 Nosotros no empezamos a pintar. ✓

4. Ustedes prefieren pepino.
 ¿Prefieren ustedes pepino?
 Ustedes no prefieren pepino. ✓

5. Ella empieza el desayuno.
 ¿Empieza ella el desayuno?
 Ella no empieza el desayuno. ✓

6. Tú quieres nadar.
 ¿Quieres tú nadar?
 Tú no quieres nadar. ✓

7. Mi tía y yo preferimos ajo.
 ¿Preferimos mi tía y yo ajo?
 Mi tía y yo no preferimos ajo. ✓

8. Thor y Eli quieren jugar al basketball.
 ¿Quieren Thor y Eli jugar al basketball?
 Thor y Eli no quieren jugar al basketball. ✓

9. Yo empiezo mi tarea.
 ¿Empiezo yo mi tarea?
 Yo no empiezo mi tarea. ✓

Another example from a student in grade 8:

> TAREA 12 oraciones
> 1. Yo me divierto en las vacaciones. ✓
> 2. Sophie se mira en el espejo. ✓
> 3. Nosotros nos quitamos nuestros calcetines.
> 4. Mi tía se acuesta muy temprano. ✓
> 5. Ellas se cepillan sus dientes. ✓
> 6. Mi gato se lava con su lengua. ✓
> 7. Tú te vistes muy rápidamente. ✓
> 8. Yo me peino mi pelo. ✓
> 9. Mi tío se afeita en la mañana. ✓
> 10. Juan se aburre muy fácilmente. ✓
> 11. Ellos se bañan en el océano.
> 12. El se despierta pronto. ✓

We can introduce adverbs and prepositions in grade 3 or 4 by bringing a small, stuffed mouse and a box to the class. We can place the mouse inside, to the right, next to, between, and so on. In this way the practice becomes more real for the students. We can also include some of these adverbs and prepositions as part of our repertoire. As the students get older we can also enhance our practice with activities such as the following exercise offered by Diamela Wetzl:

1) Dictation of the following sentences:

   a) *Yo voy a la escuela*
   b) *Un ratón vive en el garaje.*
   c) *El queso es para el ratón.*
   d) *Nosotros pasamos por la puerta de atrás.*
   e) *Mi cuarto está arriba, pero el garaje está abajo.*
   f) *Mi padre bebe café con leche.*
   g) *Mi hermana bebe té sin azúcar.*
   h) *En mi casa, la cocina está lejos del garaje.*
   i) *Las escaleras están cerca de la cocina.*
   j) *La puerta de mi casa está delante de un armario.*
   k) *El comedor está atrás de…*
   l) *La silla blanca, está entre la ventana y la cocina.*
   m) *Nosotros comemos el postre después de la comida.*

n) *Los estudiantes de primer grado están afuera, pero los estudiantes de quinto están dentro de la clase.*

o) *La lección de música es antes que la lección de español.*

2) Preposition identification: students circle the prepositions.

3) Write a story: students write a story using all the prepositions from the dictation. They may choose to use this dictation as a basis for their story, or they may write their own original story using most of these prepositions.

The following is a conversational exercise with practice of prepositions and adverbs:

1) *Repartiremos a los estudiantes un plano de un cuarto y una lista de adverbios y preposiciones:*

Principales adverbios (se excluyen los formados con –mente):

De lugar: aquí, ahí, allí, acá, allá; encima, debajo, arriba, abajo; atrás, dentro, fuera, adelante afuera, adentro, afuera; cerca, lejos.	¿dónde?	donde
De tiempo: ahora, entonces, hoy, ayer, mañana, antes, después, temprano, pronto, tarde, todavía, aún, ya, siempre, nunca, jamás.	¿cuándo?	cuando
De modo: así, tal, bien, mal, peor, mejor, deprisa, despacio.	¿cómo	como
De cantidad: tanto (tan), mucho (muy), poco, bastante, demasiado, algo, nada, más, menos, medio, apenas, casi.	¿cuánto?	cuanto, como

De afirmación: sí, claro, desde luego.

De negación: no, nunca, jamás, tampoco.

De duda: quizá, acaso, tal vez.

De relación con lo dicho: pues, así, por tanto, además, también, tampoco, sin embargo, no obstante.

Preposiciones

a	entre
ante	hacia
bajo	hasta
cabe	incluso
con	para
contra	por
de	según
desde	sin
durante	so
excepto	sobre
en	tras

2) *En el mismo papel los alumnos o nosotros dibujaremos una serie de objetos que pertenezcan a ese cuarto. Por ejemplo si es la sala, podemos pintar:*

Una mesita, un sofá, dos sillones, una alfombra, una librería con libros, un tocadiscos, una lámpara, dos mesitas pequeñas, una ventana, un rejoj de pared, una chimenea. (etc.)

3) *Cada alumno dibuja su plano.*

4) *Divididos en parejas, un alumno pregunta: ¿dónde está la ventana?*

«La ventana está entre la puerta y el comedor». El alumno que responde, ahora pregunta: ¿dónde está la lámpara?
«La lámpara está sobre la mesita pequeña».

Since teaching grammar is quite individual from teacher to teacher, the purpose of these examples is to illustrate how through the grades the teacher can guide the students in certain topics. Every group of students is different and it will be up to the teacher to prepare a unique, imaginative lesson to fit each class. It is important always to remember to allow the children to arrive at their own conclusions, guiding instead of teaching, so the students can discover how to use the Spanish language for themselves. It is our task as teachers to awaken these capacities in the students by evoking the right examples and by imbuing ourselves with the "power of speech" and preparation that will enliven the lesson in a memorable way.

6.1 Outline of Suggested Grammatical Topics by Grades

GRAMMAR TOPIC: 1 = introduction; 2 = practice & application; 3 = review & mastery

PARTS OF SPEECH:	\	\	GRADES:	\	\
	4	5	6	7	8
ARTICLE (Definite/	3	3	3	3	3
indefinite)	1	3	3	3	3
Gender	1	2	3	3	3
Number/Plural- Singular	1	2	3	3	3
Formation and use of contractions: al, del		1	2	3	3
Demonstratives: esta, esa, aquella		1	2	3	3
NOUN					
Gender of nouns	1	2	3	3	3
Number (singular and plural)	1	2	3	3	3
Agreement in gender and number with articles	1	2	3	3	3
ADJECTIVE					
Adjective of quality (colors, etc.)	2	2	3	3	3
Numbers	1	2	3	3	3
Interrogatives	1	2	3	3	3
Comparatives and superlatives			1	2	3
Agreement in gender, number w/ article + noun	1	2	3	3	3
Position of adjectives	1	1	2	3	3
Possessive adjectives		1	2/3	3	3
PRONOUN					
Personal	1	3			
Possessive	1	2	3	3	3
Reflexive	1	2	3	3	3
Pronouns as direct objects				2	3
Pronouns as indirect objects				2	3

Teaching Grammar: From the Picture to the Concept

PARTS OF SPEECH:		GRADES:			
VERB					
Regular Simple Present AR	1	2/3	3	3	3
AR / ER / IR		2	3	3	3
Irregular stem-changing verbs, simple present				–	–
TENER ESTAR	2	3	3	3	3
Tengo que…			3	3	3	3
SER—ESTAR	1	2	3	3	3
Dormir, jugar, oir, querer, volver…			1	2/3	3	3
IR			1	2/3	3	3
Dar, ver, decir, venir				2/3	3	3
Hacer, salir, traer..				2/3	3	3
Regular, simple past				1	3	3
Regular, Pretérito Indefinido IR						3
Irregular, Pretérito Indefinido Hacer, oir, querer, estar, volver, poner, ver, dar, venir….				2	3	2
Regular, imperfect tense					1	2
Comparing uses of the above tenses					1	2
Future tense, ir a + infinitive					1	2
Irregular, Simple Past: ser, tener					1	2
gustar construction	1	2	3	3	3
Reflexive verbs			1	1	2	3
Interrogative/ Negative Sentence	1	2	3	3	3

6.2 Overviews and Suggestions for Milestones and Cultural Topics through the Grades for Spanish

Grades 1 and 2

During these grades the teacher strives to bring rhythm into the lesson. The powers of imitation are very strong in the young students and each lesson incorporates the three aspects previously explained. First, a repertoire containing speech, movement, poetry, singing, body geography, etc. in a rhythmic way. Then when children sit down, the teacher presents the content of the lesson in imaginative picture form through a story. Eventually, the students will move from listening and comprehending to reenacting and telling and retelling the story chorally. This very important step; going from listening and comprehending to speaking allows students to live into the images of the language without translation, just as babies learn their mother tongue. Dialogues are presented through finger games and little "mini-plays." The vocabulary of everyday surroundings such as clothes, body geography, and objects around the classroom is taught through questions and answers that help the children form sentences that describe scenes or objects around the class. Toward the end of the lesson, the teacher brings additional activities through circle games, songs, dances, and other activities involving more movement.

At the end of grades 1 and 2, children should be able to:

- identify and name colors and respond to questions such as: «¿Es verde?», «Sí es verde»
- state their name
- state their age
- count using numbers up to 50 or more
- identify and name body geography (main features)
- identify and name objects in the classroom and animals, and use seasonal vocabulary
- use descriptive adjectives
- respond to questions: what, how big, and how many (How many baskets are on the table? Is this a pencil or a book? Is this big, medium or small? ¿Qué animal tienes tú? ¿Es la boca?)
- act out up to 15 verbs
- answer questions regarding color and number
- chorally retell and/or re-enact stories, fairytales, and fables in grade 2
- respond to very simple questions

Teaching Grammar: From the Picture to the Concept

- respond: *Yo tengo... un perro* (etc.)
- identify and respond to questions such as «*¿Cuántos lápices hay en mi mano?*»
- understand vocabulary relating to clothing (e.g., *yo llevo un sombrero*)
- sing a good repertoire of songs
- recite chorally, even an at early age, poems from diverse authors
- speak little dialogues via finger games

Grade 3

During this age the power of imitation begins to diminish and as a result the language teacher presents material that will allow more challenge in the classroom. The lesson continues to be planned in a threefold way, but the teacher incorporates many new elements and expands the students' vocabulary. For instance, the students learn as many as thirty or more verbs in the context of an activity: with the seeds I plant, with the grinder I grind, with my hands I work, etc. The repertoire of descriptions around the classroom is also enhanced by many more adjectives, for example, " the day is clear, the night is dark, the shoes are thirty, the shoes are clean. The children need to experience the vocabulary in images and these images and descriptions are always presented within the context of a situation.

During this age the story content reflects the topic of the morning lesson, and stories such as "Pelle's New Suit," "The Three Bears," or «*La gallina Marcelina*», and scenes from these stories are presented in class for speaking and acting. Topics such as the clock, telling the date, gardening, learning the professions, going to the market, the parts of a house, the weather, the months, manual activities, food, clothing, and family are presented with artistic illustration or real objects. During this age the students are encouraged to form their own sentences with less guidance from the teacher; for instance: "The blackboard is long," "I paint with the brush," "The classroom has three doors."

Topics

- telling name and age and where one lives
- counting up to 100
- telling the time
- expanding body geography vocabulary (*La lengua, la espalda*)
- clothes: individually they describe what they are wearing
- professions and actions expanded up to 30 or 40 new verbs. (The secretary answers the phone, the carpenter works with wood, the artist paints pictures, the cook cooks, etc.)
- vocabulary from the farm and animals: from the wool of the sheep to the pants and sweater, etc.

- parts of the house, rooms, and an activity (e.g., from the clay/wood to building a house)
- months, days of the week, seasons (descriptions of illustrations)
- the weather, days of the week, months, time
- fruits, vegetables, and relevant verbs: cut, prepare, eat
- food from the market: grains, drinks, meats, etc., and shopping in the market
- poems from the third grade curriculum
- the family
- more adjectives describing opposites: narrow–wide, dirty–clean, clear–dark, easy-difficult, etc.
- more vocabulary from the surroundings
- position: adverbs and prepositions

At the end of grade 3, students should be able to:

- answer up to 50 questions about any of the topics previously mentioned with a sentence
- describe an illustration in simple sentences
- recite poems chorally
- comprehend stories with illustrations and act out activities
- tell time
- describe the weather and the seasons
- describe pictures or the classroom with adjectives: «*La puerta está cerrada*».
- talk about some basic foods in the market
- name immediate family members
- name farm animals
- name simple farm activities: *cocinar, plantar, regar, cosechar,* etc.
- name some professions: *carpintero, pintor, cocinero, granjero, policía,* etc.
- tell the date
- name some of the rooms in the house
- identify all the clothes the students normally wear
- identify around thirty verbs
- know oposites: *frío-calor, claro-oscuro, fácil-difícil, seco-mojado,* etc.
- respond to questions with answers such as «*La camisa está seca*», «*el cubo está vacío?*»

Grade 4

In the fourth grade when the power of imitation begins to recede to make way for a new level of thinking, the teacher addresses some basic grammatical phenomena in a more conscious way. In Spanish grammatical rules, verb conjugation and syntax are introduced while expanding vocabulary. We bring the awareness of the differences in placement of words in a Spanish sentence. The practice of oral language continues in simple questions and answers in complete sentences.

In the Waldorf curriculum, the children learn to read by first writing material they have already learned. In the foreign language class, the transition to reading takes place in the fourth grade. We generally proceed from the whole to the parts: from the sentence to the word to the letter. It is possible for teachers to prepare readers with age-appropriate histories and fragments. Retelling stories becomes an important component of the lesson, as now the recapitulation is no longer choral, but individual. The students develop their own simple sentences in short compositions and will be asked to read them or report on several topics. Although many vocabulary themes will be reviewed and expanded, new topics from the fourth grade curriculum such as the city, the neighborhood, animal world and their own family, will be a central focus during this year.

Grade 4

Vocabulary Topics	• review and expand vocabulary related to: animals, family, food, house, weather, time, and clothes • expand vocabulary in the house to the objects in each room (e.g., in the kitchen: the dishwasher, the refrigerator, stove, etc.) • family: add more family members, such cousins, nephew, etc. • animals: add new animals from animal reports • food, the students learn to order in a restaurant • weather and seasons: individual descriptions (today is cold; it isn't raining but there are clouds in the sky, so today I am wearing…) • the students confidently describe the various clothing in their closets • «El cuerpo humano» • descriptions from the neighborhood • vocabulary from their town • some idioms (*Tengo frío, tengo calor…*) • the students should have a vocabulary of around 40 verbs

	Students should be able to
Speaking and poetry	- recite poems and parts of a play
- report orally their own short sentences: for example, *Yo camino a la escuela y toco el violín.*
- order food in a restaurant
- recall in sentences readings such as "The Turnip," "The Three Bears," etc.
- give a description of the seasons and clothes, both orally and written
- give reports about themselves or an animal
- give a description of their house or a room inside their house
- identify all the personal pronouns
- recite or act out some small parts individually, although the class continues to recite poems chorally
Reading, writing, and recall	- The students learn to read via writing. They first begin to write some sentences describing their thoughts and then they read these sentences aloud. The teacher can also present the class with a reader containing familiar poems, stories and simple texts. The students should be able to recall parts of the story. For instance, in the "The Three Bears," they should be able to describe «*la silla grande de papá oso*» (etc.)
- In writing, the students begin their own individual compositions, describing themselves, the seasons, their family, their city, or their animal with a few sentences.
Grammar and syntax	- Parts of the sentence
- introduction of the gender and number of the nouns : feminine, masculine, plural and singular
- define articles: *El, la, los, las* (introduction of «*artículos indeterminados*»)
- personal pronouns
- conjugation of regular AR verbs in the present tense
- conjugation of verb *tener*
- introduction *ser* and *estar*
- idioms: *tengo frío, tengo calor, tengo hambre, tengo sed*
Culture	- life in the Missions and the Rancho time; visiting a Mission and ordering food in a Mexican restaurant
- Christmas: *posadas, Reyes Magos*, other Hispanic festivals
- songs and dances

Grade 5

Group recitation and singing occupy less time, as conversation, reading, writing, retelling, and short grammar exercises move to the foreground. Greater focus is put on writing and the children's book work, as well as the introduction of certain organization and study skills. Singing traditional songs and reciting poems, however, remain an important part of the lesson.

In the Waldorf school language lesson, storytelling in the younger grades and stories told through narration or literary fragments in the upper grades are at the heart of the lesson. Stories invite speaking possibilities through recall of events and writing opportunities through the answering of questions; each type of exercise has been shown to attune the ear to a language's particular sounds and nuances of expression, as well as to improve overall comprehension and language acquisition. A good reader with a representative selection of stories will also facilitate conversation through the telling and retelling the stories.

As the children begin to gain a conscious knowledge of grammatical structures, the language lesson also includes not only a rhythmical grammatical instruction though reciting conjugations, but also a sentence and vocabulary-building practice. Introducing conjugation in the present tense of the regular verbs, practice of sentence structure, and creating self-composed sentences, now occupies a good part of the lesson.

In addition, the students create their own books with poems and short stories, which complement the reader and handout materials, and reflect the students' original work.

Culture, an integral aspect of the language lesson, is explored through poetry, literature and geography as well as school festivals such as *Día de los muertos*.

Grade 5

Vocabulary topics	• review familiar vocabulary. Expand to landscapes and buildings • more descriptive adjectives • what I do during the day, and the time • school and friends • the schedule • expand vocabulary around the house • activities during each season • *yo voy a las montañas., mi madre va a la oficina...* • description: *yo soy, mi casa es, mi animal es...* • dialogues • review and enhance body-part vocabulary • review of food: *yo quiero comer...* • «yo tengo que»... *limpiar mi cuarto, hacer la tarea, etc.* • idioms: *tengo miedo, tengo frío...* • vocabulary from stories • the city and the neighborhood: *El ayuntamiento, la calle, el banco, el parque...*
Speaking and recitation	• recite poems with more consciousness of their surrounding; take small parts in plays • poems from nature, landscape, seasons, the elements • write compositions of seven to ten lines: *Me llamo Erin, vivo en California y voy a la escuela Waldorf. Yo tengo un perro y un gato.... Mi gato se llama y es...mi padre...mi hermano* (etc.) • respond to a number of questions about family, house, animal, school • Using the verb SER, describe themselves, family, pet, house, etc. • write short paragraphs in Spanish about what they have read and recall
Reading, writing and retelling	• Follow a reader and longer stories. The main focus will be in retelling. After the class has read several paragraphs, students should be able to describe in a few sentences what they have understood. For instance: «*La familia visita México. Ellos van en un taxi a la ciudad*». • compositions a bit more descriptive and longer, depending on the student's ability • respond in writing to the questions from the reading • write their own compositions of approximately 10 sentences about themselves and their surroundings

Culture	- focus on the geography of Mexico and talk about its stories and legends
- *Las posadas., Día de los Reyes Magos, Día de los Muertos*
- songs and dances; Hispanic festivals in classes and school assemblies
Grammar and syntax	- defined and undefined articles
- introduction of *estar* as "location"— parts of the house
- **present tense of AR/ ER/ IR** endings. (Review of AR and introduction of ER/ IR) Understand and apply present tense conjugation of AR verbs in sentences and awareness of ER/IR endings.
- sentence agreement: article, noun, and adjective
- review of personal pronouns
- ser description: «*yo soy, mi casa es, mi animal es*»...
- introduction of some irregular verbs: *Jugar, dormir, ir, querer*
- review of food: *yo quiero comer...*
- *yo tengo que...*
- idioms: *tengo miedo, tengo frío...*
- interrogative pronouns
- new prepositions and adverbs
- comparatives
- **formulating and negating questions**
- Vocabulary of reflexive verbs: *Por la mañana me levanto, me lavo la cara, me cepillo los dientes,* etc.
- comprehending and speaking sentences regarding food: Me gusta / no me gusta
- **verbs: review and add 50 to 60 new ones**
- Parts of the sentence
- Concordance of the subject and object

Grade 6

As the faculty of thinking awakens, the learning of the language undergoes a considerable change. The students display a real desire to communicate and require more individualized attention for practice time. Group recitation and speech exercises occupy less time, whereas areas of conversation, reading, retelling, writing, and short grammar exercises step to the foreground. The student now wants to conscientiously grasp and master the modern language. Consequently new elements are added to the lesson: more individual conversations and essays and partner work.

During this age the students are introduced to geography of Europe and Latin America and Roman and Medieval History. For instance, if the students in grade 6 study Europe, the teacher can take this opportunity to bring poetry and stories from Spain. The children can retell the legends and stories from the country studied. With a newly awakened conceptual thinking, the children can discover principles in the language and write them down in a separate book.

The story content will help the students develop vocabulary of development of diverse themes. They will have the opportunity to re-tell the stories. At the same time, during the recall the teacher can also introduce and practice a specific area of grammar. At the end of story the students can practice questions, describe situations to each other, and write sentences about what they have read.

In grammar the expectation is that the students manage regular verbs in the present tense, and some irregular ones. They will be also introduced to the regular conjugation of the Simple Past Tense or *pretérito indefinido*. A good review of sentence structure (article-noun-adjective agreement), possessive adjectives, and other grammatical topics is the main focus during this year.

Grade 6

Speaking: oral comprehension and poetry	• Students should be able to express to each other the practiced sentences. They should be able to recall parts of the stories read. They also should be able to understand commands from the vocabulary described for this grade and express some simple thoughts. The students should be able to formulate and negate sentences. • Ballads named in Spanish *romances*, are quite appropriate during this time as well as epic poems.
Reading, writing, and recall	• Students should be able to follow and recapitulate legends and stories told in present and past tense. They should be able to write summaries of about 10 to 15 lines from a story. Vocabulary will be learned as part of the story. Specific vocabulary will be also part of each grammatical goal.

Vocabulary, grammar, and syntax	<ul><li>parts of the sentence</li><li>review and mastery: **Conjugation in the Present tense AR/ ER /IR regular** verbs</li><li>interrogative and negative sentences</li><li>*me gusta—No me gusta* using vocabulary: food, sports, adverbs</li><li>Vocabulary of reflexive verbs in the infinitive and only conjugation in the first person; introduction to the concept</li><li>conjugación en el presente of irregular verbs with change—"UE":*dormir, poner, volver, poder, jugar…* – **Ser (Descriptions), Estar** : review of location, introduction of *estar* (feelings, and state of "being") and *dar*. – vocabulary from adjectives and adverbs, between 50 and 70</li><li>**tengo que…** – review of vocabulary from chores (*limpiar, regar, sacar la basura etc…*)</li><li>enhance list of verbs, around 60 to 75</li><li>to go: **IR**, present and simple past. – vocabulary from the country, city, places: *el lago las montañas, el mar* – vocabulary: traveling</li><li>**irregular verbs in the present tense** such as: *ver, decir querer, venir,, salir, oír, traer, hacer* – vocabulary from nature, things: *paisaje, campo, bosque, mochila, carta, nota..*</li><li>review: define undefined articles and sentence agreement</li><li>review *tener* in the present tense</li><li>introduction of the simple past regular (pretérito) AR/ER/IR endings</li><li>introduction of demonstrative adjectives / possessive adjectives</li><li>introduction of reflexive verbs – vocabulary: list most common verbs from routines of the day</li><li>present tense of *saber and conocer* and application</li><li>At the end of this grade the students should be able to master preset tense and be well acquainted with the simple past. They also should be able to conjugate some basic irregular verbs in the present; form negative and interrogative sentences and be able to retell in sentences some of the stories read during class. They should be able to write summaries of from 10 to 15 lines from a story. Vocabulary will be learned as part of the story and through specific vocabulary topics added to the lesson.</li></ul>

Culture	- legends from Spain; Roman and Medieval focus
- geography of Spain and/or other Latin-American countries
- songs and dances
- *Día de los muertos*; other Hispanic festivals
- create a menu or report on a topic
- poetry from el *Romancero español and* epic poetry

Grades 7 and 8

Newly added students and large classes are often common in these grades. Splitting the class in two is therefore beneficial for all the students. The questions of dividing the group and mixing grades were widely asked during the faculty meetings with Rudolf Steiner and he advised grouping the students in the language lessons according to ability beginning in class 7 (Karl Stockmeyer, "Schools and Lessons in General").

During this age the students experience a real desire to communicate, and more individualized attention to practice is needed. Students now want to consciously grasp and master the modern language. Therefore, individual conversations, essays, and partner work are going to be even more central in their lessons. Divided into pairs, students have the opportunity to discuss many topics, describing or retelling stories they have read in a free exchange, asking questions, or expressing their opinions of situations while incorporating the vocabulary presented in class. At this age, students enjoy experimenting with the language and being able to retell or freely express their thoughts. Allowing them to create their own stories and summaries bolsters their sense of progress and achievement. Many students have acquired some fluency in the language, which creates a strong foundation for high school.

In the realm of grammar, ample review is essential, focusing on conjugation of verbs and vocabulary. This allows the students to solidify grammatical concepts and to practice forming sentences using past tense of mainly regular verbs and present tense with regular and irregular verbs. As we advance in grammar, we can cover present progressive tense and reflexive verbs in the present tense. The students also deepen their practice with demonstrative and possessive adjectives and with some of the irregular verb conjugations in the present and the past tenses. Slowly, students also begin to discriminate between the simple past and the imperfect tenses, and also occasionally to use the present progressive in their reports. Although at this age they still need more practice with irregular-ending verbs, the students should be able to acquire a good feeling for the use of these conjugations and the stem-changing in their speech. At this age, the students like to see their progress, and homework and testing are an important aspect for them to determine their academic standing.

Particularly in the grade 8, language teachers present biographies as part of the lessons. Teachers select texts concerned with questions of one's own destiny, with ideals and human worth, but which also offer adventure and suspense. Often literature such as adaptations of *Don Quijote de la Mancha* and biographies of idealistic people such as César Chávez, José Martí, or Simón Bolívar offer a source of inspiration for the students and good material for the language class.

The focus on a variety of cultural aspects is integral to our language lessons, including poetry, songs, and readings, as well as the preparation of festivals. The students like to express themselves in a variety of ways, with a good accent and wit, when presenting a topic to the audience. In addition, the class can read and prepare presentations about the ancient cultures of Mesoamerica and South America.

Grade 7

Speaking and retelling oral comprehension and poetry	• follow the lesson employing only Spanish with the advanced group • give descriptions about people, places, and likes and dislikes with their desk partners or individually • oral report on a Latin American country • give an oral presentation about a reading or a topic chosen in front of the class for about 10 minutes in Spanish • be well acquainted with many vocabulary topics pertaining to food, places, family, parts of the house, traveling, etc. All these topics need to be enhanced in addition to the story content given to the class. • retell freely passages from the readings in the present tense and begin to use past tense in their descriptions; occasionally use reflexive verbs, demonstrative and possessive adjective in their explanations • recite individual parts understanding the mood and the content of the poems • added poetry describing the moods of the authors
Reading and writing	• independent reading of short stories • be able to understand the story read without much help from the teacher • in witting, give summaries in Spanish of the story read • independently write a summary of about 15 or more lines on a given topic

Vocabulary, grammar, and syntax	• review and mastery: conjugation in the present tense of most common irregular verbs (e.g. *traer, pensar, empezar, jugar, hacer, poner, dormir, hacer, traer,* etc.)
	  – vocabulary from places, things, traveling, etc.
	• mastery of regular conjugation in the simple past tense (*préterito*)
	• reflexive verbs, conjugation: *Yo me lavo, tú te lavas, él se lava*
	  – vocabulary: clothing, adding new items
	• review and mastery of *saber* and *conocer*: conjugation and use in conversation
	• present progressive: *ando–iendo*
	  – vocabulary: list of verbs from 60 -100 or more
	• *ser* and *estar* present tense and simple past
	  – vocabulary: antonyms and places in the house
	• simple past (*pretérito*) and uses of *ser* and *ir*
	  – vocabulary: places, professions
	• *tener*: present tense and simple past
	• simple past or *pretérito indefinido* of **Ir–Ser–Estar**
	• review and mastery of demonstrative and possessive adjectives
	• direct pronouns and indirect pronouns and *gustar*
	• know adverbs of intensity, place, time, condition and prepositions
	• Parts of the sentence
	• comparatives: *más que, menos que*

Cultural topics	• Latin America: geography and history: Aztecs, Mayas, Incas • legends, stories, and literary extracts • leading role in the assembly *for Día de los muertos* • poetry from Latin-American authors • geography of Latin America • stories, legends, and dialogues

Grade 8

Speaking and retelling Oral comprehension and poetry	• follow the lesson in Spanish; give descriptions of people, places, likes and dislikes with desk partners or individually. • oral report on a biography • give an oral presentation to the class about a reading or a chosen topic for about 10 minutes • be well acquainted with many vocabulary topics pertaining to: food, places, family, parts of the house, traveling, etc. All these topics need to be enhanced in addition to the story content given to the class. • freely retell passages from the readings in the present tense and begin to use past tense in descriptions • occasionally use reflexive verbs, demonstrative and possessive adjectives, and present progressive in explanations • recite individual parts with an understanding of the mood and content of the poems • add poetry describing the moods, social situations, or the feelings of the authors
Reading and writing	• be able to read short stories • be able to individually read a story without much help from the teacher • be able to freely render the content of the story read • in writing, be able to summarize in Spanish of the story read • independently create original stories

Grammar, syntax and conversation	• review and mastery of: conjugation in the present tense of most common irregular verbs—e.g., *traer, pensar, empezar, jugar, hacer, dormir, hacer, traer,* etc.
	  – Vocabulary from places, things, traveling
	• review and mastery of regular conjugation in the simple past tense
	• review and mastery of reflexive verbs, conjugation, and uses in essays and conversation
	  – vocabulary: add items of clothing: *pulsera, collar, medias*
	• review and mastery of *saber* and *conocer*: conjugation in the present tense and uses
	• review and mastery of present progressive: *ando— iendo*
	  – vocabulary: review up to 130 verbs
	• *ser and estar* present tense and simple past
	  – vocabulary: antonyms and places in the house; also health: *me duele la cabeza, la ambulancia, el hospital, la enfermera…*
	• Introduction in the imperfect tense
	• review: Simple past and uses of *ser and ir*
	  – vocabulary: places (*campo y ciudad*), professions
	• review: *tener*, present tense and simple past
	• simple past or *pretérito indefinido* of **ir–ser–estar**
	• introduction to the imperfect tense: Irregular *ser, ir*
	• discrimination between simple past and imperfect tense
	• review and mastery of demonstrative and possessive adjectives
	  – Vocabulary: things around the classroom, house… direct pronouns and introduction of indirect pronouns
	• adverbs of intensity, place, time, condition and prepositions
	• comparatives *más que, menos que…*
	• introduction of future tense
	• introduction of *pretérito indefinido* in grade 8 of most common irregular verbs: *andar, poner, hacer, decir, oír, poder,* etc.

Culture	• Latin American geography and history • legends, stories, and literary extracts • leading role in the assembly *for Día de los muertos* • biograpghies such as Simón Bolívar, César Chávez, Benito Juárez, José Martí, and Frida Kahlo • poetry from Latin-American authors • stories, legends, and dialogues • Cervantes and *Don Quijote*

7

POETRY AND RECITATION THROUGH THE GRADES

«Un poeta es el que desnuda con el lenguaje rítmico su alma. El ritmo, además, le sirve como el bieldo, al aventar en la era para apresar su pensamiento, separando a la brisa del cielo soleado el grano de la paja».

"A poet is a person who bares his soul through the use of the rhythm of language. The rhythm of language, serves to capture the poet's thoughts, much like the winnowing fork, as the breeze of sunny skies threshes the grain and separates it from the chaff."[1]

—Miguel de Unamuno

The Gospel of St. John states that the Word was God, and God was the Word. Rudolf Steiner applies this concept to the development of human consciousness. As he points out in *The Genius of Language*,[2] we as human beings have the capacity to be elevated as co-creators when consciousness is brought into our voice. This powerful notion empowers us not only with the potential to create the outer world, but also with the potential to be shaped by it. All of this is made possible through the *air organization* in our circulatory system. The air organization, or movement of air within our body, helps to form our body, the corporeal vehicle through which we encounter the world. Once we encounter the world, our external gestures are the expressions of this encounter with the forms and shapes around us as well as what is within us, and at the same time, we begin to express an audible articulation of both inner and outer gestures when we learn to speak. When **language** imitates the outer world, **consonants** are formed. Of course, we also experience inward feelings and these feelings are expressed in our **vowels**. Language imitates the outer world or what we experience from this encounter through our senses as feelings and perceptions, and thus both inner and outer are parts of our experiences of language.

---

1 Translation by Diamela Wetzel.

2 "[Steiner] sought the spiritual capacity of human beings to use their thinking, feeling, and willing through their voices to transmit contents of consciousness and to use their words as live entities that can eventually elevate us to the status of being co-creators with the spiritual world" (Adam Makkai, afterword).

Vowel character in language denotes everything formed inwardly, everything that is being felt inwardly and that presses itself into the sound out of what we are experiencing in our feeling and will. Hence, we will find in all the vowels, and vowel forms, the feelings and will impulses that are called forth in us by the outer world and, in a way, are thrust into our larynx. In everything to do with consonants we will find gestures modeled on what we perceive in the outer world.[3]

"It is always possible to trace consonants back to an imitation of external objects."[4] Steiner explains that the forces that build up the human body metamorphose at a certain point into two essentially human activities: speaking and thinking. Speaking is formed by the coming together of vowels and consonants to form sounds that affect us by penetrating through the senses and the nervous system. The sounds heard are imprinted into the building forces of the human heart, which awaken the blood in the feeling life of the human being and in turn activate the inner will to imitate the sound, echoing speech that forms language.

The building forces that built the embryo metamorphose into thinking that calls forth a relationship to language and the world. Vowels and consonants that come together to create speech combine first into the syllabic sounds, then into words that become thought-carrying sentences and phrases that convey meaning. It is the working together in the soul of the building forces of feeling which activate the will and in this process develop sympathy, and the building forces of thought which activate thinking and develop antipathy that form language imbued with words and meaning. Language, therefore, is an active human creation, an artistic activity that supports the development of imaginative thinking in us.

Speech is rooted in breathing in the midsection of the human organism, and it is necessary to look at the connection of speaking to human thinking. There have been various theories of speech formation, and in many is the idea that thinking becomes the first expression of the outer world. Based on this notion, language acquisition tactics are often dependent upon drills that require a mechanical and systematic learning. Currently, language teachers in the Waldorf schools struggle with questions of media in the classroom or with different techniques for language acquisition that are not what we have come to accept as the human-centered Waldorf approach. If we want to permeate human nature with the essence of Waldorf education, we cannot compromise.

For language teachers it can be too easy to cross the line, especially when immediate results are promised following a particular language teaching technique. This does not mean that we cannot make good use of innovations, but we must do so by understanding why we are

---

3 Steiner, *The Genius of language*, pp. 80–81.
4 Steiner, *Practical Advice to Teachers*, p. 22.

employing them if we are to keep the traditional methods in perspective. It is essential for new teachers to understand that Steiner sees in language formation the need to bring mental images into our speech so it becomes a living reality. Many "language methods" do not perceive language as a living reality, but as patterns, drills, or mechanical responses to commands. The danger is that speech can become abstract and materialistic, losing its pictorial aspect as a result of an unconscious element of will. When this happens, we cannot feel the living soul qualities in our spoken words. We remain abstract not only in our way of understanding, but also in our speaking. The nature of our speech is determined first through our feeling or emotion, which arises as an expression of the meeting of antipathy and sympathy in the rhythmic system of heart and lungs. In the head this same activity results in an image.[5] "When you speak, you have a constant breast activity that you accompany with an image through the head activity. This makes it obvious that speaking is based on the constant rhythm of sympathetic and antipathetic activity, just as feeling is. Indeed, speech originates in feeling."[6]

There are many reasons why Steiner emphasizes teaching poetry as a way of experiencing speech—not just for the experience of the language itself, but also for the *formative qualities* acting in the growing children. These formative qualities are embodied in the sound, tone, rhythm, and the combination of vowels and consonants. This is why a poem cannot be analyzed, but only felt. When we recite, we do so with the whole body, experiencing the rhythm, intonation, vowels, and consonants to the tips of our fingers. When children receive such living speech, they become both unified and separated from their surroundings.

---

5   See Steiner, *Foundations of Human Experience*, pp. 58ff.
6   Steiner, *Practical Advice to Teachers*, p. 18.

7.1 Teaching Poetry in Lower Grades (Grades 1, 2, and 3)

Beginning in infancy, children enjoy clapping and chanting. Nursery rhymes, poems, and chants provide a deep connection with simple activities through speech. Each culture has its characteristic expressions, each one original and beautiful, and as children enter school, when the power of imitation is still very strong, the language teacher can present a rich repertoire containing poems, rhymes, and chants, with different gestures and intonation, so the children experience the spirit of the language through the flowing sounds and the gestures without translation.

There are many beautiful poetry options for the youngest students, poems such as «*El Sol Es De Oro*», by Salvador de Madariaga, «*La Ardilla*», by Amado Nervo, «*El burro Flautista*», by Tomás de Iriarte, or «*Enanitos*», by Germán Berdiales, to name a few. It is essential that teachers memorize the poem so they can live fully in the gestures and the images of the content. Through the our living connection, the gesture unfolds, thus allowing the children to capture much of the speech and the rich content in images. Children have a capacity to absorb language with their whole body; therefore, it is not surprising that after only a few lessons, students are able to follow us, verse by verse, repeating and moving with gestures.

Through the power of the voice and gestures, language teachers will be able to capture with their "I" all the attention of the students, and disciplinary measures will be unnecessary. First, the teacher speaks a line of the verse, then the students repeat it, and then they say it all together. For instance:

El sol es de oro[7]

Immediately the teacher adds: «*la luna es de plata*». First the teacher speaks, then students, and then both together. We add the last line: «*las estrellitas de hojalata*».

El sol es de oro;
la luna es de plata;
las estrellitas,
de hojalata.

In the first lesson the students repeat the first verse and follow the movements of the teacher. During the second lesson, the teacher can add in the same fashion: «*vino un gran platero que quiso comprarlas*».

---

7   The complete poems are in 7.1. "Selection of Poems and Stories in Rhyme for the Lower Grades."

Vino un gran platero,
que quiso comprarlas:
¿Cuánto das por ellas?

— Mil onzas labradas:
Para tantas joyas,
es poco dinero.
vete con tus onzas,
mísero platero.

El sol es de oro;
la luna es de plata;
las estrellitas,
de hojalata.

By now the students understand that the poem talks about the Sun, the Moon, and the stars, just because of the gestures and the power of the teacher's voice. However, the meaning of the next line is not so obvious, so much depends on the teacher's theatrical expression or the image given to the students. For instance, if you refer to the line «*vino un gran platero que quiso comprarlas*», you can say, "No, no, he has to hold his silver bag higher," or "He is a proud silversmith." The children right away take up your cues, thus allowing you to move forward: *¿Cuánto das por ellas?* (etc.). By the end of the third lesson, the students will be easily able to repeat two stanzas from the poem. In the following lessons, the poem will be part of "their repertoire." When the students can recite most of it by "hearing," the poem becomes a vivid story that they have been able to penetrate through the gestures, sound, and images provided by the teacher. Now the students are ready to reenact the poem, since this particular poem tells a story (see 5.2, "Storytelling"). Illustrations are always helpful when reenacting stories; in the following pages are a few examples.

Very often a few props are sufficient for staging the acting-out of the poem. For instance, a crown representing the Sun, another crown for the Moon, and some for the stars, a cape for the "silversmith with his bag of coins," an apron and a hat for the gardener, and a nice tunic for the maiden. These items can be enough to begin the "play" immediately following the usual repertoire. Music from a lyre or xylophone and a few students volunteering, can add another dimension to the poem:

Vino un jardinero,
que quiso comprarlas.
—¿Cuánto das por ellas?

—Mil rosas de Arabia.

—Para tantas joyas,
tus rosas son pocas,
vete, jardinero,
vete con tus rosas.

Vino una doncella:
tez de terciopelo,
los ojos brillantes
como otros dos cielos.
—Doncella preciosa,
¿Cuánto das por ellas?
   —Salvador de Madariaga (1886–1978), fragmento

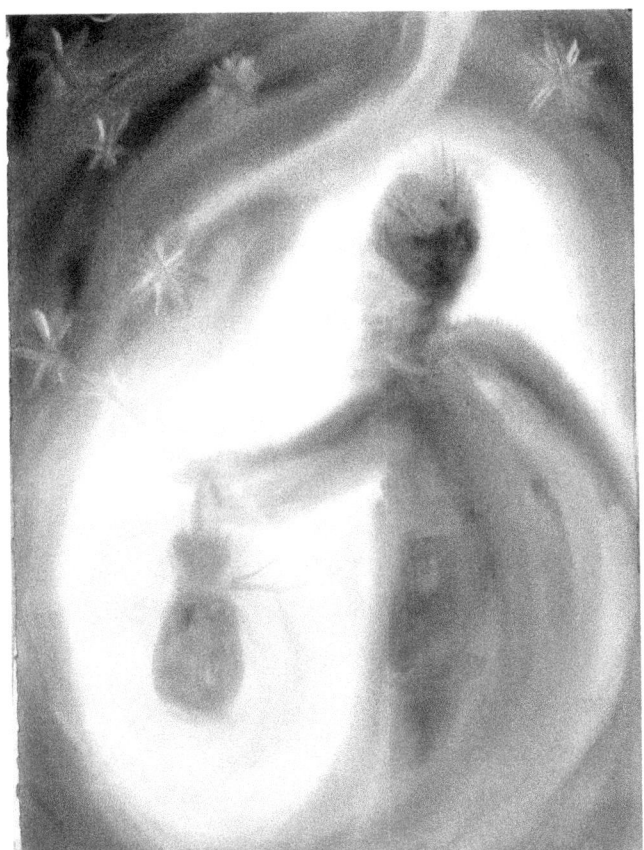

Maiden from Estrellitas de Hojalata

A Selection of Poems and Stories in Rhyme for the Lower Grades

El burro, el mantel y el palo

Versión en verso. La escinificación se encuentra en la sección de "Selection of Stories for Lower Grades." La historia en versos se puede recitar durante la sección de «Repertorio» con gestos.

CHORUS AND MOTHER:	Pedrito, Pedrito ve al río a pescar pues no hay comidita para cenar.
CHORUS:	Pedrito fue al río y un gran pez pescó era un pez dorado que así le habló:
GENIE:	El poderoso genio del río soy, si tÚ me liberas un premio te doy.
PEDRITO:	Pedrito en el río al pez liberó, una poción mágica de él recibió.
CHORUS:	Dos gotas de esencia el pez derramó, y un burro prodigioso se le apareció.
CHORUS:	Pedrito le dijo:
PEDRITO:	Burro burrito, dame el dinero que yo necesito.
CHORUS:	Monedas de oro el burro escupió y el chico contento con él se marchó. En el camino de vuelta a su casa, y cuando por una posada pasa, al burro le dice:
PEDRITO:	Burro burrito, dame el dinero que yo necesito.

CHORUS:	*Monedas de oro el burro escupió.*
	Y el posadero ambicioso todo lo vió,
	y mientras Pedrito un pan comía,
	el cambio de burro el dueño hacía.
	De vuelta a su casa, sin cambio notar,
	a su madre el burro quería mostrar;
	y al burro le dijo:
PEDRITO:	*Burro burrito, dame el dinero que yo necesito.*
CHORUS:	*El burro cambiado un rebuzno dio,*
	y su madre, enfadada, a él repitió:
CHORUS AND MOTHER:	*Pedrito, Pedrito ve al río a pescar*
	pues no hay comidita para cenar
CHORUS:	*Pedrito en el río un pez de oro pescó*
	y el pez dorado de esta forma habló:
GENIE:	*El poderoso genio del río soy,*
	si tÚ me liberas un premio te doy.
CHORUS:	*Pedrito en el río al pez liberó,*
	una poción mágica de él recibió.
	Unas gotas de esencia el pez derramó,
	y un mantel mágico apareció.
	El genio dijo:
GENIE:	*«Mantel, mantelito, dame la comida que yo necesito».*
CHORUS:	*En un banquete opulento se tranformó*
	y el chico contento a su casa marchó.
	En el camino de vuelta a su casa,
	y cuando por una posada pasa,
	dice al mantel:

PEDRITO: *Mantel, mantelito, dame la comida que yo necesito.*

CHORUS: *En un banquete opulento se tranformó.*
                           Y el posadero ambicioso todo lo vió,
                           y mientras Pedrito una siesta dormía,
                           el cambio del mantel el dueño hacía.
                           De vuelta a su casa, sin cambio notar,
                           a su madre el mantel quería mostrar;
                           y al mantel le dijo:

PEDRITO:	*Mantel, mantelito, dame la comida que yo necesito.*
CHORUS:	*El mantel ordinario nada ofreció,* *su madre, enfadada, a él repitió:*
MOTHER:	*Pedrito, Pedrito ve al río a pescar* *pues no hay comidita para cenar.*
CHORUS:	*Pedrito en el río un pez de oro pescó* *y el pez dorado de esta forma habló:*
GENIE:	*El poderoso genio del río soy, si tu me liberas un premio te doy.*
CHORUS:	*Pedrito en el río al pez liberó,* *y un palo curioso de él recibió.* *En el camino de vuelta a su casa,* *por una posada pasa.* *El posadero ambicioso,* *cambia el palo curioso* *y sin miedo dice:*
INNKEEPER:	*Palo, palito, dame los palos que yo necesito.*
CHORUS:	*Palos y palos el palo le dió,* *Y el posadero gritando a todos llamó.* *Primero devolvió el burro prodigioso.* *Después, el mágico mantel.* *Y el palo curioso, dejo de dar palos,* *al posadero ambicioso.*

          (oral tradition; adapted by Elena Forrer)

Romance de la noche

This poem can be performed in grade 1 or grade 2 as a play. A few months before the performance, the class can learn the recitation chorally at the beginning of the lesson as part of the repertoire. With gestures they can follow the teacher for some weeks, as some parts have been learned by heart. (After they are seated, the teacher can show the children several illustrations referring to the night, the Sun, the Moon, and the stars, and later ask questions about them. When most of the poem is ready, the play begins. Immediately, we can ask a student to be the Sun and another the night dressed in a black shawl covered with stars. Now the children begin to enter into an imagination as the parts of the poem are recited. During the following weeks, we can incorporate this recitation during our repertoire, and over consecutive days, we add more parts; for example, more children can be the stars and another the Moon. In the following weeks, a silk representing the sky can be added, which can be used to depict sunrise and sunset. I always like to add a song when the play begins to take form. Since I did not have a particular song for this poem, I adapted the music «*Pimpón es un Muñeco*» with the lyrics giving below.

NARRADORS:	*La noche tenía frío* *y se fue al sol con la queja.* *El sol, que es buena persona,* *Le dijo:*
SOL:	*Pues ten paciencia,* *y te haré yo una toquilla* *toda de linda calceta;* *las agujas, las del tiempo;* *los dedos, mis rayos sean:* *la lana un hilo de luz,* *y la Luna la madeja.* *Allí donde caiga un nudo* *he de poner una estrella.*
NARRADORS:	*El sol cumplió su palabra.* *Cuando terminó de hacerla,* *la noche quedó asombrada* *de toquilla tan espléndida.*

*Al echársela a los hombros,
la noche, que es friolera,
seguía teniendo frío;
pero al mirarse, por verla,
en el espejo del mar,
se quedó tan satisfecha*

*luciendo sobre la espalda
una toquilla de estrellas,
que se aguantó todo el frío
con tal de ir tan peripuesta;
y, como es agradecida,
se fue a ver al sol, dispuesta
a dar las gracias, muy fina,
por aquella gentileza.*

*Pero nunca se encontraban
sobre la celeste cresta,
porque cuando el sol subía,
ella bajaba la cuesta,
hasta que gritando fuerte,
a través de toda la esfera,
ella dijo:*

LUNA: *¡Gracias, rubio!
Y él dijo:*

Sol: *¡A tus pies, morena!*
—SALVADOR DE MADARIAGA (1886–1978)

SONG: "MUSIC FROM PIMPÓN ES UN MUÑECO"

*La noche tiene frío,
la noche tiene frío
y pide al buen sol, al buen sol;*

*Una toquilla gruesa
de lana y algodón, algodón.*

*Cuando las estrellas
comienzan a salir, a salir,*

*el sol se va a la cama
se acuesta, y a dormir a dormir.*

(popular; adapted by E. Forrer)

Las tres cabritas en verso

Esta recitación se puede incluir como parte del «Repertorio» con gestos. También el maestro puede variar la recitación recreando la historia con los dedos de la mano pretendiendo que son las cabritas. Cuando las clase ha memorizado la historia, se puede escenificar de acuerdo con las instrucciones ofrecidas en la sección de "Storytelling."

*Las tres cabritas traviesas hierba fresca querían comer.
Las tres cabritas traviesas le temían al ogro cruel.*

*Trin, trin, trin, trin
Pateaba con sus pezuñas.*

*¿Quién patea sus pezuñas y cruza mi puente?
Soy yo, la cabrita pequeñita.
Pues yo soy el ogro cruel y te quiero comer.*

*No, no me comas. Cabra mediana está más gordita y es más sabrosa.
Está bien, te puedes marchar.*

*Tran, tran, Tran, tran
Pateaba sus pezuñas.*

*¿Quién patea sus pezuñas y cruza mi puente?
Soy yo, la mediana de las cabritas.*

Pues yo soy el ogro cruel y te quiero comer.

*No, no me comas. Cabra grande está más gordita y es más sabrosa.
Está bien, te puedes marchar.*

*Tron, tron, tron, tron.
Pateaba sus pezuñas.*

*¿Quién patea sus pezuñas y cruza mi puente?
Soy yo la más grande las cabritas.*

Pues yo soy el ogro cruel y te quiero comer.

*¡No me comerás! Tengo dos cuernos como lanzas y con ellos te empujaré.
Cabra grande al ogro empujó y el ogro, al río se cayó.*

(oral tradition; adapted by Elena Forrer)

DAME LA MANO

This poem by Gabriela Mistral has a beautiful melody found on the Internet. It works well in grades 2 and 1. The children first learn the song and then the teacher begins by walking between the rows of the class while singing the melody and tapping the children's head randomly. The first child holds the teacher's hand, and all the children begin to form a line moving around the classroom. When all the children are connected and moving between the rows, they can sit down after they pass their own desk.

Dame la mano y danzaremos;
dame la mano y me amarás.
Como una flor los dos seremos,
como una flor y nada más...

El mismo verso cantaremos,
al mismo paso bailarás.
Como una espiga ondularemos,
como una espiga, y nada más.

Te llamas Rosa y yo Esperanza;
pero mi nombre olvidarás,
porque seremos una danza
en la colina, y nada más.
—Gabriela Mistral (1889–1957)

Una historia

Oculta en el corazón
de una pequeña semilla,
bajo la tierra una planta
en profunda paz dormía.
—¡Despierta!—Dijo el calor.
¡Despierta!— La lluvia fría.
la planta que oyó el llamado,
quiso ver lo que ocurría;
se puso un vestido verde
y estiró el cuerpo hacia arriba.
De toda planta que nace
ésta es la historia sencilla.
     —Manuel F. Juncos (1846–1927)

Para mi triguito

Agua de San Marcos
rey de los charcos.
Para mi triguito
que está muy bonito.
Para mi cebada
que está ya granada.
Para mi melón
que ya tiene flor.
Para mi sandía
que ya está florida.
Para mi aceituna
que ya tiene una.

(popular)

ENANITOS

Cuando está la luna
sobre el horizonte
muchos enanitos
juegan en el monte.

A las esquinitas
y a la rueda, rueda
juegan los enanos
bajo la arboleda.

Muy blanca la barba,
muy rojo el vestido,
los enanos juegan
sin hacer ruido.

Y así, como blandos
ovillos de lana,

por el campo corren
hacia la montaña.

—GERMÁN BERDIALES (1896–1975)

El invierno

This is a delightful poem for reenacting. After the children have learned a few verses, one can be chosen as "Father Winter" and the other can just be the child. It can also be acted out with gestures holding the palm of the hand as the door, a thumb as "Father Winter," and the pinky as the child.

Ha llegado un viejecito
despacito, despacito.

Con la nariz colorada
y larguísima barba.

Lleva un gorro hasta las cejas
que le tapa las orejas,
y un traje grueso de lana
cubierto de nieve blanca.

Llama—¡Tam, tam!— a una puerta.

¿Quén es?— un niño contesta.
El invierno soy, ¡abridme,
que estoy helado de frío!

Anónimo

Sopla, sopla el viento del Norte
sopla, sopla el viento Norte
Esta noche va a nevar.
—¿Qué va a hacer el jilguero?
¿El jilguerito que hará?
Se sentará en el granero
y allí se calentará.
En el manto de las alas
su cabeza esconderá.
¡Pobrecito jilguerito!
¡Vuela que te vas a helar!

(popular)

El sol es de oro

This poem is by Salvador de Madariaga. The students in grades 1 and 2 can perform it as a small play. Several weeks before performing the play, the teacher needs to work with gestures and speech. Every week the children can repeat the poem from their places with gestures. When they have learned the first part of this poem, the teacher can bring costumes for the class and help them act it out. To begin, the class forms a semicircle and some students are chosen to act out different characters with capes and props in front of the class. They will step forward according to their part, acting with movements as the class recites, and reciting in chorus.

CAST OF CHARACTERS: The Sun, the Moon, two or three stars, silversmith, gardener, and maiden.

(Children stand in a semicircle in front of the audience. The Sun, the Moon, and the stars come up to the front when they are named in the recitation.)

CHORUS:
El sol es de oro;
la luna es de plata;
las estrellitas,
de hojalata.

(Music of a lyre or xylophone. The silversmith steps to the front looking at the stars.)

CHORUS:
Vino un gran platero,
que quiso comprarlas:
¿Cuánto das por ellas?

SILVERSMITH:
—Mil onzas labradas:

CHORUS:
Para tantas joyas,
es poco dinero.
Vete con tus onzas,
mísero platero.

(The Silversmith returns to the semicircle.)

CHORUS:	*El sol es de oro;*
	la luna es de plata;
	las estrellitas,
	de hojalata.

(Music. A gardener appears from the other side.)

CHORUS:	*Vino un jardinero,*
	que quiso comprarlas.
	—¿Cuánto das por ellas?
GARDENER:	*—Mil rosas de Arabia.*
CHORUS:	*—Para tantas joyas,*
	tus rosas son pocas,
	vete, jardinero,
	vete con tus rosas.

(Gardener leaves with his roses. Music. A maiden appears in the center.)

CHORUS:	*Vino una doncella:*
	tez de terciopelo,
	lo ojos brillantes
	como otros dos cielos.
	—Doncella preciosa,
	¿Cuánto das por ellas?

(Maiden approaches as the Sun, the Moon, and the stars form a circle while moving their hands and turning.)

CHORUS:	*Mientras lo decía,*
	miró al firmamento:
	y sol, luna, estrellas,
	tomando sus ojos
	por otros dos cielos,
	radiantes de gozo
	se metieron dentro.

(Música de lyre o xilofón)

El sol es de oro;
La luna de plata;
y las estrellitas
de hojalata.

(At the end of the play, the students could sing «El sol se llama Lorenzo».)

—SALVADOR DE MADARIAGA (1886–1978)
(poem adapted for a play by Elena Forrer)

EL LAGARTO ESTÁ LLORANDO

El lagarto está llorando.
La lagarta está llorando.
El lagarto y la lagarta
con delantalitos blancos.
Han perdido sin querer
su anillo de desposados.
¡Ay, su anillito de plomo,
ay, su anillito plomado!
Un cielo grande y sin gente
monta en su globo a los pájaros.
El sol, capitán redondo,
lleva un chaleco de raso.
¡Miradlos qué viejos son!
¡Qué viejos son los lagartos!

¡Ay cómo lloran y lloran.
¡ay! ¡ay!, cómo están llorando.

—FEDERICO GARCÍA LORCA (1818–1936)

LA ARAÑA

An excellent fable to act out in grade 2

*La araña le dijo a la mosca
con muy corteses razones:*

*—Ven recorre mis salones,
examina este primor.*

*Pero la mosca dijo prudente
así contestó advertida:*

*—Al salón fuera enseguida;
pero no a tu comedor.*

—Manuel Ossorio Bernard (1839–1904)

La ardilla

La ardilla corre,
la ardilla vuela.
La ardilla salta
como locuela.
—Mamá, la ardilla
¿no va a la escuela?
Ven, ardillita,
tengo una jaula
que es muy bonita.
—No, yo prefiero
mi tronco de árbol
y mi agujero.

—Amado Nervo (1870–1919)

Zapatero

(Juego de manos y trabalenguas)

Zapatero remendero
que mete la aguja por el agujero.
Que ya la he metido,
que ya la he sacado.
Date la vuelta,
ya la he dado.

(popular)

La zorra y las uvas

We can tell this story to the children with the help of an illustration or a felt board. We begin by first introducing the recitation with gestures during the "repertoire." After a few lessons, we can bring the felt board and tell the story in our own words. At one point, in another lesson, we can also reenact the poem with props. The first part of the poem is more suitable for the recitation in the class.

Es voz común que a más del mediodía,
en ayunas la Zorra iba cazando;
halla una parra, quedase mirando
de la alta vid el fruto que pendía.
Cansábala mil ansias y congojas
no alcanzar a las uvas con la garra,
al mostrar a sus dientes la alta parra
negros racimos entre verdes hojas.
Miró, saltó y anduvo en probaduras,
pero vio el imposible ya de fijo.
Entonces fue cuando la Zorra dijo:
«No las quiero comer. No están maduras».

No por eso te muestres impaciente,
Si se te frustra, Fabio, algún intento:
Aplica bien el cuento,
Y di: No están maduras, frescamente.

—Félix María Samaniego (1745–1801)

Francisco de Asís: Los motivos del lobo

lobo!
Francisco salió
al lobo buscó en su madriguera.
cerca de una cueva encontró a la fiera
enorme que al verlo, se lanzó feroz
contra él. Francisco con voz dulce
alzando la mano
al lobo furioso dijo: ¡Paz hermano!
— Rubén Darío (1867–1916), *fragmento*

Los Sentidos

Niño, vamos a cantar
una bonita canción;
yo te voy a preguntar,
tu me vas a responder:
—Los ojos, ¿para qué son?
—Los ojos son para ver.
—¿Y el tacto?— Para tocar.
—¿Y el oído?— Para oír.
—¿Y el gusto?— Para gustar.
—¿Y el olfato?— Para oler.
—¿Y el alma? Para sentir,
para querer y para pensar.
— Amado Nervo (1870–1801)

El Zorro y el Cuervo

The following fable is an adaptation of Samaniego's «*El zorro y el cuervo*» for grade 2. Some of the stanzas have been omitted to facilitate the recitation.

En la rama de un árbol,
bien ufano y contento,
con un queso en el pico,
estaba el señor Cuervo.

Del olor atraído
un Zorro muy maestro,
le dijo estas palabras,
a poco más o menos:

«Tenga usted buenos días,
señor Cuervo, mi dueño;
vaya que estáis donoso,
mono, lindo en extremo.

Al oír un discurso
tan dulce y halagüeño,
de vanidad llevado,
quiso cantar el Cuervo.

Abrió su negro pico,
dejó caer el queso;
el muy astuto Zorro,
después de haberle preso,
le dijo:

«Señor bobo,
digerid las lisonjas
mientras yo como el queso».

—Félix Samaniego (1745–1801), fragmento

Segaba...

Segaba la niña y ataba
y a cada manadita descansaba.

Segaba...

Con el son de las hoces
cantan las aves
y responden las fuentes
al son del aire.

Segaba...
Segaba la niña y ataba,
y a cada manadita descansaba.

Segaba...
No sigas deprisa.
Que la que va atando es una niña.

(anónimo)

Canción del Maizal

It is possible to select a fragment of this poem for grade 3. Section III is especially conducive for recitation in the language lesson.

I

El maizal canta en el viento
verde, verde de esperanza.
Ha crecido en treinta días:
su rumor es alabanza.

Llega, llega al horizonte,
sobre la meseta afable,
y en el viento ríe entero
con su risa innumerable.

II

El maizal gime en el viento
para trojes ya maduro;
se quemaron sus cabellos
y se abrió su estuche duro.

Y su pobre manto seco
se le llena de gemidos:
el maizal gime en el viento
con su manto desceñido

III

Las mazorcas del maíz
a niñitas se parecen:
diez semanas en los tallos
bien prendidas que se mecen.

Tienen un vellito de oro
como de recién nacido
y unas hojas maternales
que les celan el rocío.
Y debajo de la vaina,

como niños escondidos,
con sus dos mil dientes de oro
ríen, ríen sin sentido…

Las mazorcas del maíz
a niñitas se parecen:
en las cañas maternales
bien prendidas que se mecen.

El descansa en cada troje
con silencio de dormido;
va soñando, va soñando
un maizal recién nacido.

—Gabriela Mistral (1889–1957)

Los dias de la semana y sus actividades:
Recitación y canción de «La Bella Hortelana»

En los lunes sembró.
En martes regó.
En miércoles cosechó.
En jueves molió.
En viernes cocinó.
En sábado amasó.
Y en domingo descansó.
              (popular)

La Bella Hortelana

Cuando siembra la bella hortelana,
cuando siembra, siembra así.
Sí, siembra poco a poco,
luego pone las manos así;
siembra así, luego pone las manos así.
Cuando riega la bella hortelana,
cuando riega, riega así;
sí, riega poco a poco,
luego pone las manos así.
Siembra así riega así, luego pone las manos así.

Cuando corta...
Cuando muele...
Cuando tortea...
Cuándo come...
              (popular song)

Poesía

La señora luna
le pidió al naranjo
un vestido verde
y un velillo blanco.

La señora luna
se quiere casar
con un pajarito
de plata y coral.

Duérmete niña
e irás a la boda
peinada de moño
y en traje de cola.

—Juana de Ibarborou (1895–1979)

El Barquito de papel

Con la mitad de un periódico
hice un barco de papel,
en la fuente de mi casa
le hice navegar muy bien.
Mi hermana con su abanico
sopla y sopla sobre él.
¡Buen viaje, muy buen viaje,
barquichuelo de papel!

—Amado Nervo (1870–1919)

La Lechera

Camino al mercado a vender
una lechera temprano
con el cántaro en la mano
soñaba en dinero obtener.

Ocho docenas de huevos
que luego pollitos se harán
y en nueva venta darán
para dos lechones buenos.

Comiendo de mis castañas
pronto gordos los veré
y una vaca compraré
que corra entre las cabañas.

Contenta la chica saltó
brincando de tal manera
que el cántaro por la ladera
la leche rodando cayó.

No hay ya leche, no hay dinero
no hay pollitos ni lechones
ni la vaca entre algodones
cuidada con tanto esmero.

¡Ay! Lechera, tu ambición
muchas ideas te ha dado
sin haberte percatado
que era todo una ilusión.

—Santiago Muelas Medrano
(1943–2011)

El Molino

De harina, blanca y fina,
mi saquito llenarás.
Muele el trigo, Catalina,
tac, tic, tac, tic, tac, tic, tac.

Qué cargada va la niña,
su saquito lleno está,
se oye el ruido del molino,
tac, tic.
        (popular)

Siembra

En febrero siembra el vero,
en marzo, el garbanzo;
en abril, el maíz;
en mayo, esperarlo;
y cuando llega San Juan,
los dineros te darán.

Desgraciado el labrador
que siembra y no coge trigo;
más desgraciado soy yo
que no me caso contigo.
    (Provincia de Cáceres España, popular)

Las tres ovejas

Tengo, tengo, tengo;
tú no tienes nada,
tengo tres ovejas
en una cabaña.

Una me da leche,
otra me da lana,
otra mantequilla
para la semana.
        (popular)

Meses

Enero, febrero, te quiero, te quiero.
marzo y abril, verde perejil,
mayo y junio, el trigo está rubio.
Julio y agosto, calor en el rostro.
Septiembre y octubre la capa me cubre.
Noviembre y diciembre, el gato que tiemble.

Treinta días tiene noviembre
con abril, junio y septiembre.
De veintinueve sólo hay uno,
los demás son treinta y uno.
        (anónimo)

Poetry and Recitation through the Grades

EL SILBO DEL DALE

Dale al aspa, molino,

hasta nevar el trigo.

Dale a la piedra, agua,

hasta ponerla mansa.

Dale al molino, aire,

hasta lo inacabable.

Dale al aire, cabrero,

hasta que silbe tierno.

Dale al cabrero, monte,

hasta dejarle inmóvil.

Dale al monte, lucero,

hasta que se haga cielo.

Dale, Dios, a mi alma,

hasta perfeccionarla.

Dale que dale, dale

molino, piedra, aire,

cabrero, monte, astro;

dale que dale largo.

Dale que dale, Dios,

¡ay!,

hasta la perfección.

—MIGUEL HERNÁNDEZ (1910–1942)

Una vieja y un viejo

Una vieja y un viejo
no tenían para comer
más que un queso,
y vino un ratón y se lo comió.

Entonces vino el gato
y se comió al ratón
que comió el queso
de la vieja y del viejo.

Entonces vino el perro y comió al gato
porque comió al ratón
que comió el queso
de la vieja y del viejo.

Entonces vino el palo y pegó al perro
porque comió al gato
porque comió al ratón
que comió el queso
de la vieja y del viejo.

Entonces vino el fuego y quemó el palo,
porque comió al perro
porque comió al gato,
porque comió al ratón
que comió el queso de la vieja y del viejo.

Entonces vino el agua y apagó al fuego
porque quemó al palo,
porque comió al perro
porque comió al gato
porque comió al ratón,
que comió el queso de la vieja y el viejo.

Entonces vino el burro y bebió el agua,
porque apagó el fuego,
porque quemó el palo,
porque comió al perro,
porque comió al gato,
porque comió al ratón
que comió el queso de la vieja y el viejo.

El burro ya durmió.
El cuento acabó.
Y la vieja y el viejo
sin queso se quedó.

(tradición oral)

Doña Primavera

Doña Primavera
viste que es primor,
viste en limonero
y en naranjo en flor.

Lleva por sandalias
unas anchas hojas,
y por caravanas
unas fucsias rojas.

Salid a encontrarla
por esos caminos.
¡Va loca de soles
y loca de trinos!

Doña Primavera
de aliento fecundo,
se ríe de todas
las penas del mundo...

No cree al que le hable
de las vidas ruines.
¿Cómo va a toparlas
entre los jazmines?

¿Cómo va a encontralas
junto de las fuentes
de espejos dorados
y cantos ardientes?

De la tierra enferma
en las pardas grietas,
enciende rosales
de rojas piruetas.

Pone sus encajes,
prende sus verduras,
en la piedra triste
de las sepulturas...

Doña Primavera
de manos gloriosas,
haz que por la vida
derramemos rosas:

Rosas de alegría,
rosas de perdón,
rosas de cariño,
y de exultación.

—GABRIELA MISTRAL (1889–1957)

7.2 Selection of Poetry and Stories in Rhyme for the Middle Grades (Grades 4 and 5)

As the children grow older, we also need to be aware of their changing needs and adapt our approach to meet them. We need to "step into their shoes" and bring vivid images of a different content. Poems speaking to the mood of nature, the environment, filial love, or poems about botany, for instance, are appropriate themes. It is important that the students sense the rhythm and the beauty of poems such as «*Caricias*» by Gabriela Mistral, «*Soy el gallo*» by A. Marquerίe, or «*Los troncos muertos*» by Juan Ramón Jiménez. These are good examples of poetry for the fourth and fifth grades.

It is helpful in the middle grades to give the students an image of the poem they are speaking, using your own words. For instance, in the first poem by Gabriela Mistral, we can speak about the special love and closeness we feel for a father or mother and the feelings we experience when we are hugged or kissed by them. If we teach the poem «*Los troncos muertos*», we can talk about life in a rural village, where we can smell and hear nature surrounding us. These images prepare the children for their recitation. As the verses unfold, often the students ask for a particular translation of a word.

As the students get older, special attention has to be given to enunciation; the power of imitation is no longer present in the children, and although the teacher will still bring some small gestures as she repeats the verses, the students will be repeating the stanzas without the gestures they used to execute in the younger grades. In each lesson, the teacher paints a deeply-felt image of the poem in the students' mother tongue. More and more the students will penetrate the sounds as rich images are brought to them without translation.

After the students have learned several stanzas from the poem, they can look at it on the board and then illustrate the images. The following is a fragment from the poem *Los troncos muertos* and a rendering of the poem from one of the students' books (the complete poem is on page 226).

LOS TRONCOS MUERTOS (FRAGMENTO)

Ya están ahí las carretas...
Lo han dicho el pinar y el viento,
lo ha dicho la luna de oro,
lo han dicho el humo y el eco...

Son las carretas que pasan
estas tardes, al sol puesto,
las carretas que se llevan
del monte los troncos muertos.

¡Cómo lloran las carretas,
camino de Pueblo Nuevo!

—Juan Ramón Jiménez

Caitlin Sullivan, San Francisco Waldorf School

ÉSTA ES LA CASA QUE JUAN CONSTRUYÓ

Esta recitación puede ser apropiada para el cuarto grado. Primero se pueden traer a la clase ilustraciones y luego disfraces.

Ésta es la casa
que Juan construyó

Y éste es el grano
guardado en la casa
que Juan construyó.

Y esta es la rata
que se comió el grano
guardado en la casa
que Juan construyó.

Y esta es la gata
que persiguió a la rata,
que se comió el grano
guardado en la casa
que Juan construyó.

Y este es el perro
que persiguió a la gata,
que cazó a la rata,
que se comió el grano
guardado en la casa
que Juan construyó.

Y esta es la vaca
del cuerno torcido
que revolcó al perro,
que persiguió a la gata,
que cazó a la rata,
que se comió el grano
guardado en la casa
que Juan construyó.

Y ésta es la muchacha
del roto vestido
que ordeñó a la vaca
del cuerno torcido.
Que revolcó al perro,
que persiguió a la gata,
que cazó a la rata,
que se comió el grano
guardado en la casa
que Juan construyó.

Y éste es el muchacho
feo y atrevido
novio de la muchacha
del roto vestido,
que ordeñó a la vaca
del cuerno torcido.
Que revolcó al perro,
que persiguió a la gata,
que cazó a la rata,
que se comió el grano
guardado en la casa
que Juan construyó.

Y éste es el cura
del pueblo llegado
que casó al muchacho
feo y atrevido
novio de la muchacha,
del roto vestido,
que ordeñó a la vaca
del cuerno torcido.

Que revolcó al perro,
que persiguió a la gata,
que cazó a la rata
que se comió el grano
guardado en la casa
que Juan construyó.

Y éste es el gallo
que al alba ha cantado
despertando al cura
del pueblo llegado,
que casó al muchacho
feo y atrevido,
novio de la muchacha
del roto vestido,
que ordeñó a la vaca
del cuerno torcido.
Que revolcó al perro,
que persiguió a la gata,
que cazó a la rata
que se comió el grano
guardado en la casa
que Juan construyó.

Este es granjero
que el grano ha sembrado
que picoteó el gallo
que al alba ha cantado,
despertando al cura
del pueblo llegado
que casó al muchacho
feo y atrevido,
novio de la muchacha
del roto vestido,
Que ordeñó a la vaca
del cuerno torcido.
Que revolcó al perro,

que persiguió a la gata,
que cazó a la rata,
que se comió el grano
guardado en la casa
que Juan construyó.

(Popular)

Los troncos muertos

Ya están ahí las carretas...
Lo han dicho el pinar y el viento,
lo ha dicho la luna de oro,
lo han dicho el humo y el eco...

Son las carretas que pasan
estas tardes, al sol puesto,
las carretas que se llevan
del monte los troncos muertos.

¡Cómo lloran las carretas,
camino de Pueblo Nuevo!

Los bueyes vienen soñando,
a la luz de los luceros,
en el establo caliente
que sabe a madre y a heno.

Y detrás de las carretas,
caminan los carreteros,
con la aijada sobre el hombro
y los ojos en el cielo.

¡Cómo lloran las carretas,
camino de Pueblo Nuevo!

En la paz del campo, van
dejando los troncos muertos
un olor fresco y honrado
a corazón descubierto.

Y cae el ángelus desde
la torre del pueblo viejo,
sobre los campos talados,
que huelen a cementerio.

¡Cómo lloran las carretas
camino de Pueblo Nuevo!

—Juan Ramón Jiménez (1881–1959)

CUENTAN DE UN SABIO QUE UN DÍA

*Cuentan de un sabio que un día
tan pobre y mísero estaba,
que sólo se sustentaba
de unas hierbas que cogía.
¿Habrá otro, entre sí decía,
más pobre y triste que yo?
Y cuando el rostro volvió
halló la respuesta, viendo
que otro sabio iba cogiendo
las hierbas que él arrojó.*

*Quejoso de mi fortuna
yo en este mundo vivía,
y cuando entre mí decía:
habrá otra persona alguna
de suerte más importuna?
Piadoso me has respondido
Pues, volviendo a mi sentido,
hallo que las penas mías,
para hacerlas tú alegrías,
las hubieras recogido*

—Calderón de la Barca (1601–1681)
(fragmento de La vida es sueño)

DIOS LO SABRÁ

*Eran Carlitos y Adela
dos hermanos cariñosos,
con los pobres bondadosos,
y aplicados en la escuela.*

*Al salir de clase un día,
frente a la iglesia pasaron,
y en la puerta se encontraron
con un pobre que dormía.*

*Despertarlo quiere el niño,
para darle el pan que tiene;
mas Adela lo detiene
y le dice con cariño:*

*—¡Ay, qué cansado estará!
Déjalo al pobre dormido.
—¿Sabrá quién lo ha socorrido?
—Él no, mas Dios lo sabrá…*

—Leonardo Lis

El Invierno

Sopla, sopla viento norte
que esta noche va a nevar
¿qué va a hacer el jilguerito?
El jilguerito ¿qué hará?
Se sentará en el granero
y allí se calentará.
En el manto de las alas
su cabeza esconderá
¡pobrecito jilguerito!
¡Vuela, que te vas a helar!
        (popular)

Mariposa

Mariposa del aire,
qué hermosa eres,
mariposa del aire
dorada y verde.
Luz del candil,
mariposa del aire,
¡quédate ahí, ahí, ahí!
No te quieres parar,
pararte no quieres.
Mariposa del aire
dorada y verde.
Luz de candil,
mariposa del aire,
¡quédate ahí, ahí, ahí!
¡Quédate ahí!
Mariposa, ¿estás ahí?
—Federico García Lorca (1898-1936)

Las campanas

Yo las amo, yo las oigo,
cual oigo el rumor del viento,
el murmurar de la fuente
o el balido de cordero.
Como los pájaros, ellas,
tan pronto asoma en los cielos
el primer rayo del alba,
le saludan con sus ecos.
Y en sus notas, que van prolongándose
por los llanos y los cerros,
hay algo de candoroso,
de apacible y de halagüeño.
Si por siempre enmudecieran,
¡qué tristeza en el aire y el cielo!
¡Qué silencio en la iglesia!
¡Qué extrañeza entre los muertos!
    —Rosalía de Castro (1837-1885)

El viento

El viento juega en los árboles
en el monte y en el valle,
hace ondular las praderas
que se visten de trigales.

El viento juega en el mar
haciendo rodar el agua,
a las olas de la mano
el viento lleva a la playa.

Cómo poder yo jugar
como el viento, como el agua,
y hacer anillos de cielo
para ponerme en el alma.

—Bernardo Gutiérrez,
poeta chileno

Plantemos el árbol

Abramos la tierra, plantemos el árbol,
será nuestro amigo y aquí crecerá,
y un día vendremos buscando su abrigo
y flores y frutas y sombra dará.

El cielo benigno dé riego a su planta,
el sol de septiembre le dé su calor,
la tierra su jugo dará a sus raíces
y tengan sus hojas verdura y frescor.

Plantemos el árbol, el árbol amigo;
sus ramas frondosas aquí extenderá,
y un día vendremos buscando sus flores
y sombras y frutas y flores dará.

—Enrique E. Rivarola, 1862

Ésta es la llave de Roma

This recitation can be played as a game after the class has memorized all the new vocabulary. The game begins with all the players seated in a circle. The first player has a key, touches the floor with the key, and passes the key to the next player while repeating the first line:

«Ésta es la llave de Roma y toma».

The second player takes the key and repeats the first line, adding the second line and then tapping the floor before passing the key:

«Ésta es la llave de Roma y toma.
En Roma hay una casa».

The game continues with all the players adding a line, tapping the floor with the key and passing the key to the next player. If the player forgets any of these things, then the game needs to start all over gain, or just that player is eliminated.

Ésta es la llave de Roma y toma.
En Roma hay una calle.
En la calle hay una casa.
En la casa hay un patio.
En el patio hay una sala.
En la sala hay una alcoba
En la alcoba hay una dama.
Junto a la dama, una mesa.
En la mesa hay una jaula.
Dentro de la jaula un loro.

Saltó el loro.
Saltó la jaula.
Saltó la mesa.
Saltó la dama.
Saltó la cama.
Saltó la alcoba.
Saltó la sala.
Saltó el patio.
Saltó la casa.
Saltó la calle. Y aquí tienes a Roma
Con todas sus siete llaves.

(anónimo)

CARICIAS

Madre, madre, tú me besas;
pero yo te beso más.
Como el agua en los cristales,
son mis besos en tu faz.

Te he besado tanto, tanto,
que de mí cubierta estás
y el enjambre de mis besos
no te deja ya mirar...

Yo te miro, yo te miro,
sin cansarme de mirar,
y que lindo niño veo,
a tus ojos asomar...
—GABRIELA MISTRAL (1889–1957)

CARACOLA

Me han traído una caracola
Dentro le canta
un mar de mapa.
Mi corazón
se llena de agua
con pececillos
de sombra y plata.

Me han traído una caracola.
—FEDERICO GARCÍA LORCA
(1898–1936)

ARROYO CLARO

Arroyo claro,
fuente serena,
quién te lava el pañuelo
saber quisiera.

—Cuatro morenas:
una lo lava,
otra lo tiende,
otra le tira rosas
y otra claveles.
(popular)

ÁRBOLES

Los sauces lloran
los álamos son de plata
los cipreses tan altos
la tristeza los mata.

Los cedros son oscuros
y el pino verde, verde.
el olmo es orgulloso,
por el llano se pierde.
(popular)

La pobre Viejecita

Érase una viejecita
sin nadita qué comer
sino carnes, frutas, dulces
tortas, huevos, pan y pez.

Bebía caldo, chocolate,
leche, vino, té y café
y la pobre no encontraba
qué comer ni qué beber.

Y esta vieja no tenía
ni un ranchito en qué vivir
fuera de una casa grande
con su huerta y su jardín.

Nadie, nadie la cuidaba
sino Andrés y Juan y Gil
y ocho criadas y dos pajes
de librea y corbatín.

Nunca tuvo en qué sentarse
sino sillas y sofás
con banquitos y cojines
y resorte al espaldar

Ni otra cama que una grande
más dorada que un altar,
con colchón de blanda pluma,
mucha seda y mucho olán.

Y esta pobre viejecita
cada año, hasta su fin,
tuvo un año más de vieja
y uno menos que vivir.

Y al mirarse en el espejo
la espantaba siempre allí
otra vieja de antiparras,
papalina y peluquín.

Y esta pobre viejecita
no tenía que vestir
sino trajes de mil cortes
y de telas mil y mil.

Y a no ser por sus zapatos,
chanclas, botas y escarpín,
descalcita por el suelo
anduviera la infeliz.

Apetito nunca tuvo
acabando de comer,
ni gozó salud completa
cuando no se hallaba bien.

Se murió del mal de arrugas,
ya encorvada como un tres,
y jamás volvió a quejarse
ni de hambre ni de sed.

Y esta pobre viejecita
al morir no dejó más
que onzas, joyas, tierras, casas,
ocho gatos y un turpial.

Duerma en paz, y Dios permita
que logremos disfrutar
las pobrezas de esa pobre
y morir del mismo mal

—Rafael Pombo (1833–1912)

Canción

Gris y morado es mi verde olivar;
blanca mi casa y azul mi mar.
Cuando tú vengas no me vas a encontrar;
yo seré un pájaro del verde olivar.
Cuando tú vengas no me vas a encontrar;
seré una llamita roja del hogar.
Cuando tú vengas no me vas a encontrar;
seré una estrella encima del mar.
—José Moreno Villa (1887–1955)

A la montaña

A la montaña
nos vamos ya,
a la montaña
para jugar.

En sus laderas
el árbol crece,
brilla el arroyo,
la flor se mece.

Qué lindo el aire,
qué bello el sol,
azul el cielo:
¡se siente a Dios!
—Alfonsina Storni
(1892–1938)

Tarde del Trópico

Es la tarde gris y triste.
Viste el mar de terciopelo
y el cielo profundo viste
de duelo.

Del abismo se levanta
la queja amarga y sonora.
La onda, cuando el viento canta,
llora.

Los violines de la bruma
saludan al sol que muere.
Salmodia la blanca espuma:
¡Miserere!

La armonía el cielo inunda,
y la brisa va a llevar
la canción triste y profunda
del mar.

Del clarín del horizonte
brota sinfonía rara,
como si la voz del monte
vibrara.

Cual si fuese lo invisible ...
cual si fuese el rudo son
que diese al viento un terrible
león.
—Rubén Darío (1869–1916)

El gallo

Yo soy el gallo más gallo
Que existe en el gallinero.
Mi cresta es como una llama,
Mis espolones de acero;
Y el arco iris envidia
Mi cola de gran plumero.
Al que busca pelea
Lo deshago como quiero.
Si digo kikirikí…,
Se estremece el mundo entero.
—Alfredo Marqueríe
(1907–1974)

Árboles

Los sauces lloran
los álamos son de plata
los cipreses tan altos
la tristeza los mata.

Los cedros son oscuros
y el pino verde, verde.
El olmo es orgulloso,
por el llano se pierde
(popular)

Los hermanos (fragmento)

Yo tengo tantos hermanos
que no los puedo contar.
En el valle, la montaña,
en la pampa y en el mar.

Cada cual con sus trabajos,
con sus sueños cada cual.
Con la esperanza delante,
con los recuerdos detrás.

Yo tengo tantos hermanos
que no los puedo contar.
—Atahualpa Yupanqui
(1908–1992)[8]

---

8   Mercedes Sosa covered the song in 1977; available on CD as "Mercedes Sosa interpreta a Atahualpa Yupanqui."

EN ABRIL, LAS AGUAS MIL (FRAGMENTO)

Son de abril las aguas mil.
Sopla el viento achubascado,
y entre nublado y nublado
hay trozos de cielo añil.
Agua y sol. El iris brilla.
En una nube lejana,
zigzaguea
una centella amarilla.
La lluvia da en la ventana
y el cristal repiquetea.
A través de la neblina
que forma la lluvia fina,
se divisa un prado verde,
y un encinar se esfumina,
y una sierra gris se pierde…
Lluvia y sol. Ya se oscurece
el campo, ya se ilumina;
allí un cerro desparece,
allá surge una colina.
Ya son claros, ya sombríos
los dispersos caseríos
los lejanos torreones.
Hacia la sierra plomiza
van rodando en pelotones
nubes de nata y ceniza.
—Antonio Machado (1875–1937)

7.3 POETRY AND RECITATION IN THE UPPER GRADES

As the students approach adolescence, they gain more individuality. In the sixth, seventh and eighth grades, the teacher will want to choose poems that enrich the souls of the maturing children, poems that will speak to them as they practice it through repetition. The students of this age need a clear image of what they are saying so they can also enter into the sound. Many teachers wonder if during this time they should distribute a written copy of the poem to all the students in class; however, as the students become more conscious of the written word, they do not rely any longer on the sound, but are rather trapped in the reading. My experience has been that as the students bring a "thinking" quality into the recitation, their speech becomes sluggish and dull and their enunciation and pronunciation are not nearly as pure as when they speak without the paper. Often when the students themselves realize this effect, they prefer not to follow the reading, instead they want to feel the poem through the rhythm and the sound.

Although with short poems, the students are comfortable just speaking them by heart, I have found that it is helpful for the students when learning long poems such as the poems mentioned below, to first learn a good portion following the teacher but then, after a number of lessons only reciting the poem by heart, to give them a copy, so different parts can be assigned to different students or a particular image can be brought to their attention. Then, as the students begin talking about the image the poet has brought forward, they themselves can also bring "consciousness" and an opinion to the topic.

For instance, if they are learning the poem by Nicolas Guillén, «*Los abuelos*», the students first feel the language chosen by the author. They hear the beat of the African drums in the contrasting images of the heritage of the two *abuelos*: the Afro-Cuban and the European. As the students begin to hear the contrast in the description, and when the content in the duality becomes apparent, divide the class into two groups, one reciting the stanzas for one of the grandfathers and the other half, for the other. When I taught this particular poem, the students were able to transport themselves with the sounds, and while many preferred to rely purely on the sound and leave behind a copy, others needed to use the written poem as a guide to keep them moving through the long recitation. This poem allowed for difficult but powerful images to ignite the curiosity of the students and led us into the students' first real literary discussions in a second language.

In the upper grades, success will depend upon how capable the teacher is in involving the students in the images of the poem, and in giving them an inner vision. If for instance, if you choose to teach the poem by José Martí, «*Los zapaticos de rosa*», the students in the eighth or seventh grade can peer into the social divisions at the turn of the nineteenth century while following the course of this lovely story bathed in sound and color. You would need to prepare the poem so the different stanzas are clearly assigned in parts. The first day you might give a summary of the context of the poem; I have used the book illustrated by Lulu Delacre, to introduce a description of the poem.[9] In the following days, without a written copy, the class can begin reciting the beginning of the poem:

Hay sol bueno y mar de espuma,
y arena fina, y Pilar
quiere salir a estrenar
su sombrerito de pluma.

«¡Vaya la niña divina!»
dice el padre y le da un beso:
«¡Vaya mi pájaro preso
a buscarme arena fina!»

«*Yo voy con mi niña hermosa*»,
le dijo la madre buena:
«*¡No te manches en la arena*
los zapaticos de rosa!»

Fueron las dos al jardín
por la calle del laurel:
la madre cogió un clavel
y Pilar cogió un jazmín.

---

9 Marti and Delacre, "Los zapaticos de Rosa."

After a few classes, you can prepare parts and distribute copies to the students as follows.[10]

> NARRATORS: *Hay sol bueno y mar de espuma*
> *y arena fina, y Pilar*
> *quiere salir a estrenar*
> *su sombrerito de pluma.*
>
> PADRE: *¡Vaya la niña divina!*
>
> NARRATORS: *Dice el padre y le da un beso:*
>
> PADRE: *¡Vaya mi pájaro preso*
> *A buscarme arena fina!*
>
> MADRE: *Yo voy con mi niña hermosa,*
>
> NARRATORS: *Le dijo la madre buena:*
>
> MADRE: *¡No te manches en la arena*
> *Los zapaticos de rosa!*
>
> NARRATORS: *Fueron las dos al jardín*
> *por la calle del laurel:*
> *la madre cogió un clavel*
> *y Pilar cogió un jazmín.*

For the sixth grade, the age of chivalry, or what we call romances, is a great source of poetry. It provides the students with satisfying individual parts. Romances such as «*Las tres cautivas*» or «*La vuelta del cid*» or «*Las señas del esposo*» can be excellent poems for this grade.

In the upper grades, the poems often serve as a bridge for the teacher to talk about geographical, social or historical topics. It is always helpful to give the students an historical context in their mother tongue. For instance, the teacher can explain life in Medieval Muslim Spain. These presentations require some research and can be enhanced through pictures of Spanish Moslem palaces and castles or a map of Spain to illustrate the story geographically.

The following ballad or romance «*La vuelta del Cid*» gives us a particularly good example of what is described above. This famous poem describes the night of el Cid's victorious return to Castile from the kingdom of Valencia. We can talk about how el Cid befriended Moslem kings

---

10   The example given here illustrates only the beginning of the poem.

and Christian kings throughout his life, while maintaining his loyalty to both, a great social gesture that speaks especially to the socially awakened in a sixth grade class.

Here we can have the class reciting chorally the first stanzas from «*La vuelta del Cid*»: Then have a student or students repeat the individual part for El Cid:

Victorioso vuelve el Cid
a San Pedro de Cardeña,
de las guerras que ha tenido
con los moros de Valencia.

Las trompetas van sonando
por dar aviso que llega,
y entre todos se señalan
los relinchos de Babieca.

—Salí de ti, templo santo,
desterrado de mi tierra;
mas ya vuelvo a visitarte
acogido en las ajenas.

Desterrome el rey Alfonso
porque allá en Santa Gadea
le tomé su juramento
con más rigor que él quisiera…

¡Oh, envidiosos castellanos,
cuán mal pagáis la defensa
que tuvisteis en mi espada
ensanchando vuestra cerca!

El abad y monjes salen
a recibirle a la puerta,
dando alabanzas a Dios
y al Cid mil enhorabuenas.

Apeóse del caballo,
y antes de entrar en la iglesia
tomó el pendón de sus manos,
y dice de esta manera:

¿Veis?, aquí os traigo ganado
otro reino y mil fronteras,
que os quiero dar tierras mías
aunque me echéis de las vuestras.

Pudiera dárselo a extraños;
mas, para cosas tan feas,
soy Rodrigo de Vivar,
castellano a derechas.

(romancero)

Poetry will often be part of our whole lesson. If for instance we are going to cover a particular topic, such as a geographic region, medieval history, or biography we can plan, we can plan ahead for the integration of this topic though poems, music, and stories. The content of the lesson will be woven as a whole, and will not focus solely on a poem.

La canción del pirata

Con diez cañones por banda,
viento en popa a toda vela,
no corta el mar, sino vuela,
un velero bergantín:
Bajel pirata que llaman,
por su bravura el Temido
en todo mar conocido
del uno al otro confín.

La luna en el mar riela,
en la lona gime el viento,
y alza en blando movimiento
olas de plata y azul;
y ve el capitán pirata,
cantando alegre en la popa,
Asia a un lado; al otro, Europa;
y allá a su frente, Estambul.

«Navega, velero mío,
sin temor;
que ni enemigo navío,
ni tormenta, ni bonanza,
tu rumbo a torcer alcanza,
ni a sujetar tu valor».

Veinte presas, hemos hecho
a despecho, del inglés
y han rendido cien naciones
sus pendones a mis pies».

* Que es mi barco mi tesoro,
que es mi Dios la libertad,
mi ley la fuerza y el viento,
mi única patria la mar.

«Allá muevan feroz guerra,
ciegos reyes
por un palmo más de tierra;
que yo tengo aquí por mío,
cuanto abarca el mar bravío,
a quien nadie impuso leyes.

Y no hay playa,
sea cualquiera,
ni bandera,
de esplendor,
que no sienta
mi derecho
y dé pecho
a mi valor».

* Que es mi barco mi tesoro…

A la voz de «¡Barco viene!».
es de ver
cómo vira y se previene,
a todo trapo escapar;
que yo soy el rey del mar,
y mi furia es de temer.

En las presas
yo divido
lo cogido
por igual;
sólo quiero
por riqueza
la belleza
sin rival.

Que es mi barco mi tesoro…

¡Sentenciado estoy a muerte!
Yo me río;

no me abandone la suerte
y al mismo que me condena,
colgaré de alguna entena,
quizá en su propio navío.

Y si caigo,
¿qué es la vida?
Por perdida
ya la di,
cuando el yugo
del esclavo
como un bravo
sacudí.

* *Que es mi barco mi tesoro...*

«Son mi música mejor
aquilones;
el estrépito y temblor
de los cables sacudidos,
del negro mar los bramidos
y el rugir de mis cañones.

Y del trueno
al son violento,
y del viento
al rebramar,
yo me duermo
sosegado,
arrullado
por la mar».

Que es mi barco mi tesoro,
que es mi Dios la libertad,
mi ley la fuerza y el viento,
mi única patria la mar.

—José de Espronceda (1808–1842)

Las señas del esposo

—Soldadito, soldadito
¿De dónde ha venido usted?
—He venido de la guerra,
de la guerra de Aranjuez.
—¿Ha visto usted a mi marido
una vez en Aranjuez?
—Si le he visto, no me acuerdo:
déme usted las señas de él.

—Mi marido es alto y rubio,
alto y rubio y aragonés,
en la punta de la lanza
lleva un pañuelo bordés,
se lo borde cuando niña,
cuando niña lo bordé;
uno se lo estoy bordando
y otro que le bordaré.

Siete años llevo esperando,
Y otros siete esperaré,
Si a los catorce no viene,
Monjita me meteré.
—Calla Isabelita, calla,
calla, por Dios, Isabel,
que yo soy tu querido esposo,
tú, mi querida mujer.

(anónimo)

El día de los torneos

This Romance can be part of a performance with grade 6 in the same way as «*Conde Olinos*» or «*Las tres cautivas*». During the beginning of the lesson the students can recite the story, and later they can be acted out. Another way to present this poem is as a shadow play as suggested in the book *Senderos*. By doing so, recorder music from the time can be incorporated. The shadow cuts are very easy and inexpensive and a simple onionskin paper with a frame can be the screen.

*El día de los torneos
pasé por la morería,
y vi. una mora lavando
al pie de la fuente fría.*

*—Apártate, mora bella,
apártate, mora linda,
que va a beber mi caballo
de esa agua cristalina.*

*—No soy mora, caballero,
que soy cristiana cautiva;
me cautivaron los moros
el día de Pascua Florida.*

*—¿Te quieres venir conmigo?
— De buena gana me iría, me iría;
mas los pañuelos que lavo
¿en dónde los dejaría?*

*—Los de seda y los de Holanda
aquí, en mi caballo, irían,
y los que nada valieren,
la corriente llevaría.*

*La hizo subir al caballo,
y a su casa la traía.*

*—¿De qué te ríes, morita?
—No me río del caballo,
ni tan poco del que guía,
me río al ver esta tierra,
que es toda patria mía.*

*Al llegar a aquellos montes,
ella a llorar se ponía.*

*—¿Por qué lloras, mora bella?
¿Por qué lloras, mora linda?
—Lloro porque en estos montes
mi padre a cazar venía.
—¿Cómo se llama tu padre?
—Mi padre Juan de Oliva.*

*—¡Válgame la fe de Dios
y también la de María!
¡Pensaba que era una mora,
y llevo una hermana mía!
¡Abra usted, madre, las puertas,
ventanas y celosías,
que aquí le traigo la rosa
que esperaba noche y día.*

(popular)

El conde Olinos (Shadow Play)

*Madrugaba el conde Olinos,
mañanitas de san Juan,
a dar agua a su caballo
a las orillas del mar,*

*Mientras el caballo bebe,
se oye un hermoso cantar;
las aves que iban volando
se paraban a escuchar.*

*Desde las torres más altas
la Reina le oyó cantar.
—Mira hija, como canta
la sirenita del mar.*

*—No es la sirenita, madre,
que ésta tiene otro cantar;
es la voz del conde Olinos
que por mí penando está.
—Si es la voz del conde Olinos
yo le mandaré matar;
que para casar contigo
le falta sangre real.*

*—No le mande matar, madre,
no le mande usted matar;
que si mata al conde Olinos
a mí la muerte me va.*

Guardias mandaba la Reina
al conde Olinos buscar,
que le maten a lanzadas
y echen su cuerpo a la mar.

La infantina, con gran pena,
no cesaba de llorar.
Él murió a la media noche
y ella, a los gallos cantar.
  (tradición oral)

LAS TRES CAUTIVAS

En el valle, valle
de la verde oliva,
donde cautivaron
tres hermosas niñas.
—¿Cómo se llamaban?
—¿Cómo se decían?
—La una Constanza;
la otra Lucía,
y la más pequeña
era Rosalinda.

—¿En qué se empleaban
estas tres cautivas?
—Constanza amasaba;
Lucía cosía,
y la más pequeña
el agua traía.

Fue un día por agua
a la fuente fría.
Se encontró un buen viejo
y el viejo decía:

—¡Ay, se me han perdido
tres hermosas niñas!

—¿Cómo se llamaban?
—¿Cómo se decían?

—La una Constanza;
la otra Lucía,
y la más pequeña
era Rosalinda.

—¡Abrázame, padre,
que yo soy tu hija!
Y estamos esclavas
en la Morería.
Espérame un poco,
que vengo enseguida;
voy corriendo a casa
por mis hermanitas.

—Escucha Constanza;
óyeme Lucía,
hoy he visto a padre
en la fuente fría.

Constanza lloraba;
Lucía gemía,
y la más pequeña
así les decía:

—¿Por qué estáis llorando?
—Esto es de alegría.

(popular)

CASTILLA

El ciego sol se estrella
en las duras aristas de las armas,
llaga de luz los petos y espaldares
y flamea en las puntas de las lanzas.

El ciego sol, la sed y la fatiga.
Por la terrible estepa castellana,
al destierro, con doce de los suyos,
—polvo, sudor y hierro —el Cid
cabalga.

Cerrado está el mesón a piedra y
lodo…
Nadie responde. Al pomo de la
espada
y al cuento de las picas, el postigo
va a ceder… ¡Quema el sol, el aire
abrasa!

A los terribles golpes,
de eco ronco, una voz pura, de plata
y de cristal responde… Hay un niña
muy débil y muy blanca,
en el umbral. Es toda
ojos azules; y en los ojos, lágrimas.
Oro pálido nimba
su carita curiosa y asustada.

«¡Buen Cid! Pasad… El rey nos dará
muerte,
arruinará la casa
y sembrará de sal el pobre campo
que mi padre trabaja…
Idos. El Cielo os colme de venturas…
En nuestro mal ¡oh Cid! No ganáis
nada».

Calla la niña y llora sin gemido…
Un sollozo infantil cruza la escuadra
de feroces guerreros,
y una voz inflexible grita: «¡En
marcha!».

El ciego sol, la sed y la fatiga.
Por la terrible estepa castellana,
al destierro, con doce de los suyos
—polvo, sudor y hierro—, el Cid
cabalga.

—MANUEL MACHADO (1874–1947)

El congreso de ratones

*Juntáronse los ratones
para librarse del gato,
y después de un largo rato
de disputas y opiniones,
dijeron que acertarían
en ponerle un cascabel;
que, andando el gato con él,
librarse mejor podían.*

*Salió un ratón barbicano,
colilargo, hociquirromo,
y encrespando el grueso lomo,
dijo al senado romano,*

*después de hablar culto un rato:
—¿Quién de todos ha de ser
el que se atreva a poner
ese cascabel al gato?*

—Lope de Vega (1562–1635)

El tren que pasa

*Va cayendo la tarde,
tranquila y despejada.
Estoy en pleno campo;
mi perro me acompaña.
Voy a cruzar la vía
para seguir la marcha.
Me detiene el aviso
de un silbato a distancia.*

*Un tren que se acerca,
Avanza, ¡avanza!, ¡¡avanza!!
Llega, tendida al aire
Su cabellera blanca.
Pasa un lujuso expreso...
Un rebaño se espanta...
Es el campo que se asusta
De la ciudad que pasa.*

—Carlos Fernández Shaw (1865–1911)

EL VIEJO Y LA MUERTE

Entre montes, por áspero camino,
tropezando con una y otra peña,
iba un viejo cargado con su leña,
maldiciendo su mísero destino.

Al fin cayó, y viéndose de suerte
que apenas levantarse ya podía,
llamaba con colérica porfía
una, dos y tres veces a la Muerte.

Armada de guadaña, en esqueleto,
la Parca se le ofrece en aquel punto;
pero el viejo, temiendo ser difunto,
lleno más de terror que de respeto,
trémulo la decía y balbuciente:

—«Yo...señora...os llamé desesperado;
pero...
—«Acaba; ¿qué quieres, desdichado?».

—«Que me cargues la leña solamente».

Tenga paciencia quien se cree infeliz;
que aun en la situación más lamentable
es la vida del hombre siempre amable:
el viejo de la leña nos lo dice.

—Félix María Samaniego (1745–1801)

¡QUIÉN SABE!

Indio que asomas a la puerta
de esa tu rústica mansión:
¿para mi sed no tienes agua?
¿Para mi frío, cobertor?
¿Parco maíz para mi hambre?
¿Para mi sueño mal rincón?
¿Breve quietud para mi andanza?
-¡Quién sabe señor!

Indio que labras con fatiga
tierras que de otros dueños son:
¿ignoras tú que deben tuyas
ser, por tu sangre y tu sudor?
¿Ignoras tú que audaz codicia,
siglos atrás te las quitó?
¿Ignoras tú que eres el amo?
-¡Quién sabe señor!

Indio de frente taciturna
y de pupilas sin fulgor:
¿qué pensamiento es el que escondes
en tu enigmática expresión?
¿Qué es lo que buscas en tu vida?
¿Qué es lo que imploras a tu Dios?
¿Qué es lo que suena tu silencio?
-¡Quién sabe señor!

—José Santos Chocano (1875–1934)

Los dos príncipes

El palacio está de luto
en el trono llora el rey,
y la reina está llorando
donde no la puedan ver:

En pañuelos de holán fino
lloran la reina y el rey:
los señores del palacio
están llorando también.

Los caballos llevan negro
el penacho y el arnés:
los caballos no han comido,
porque no quieren comer:

El laurel del patio grande
quedó sin hoja esta vez:
Todo el mundo fue al entierro
con coronas de laurel:

—¡El hijo del rey se ha muerto!
¡Se ha muerto el hijo del rey!

En los álamos del monte
tiene su casa el pastor:
La pastora está diciendo
—«¿Por qué tiene luz el sol?».

Las ovejas, cabizbajas,
viene todas al portón:
¡Una caja larga y honda
está forrando el pastor!

Entra y sale un perro triste:
canta allá adentro una voz
—«¡Pajarito, yo estoy loca,
llévame donde él voló!».

El pastor coge llorando
la pala y el azadón:
abre en la tierra una fosa:
echa en la fosa una flor:

—¡Se quedó el pastor sin hijo!
¡Murió el hijo del pastor!

—José Martí (1853–1895)

EL ENEMIGO

*Un ruido de cadenas y caballos
se acerca por el valle.*

*Negras espadas, tétricos arados
quieren tu espalda pura,
¡Oh rosa delgada!
¡Oh virgen campesina!*

*Lívidos tribunos, altos centuriones,
vienen con rojas enseñas,
vienen con tercas amapolas,
y con palacios de lanzas
resplandecientes.*

*Un ruido de caballos y cadenas
se acerca por el valle.*

*¡Afilad las lanzas y los dardos!
¡Reforzad las torres y los muros!
que los romanos vienen
con látigos de hierro enloquecido
y lobos de basalto.*

—Juan Eduardo Cirlot (1916–1973)

NUMANCIA

A Blas Taracena

*Era en Numancia, al tiempo que declina
la tarde del agosto augusto y lento,
Numancia del silencio y de la ruina,
alma de libertad, trono del viento.*

*La luz se hacía por momentos mina
de transparencia y desvanecimiento,
diafanidad de ausencia vespertina,
esperanza, esperanza del portento.*

*Súbito, ¿dónde?, un pájaro sin lira,
sin rama, sin atril, canta, delira,
flota en la cima de su fiebre aguda.*

*Vivo latir de Dios nos goteaba,
risa y charla de Dios, libre y desnuda.
Y el pájaro, sabiéndolo, cantaba.*

—Gerardo Diego (1896–1987)

Más Allá

Por un áspero camino,
un cansado peregrino
busca la felicidad;
y cuantos al paso halla,
todos le dicen que vaya
más allá.

Y cruza por los estrados
de los palacios dorados
buscándola con afán;
y entre el rumor de la orgía
siempre una voz le decía:
más allá.

A gentes de las montañas
pregunta si, en sus cabañas,
con ellos habita en paz;
y ellos bajan la cabeza
y le dicen con tristeza:
más allá.

Penetra con desaliento
por los claustros de un convento,
y se postra ante un altar;
y entre el rumor de las preces
oye a veces, solo a veces:
más allá.

Al fin, en el camposanto,
con ojos llenos de llanto,
busca la felicidad;
y una figura huesosa
le dice abriendo la fosa:
más allá.

—Juan Ruiz de Alarcón (1580–1639)

Anoche cuando dormía

Anoche cuando dormía
soñé, ¡bendita ilusión!,
que una fontana fluía
dentro de mi corazón.
Di, ¿por qué acequia escondida,
agua, vienes hasta mí,
manantial de nueva vida
de donde nunca bebí?
Anoche cuando dormía
soñé, ¡bendita ilusión!,
que una colmena tenía
dentro de mi corazón;
y las doradas abejas
iban fabricando en él,
con las amarguras viejas
blanca cera y dulce miel.
Anoche cuando dormía
soñé, ¡bendita ilusión!,
que un ardiente sol lucía
dentro de mi corazón.
Era ardiente porque daba
calores de rojo hogar,
y era sol porque alumbraba
y porque hacía llorar.
Anoche cuando dormía
soñé, ¡bendita ilusión!,
que era Dios lo que tenía
dentro de mi corazón.
   —Antonio Machado (1875–1939)

Extracto de proverbios y cantares XXIX

Caminante, son tus huellas
el camino, y nada más;
caminante, no hay camino,
se hace camino al andar.
Al andar se hace camino,
y al volver la vista atrás
se ve la senda que nunca
se ha de pisar.
Caminante, no hay camino,
sino estelas en la mar.
   —Antonio Machado (1875–1939)

ENSUEÑOS

Yo voy soñando caminos
de la tarde. ¡Las colinas
doradas, los verdes pinos,
las polvorientas encinas!...
¿Adónde el camino irá?
Yo voy cantando, viajero
a lo largo del sendero...
—la tarde cayendo está—.
«En el corazón tenía
la espina de una pasión;
logré arrancármela un día:
«ya no siento el corazón».

Y todo el campo un momento
se queda, mudo y sombrío,
meditando. Suena el viento
en los álamos del río.

La tarde más se oscurece;
y el camino que serpea
y débilmente blanquea
se enturbia y desaparece.

Mi cantar vuelve a plañir:
«Aguda espina dorada,
quién te pudiera sentir
en el corazón clavada».

—ANTONIO MACHADO (1875–1939)

RIMA NÚMERO XIII

—Allá está la cumbre.
¿Qué miras?—Un astro.
—¿Me amas?—¡Te adoro!
¿Subimos?—¡Subamos!

—¿Qué ves?—Una aurora
fugitiva y pálida.
—¿Qué sientes?—Anhelo.
—Esa es la esperanza.

—¡Qué alientos de vida!
¡Qué fuego de sol!
¡Qué luz tan radiante!
—¡Ese es el amor!

—¿Qué ves a tus plantas?
—Un profundo abismo.
¿Tiemblas?—Tengo miedo...
—¡Ese es el olvido!

Pero no tiembles ni temas:
bajo el sacro cielo azul,
para el que ama no hay abismos
porque tiene alas de luz.

—RUBÉN DARÍO (1867–1916)

Melancolía

Hermano, tu que tienes la luz, dime la mía.
Soy como un ciego. Voy sin rumbo y ando a tientas.
Voy bajo tempestades y tormentas,
ciego de ensueño y loco de armonía.

Ese es mi mal. Soñar. La poesía
es la camisa férrea de mil puntas cruentas
que llevo sobre el alma. Las espinas sangrientas
dejan caer las gotas de mi melancolía.

Y así voy, ciego y loco por este mundo amargo;
a veces me parece que el camino es muy largo,
y a veces que es muy corto...

Y en este titubeo de aliento y agonía,
cargo lleno de penas lo que apenas soporto.
¿No oyes caer las gotas de mi melancolía?

—Rubén Darío (1867–1916)

Invierno

Sufre, si quieres gozar
baja, si quieres subir;
pierde si quieres ganar;
muere, si quieres vivir.

Los días son fríos
las noches son largas,
y el viento del norte
silba en la ventana.

—Antonio Trueba (1821–1889)

Romance del enamorado y la muerte

Yo me estaba reposando
anoche como solía,
soñaba con mis amores,
que en mis brazos se dormían.
Vi entrar señora tan blanca
muy más que la nieve fría.

—¿Por dónde has entrado, amor?
¿Cómo has entrado, mi vida?
Las puertas están cerradas,
ventanas y celosías.

—No soy el amor, amante:
La muerte que Dios te envía.
—¡Hay muerte tan rigurosa,
déjame vivir un día!

—Un día no puedo darte,
—una hora tienes de vida.
Muy deprisa se levanta,
más deprisa se vestía.

Ya se va para la calle,
en donde su amor vivía.
—¡Ábreme la puerta, blanca,
ábreme la puerta niña!

—¿La puerta cómo he de abrirte
si la ocasión no es venida?
Mi padre no fue a palacio,
mi madre no está dormida.

—Si no me abres esta noche,
ya nunca más me abrirías;
la muerte me anda buscando,
junto a ti vida sería.

—Vete bajo la ventana
donde bordaba y cosía,
te echaré cordel de seda
para que subas arriba,
si la seda no alcanzare,
mis trenzas añadiría.

Ya trepa por el cordel,
ya toca la barandilla,
la fina seda se rompe,
él como plomo caía.

La Muerte le está esperando
abajo en la tierra fría:
Vamos, el enamorado,
la hora ya está cumplida.

(anónimo)

No sé por qué piensas tú

No sé por qué piensas tú,
soldado, que te odio yo,
si somos la misma cosa
yo,
tú.
Tú eres pobre, lo soy yo;
soy de abajo, lo eres tú;
¿de dónde has sacado tú,
soldado, que te odio yo?

Me duele que a veces tú
te olvides de quién soy yo;
caramba, si yo soy tú,
lo mismo que tú eres yo.

Pero no por eso yo
he de malquererte, tú;
si somos la misma cosa,
yo,
tú,
no sé por qué piensas tú,
soldado, que te odio yo.

Ya nos veremos yo y tú,
juntos en la misma calle,
hombro con hombro, tú y yo,
sin odios ni yo ni tú,
pero sabiendo tú y yo,
a dónde vamos yo y tú…
¡no sé por qué piensas tú,
soldado, que te odio yo!

—Nicolás Guillén (1902–1989)

Poesía de Nicolás Guillén

Nicolás Guillén was one of the most famous Cuban poets. He was born in 1902. Although he cultivated many styles, Guillén was inspired by Afro-Cuban folklore, its music, and its rhythms. By using various resources, he created a new style of poetry that represented the black culture. He incorporated rhythm and musicality into his poems by adding onomatopoetic words that imitate the sounds of drums, honoring the culture of his African descent.

The following poem by Nicolás Guillén was probably presented to honor grandparents during their special day and to honor holidays such as Martin Luther King Day. This powerful recitation can be presented with bongos and other Cuban percussion instruments.

BALADA DE LOS DOS ABUELOS

Sombras que sólo yo veo,
me escoltan mis dos abuelos.
Lanza con punta de hueso,
tambor de cuero y madera:
mi abuelo negro.
Gorguera en el cuello ancho,
gris armadura guerrera:
mi abuelo blanco.
Pie desnudo, torso pétreo
los de mi negro;
pupilas de vidrio antártico
las de mi blanco!
Africa de selvas húmedas
y de gordos gongos sordos...
—¡Me muero!
(Dice mi abuelo negro.)
Aguaprieta de caimanes,
verdes mañanas de cocos...
—¡Me canso!
(Dice mi abuelo blanco.)
Oh velas de amargo viento,
galeón ardiendo en oro...
—¡Me muero!
(Dice mi abuelo negro.)
¡Oh costas de cuello virgen
engañadas de abalorios...!
—¡Me canso!
(Dice mi abuelo blanco.)
¡Oh puro sol repujado,
preso en el aro del trópico;
oh luna redonda y limpia
sobre el sueño de los monos!
¡Qué de barcos, qué de barcos!

¡Qué de negros, qué de negros!
¡Qué largo fulgor de cañas!
¡Qué látigo el del negrero!
Piedra de llanto y de sangre,
venas y ojos entreabiertos,
y madrugadas vacías,
y atardeceres de ingenio,
y una gran voz, fuerte voz,
despedazando el silencio.
¡Qué de barcos, qué de barcos,
qué de negros!
Sombras que sólo yo veo,
me escoltan mis dos abuelos.
Don Federico me grita
y Taita Facundo calla;
los dos en la noche sueñan
y andan, andan.
Yo los junto.

—¡Federico!
¡Facundo! Los dos se abrazan.
Los dos suspiran. Los dos
las fuertes cabezas alzan;
los dos del mismo tamaño
bajo las estrellas altas;
los dos del mismo tamaño,
ansia negra y ansia blanca,
los dos del mismo tamaño,
gritan, sueñan, lloran, cantan.
Sueñan, lloran, cantan.
Lloran, cantan.
¡Cantan!

EL RATONCILLO

Dos ratones viejos
dan sabios consejos
a su ratoncillo:

«Sé diablo, sé pillo,
corre por doquiera;
pero huye al momento
huye como el viento,
de toda trampera.
¡Tiene ese aparato
un alma de gato!».

Corre el ratoncillo,
y un dulce olorcillo
guía su carrera
hasta la trampera.

«¡Pues ya es disparate
—Clama el botarate—
Llamar a esto un gato!...
¡Yo no tengo miedo!...
Bien mirarla puedo
de lejos un rato!».

Se para, la mira,
su perfume aspira;
con audacia loca
se acerca, la toca;
junto a ella se sienta;
descubre allí preso
un trozo de queso;
lo huele, lo tienta,
el queso se zampa...
¡Y cae en la trampa!

—Carlos Octavio Bunge
(1875–1918)

LA CANCIÓN DEL CAMINO

Aunque voy por tierra extraña
solitario y peregrino
no voy solo, me acompaña
mi canción en el camino.

Y si la noche está negra,
sus negruras ilumino:
canto y mi canción alegra
la oscuridad del camino.

La fatiga no me importa,
porque el báculo divino
de la canción hace corta
la distancia en el camino.

Ay, triste y desventurado
quién va solo peregrino
y no marcha acompañado
¡Por la canción del camino!

—Federico A de Icaza (1863–1925)

Poesía dedicada a Simón Bolívar

Político, militar, héroe, orador y poeta.
Y en todo grande. Como las tierras libertadas por él,
que no nació hijo de patria alguna
sino que muchas patrias nacieron hijas de él.

Tenía la valentía del que lleva una espada.
tenía la cortesía del que lleva una flor,
y entrando en los salones arrojaba la espada,
y entrando en los combates arrojaba la flor.
Los picos del Ande no eran más a sus ojos,

que signos admirativos de sus arrojos.
Fue un soldado poeta. Fue un poeta soldado.

Y cada pueblo libertado, era una hazaña del poeta
y era un poema del soldado.
¡Y fue crucificado!

—Luís Llorens Torres (1876–1944)

El Ombú

Cada comarca en la Tierra
tiene un rasgo prominente
el Brasil, su sol ardiente;
minas de plata, el Perú;
Montevideo, su cerro;
Buenos Aires –patria hermosa-,
tiene su pampa grandiosa;
la pampa tiene el ombú.
Esa llanura extendida,
inmenso piélago verde,
donde la vista se pierde,
sin tener donde posar;
es la pampa misteriosa
todavía para el hombre,
que a una raza da su nombre,
que nadie pudo domar.
No tiene grandes raudales
que fecunden sus entrañas
pero lagos y espadañas
inundan toda su faz,
que dan paja para el rancho,
para el vestido dan pieles,
agua dan a los corceles,
y guarida a la torcaz.
Esa llanura extendida
inmenso pielogo verde
donde la vision se pierde
sin tener donde pasar,
es la Pampa misteriosa
todavia para el hombre,
que a una raza da su nombre,
que nadie pudo domar.

No tiene bosques frondosos
ni aves, cantoras en ellos;
pero si pajaros bellos
hijos de la soledad,
que siendo unicos testigos
del que habita esas regiones,
adivinan sus pasiones
y acompanan su orfandad.

No hay alli bosque frondosos,
pero alguna vez asoma
en lo alto de una loma
que se alcanza a divisar,
el ombu, solemne, aislado,
la gallarda, airosa planta
que a las nubes se levanta
como faro de aquel mar.

— Luis Dominguez (1819–1839)
(Recopiladora, Diamela Wetzel)

Los Volcanes de México—
Argentina—Ecuador

A través de la inmensa cordillera
corre por nuestra América Latina
el fuego aterrador con que ilumina
cada volcán su propia torrentera.

El Ixtacihuatl tiene por cimera
la nubes que flechaba Iluicamina;
y el Tupungato vela la Argentina
como un dragón al pie de su trinchera.

Los volcanes hieráticos, al paso
de los siglos, extreman su portento;
y gemelos de idéntico regazo,
dialogan bajo el mismo firmamento.

Con el águila altiva el Chimborazo
y el viejo Cotopaxi con el viento.

—Primitivo Herrera (1883–1953)

Los zapaticos de Rosa

I find this poem to be more appropriate for the upper grades because it also serves as an opportunity to talk about the social situation in Central America at the turn of the century. There are several parts that the class recites chorally. There are also assigned parts for the individual characters. Some of the narrators read in pairs or individually. This allows the whole class to also participate. A good suggestion is to bring to the class the illustrations of this poem by Lulu Delacré, so the students can follow the story. This poem promotes compassion and empathy.

NARRATORS:

Hay sol bueno y mar de espuma,
y arena fina, y Pilar
quiere salir a estrenar
su sombrerito de pluma.

PADRE:

«¡Vaya la niña divina!».

NARRATORS:

Dice el padre y le da un beso:

PADRE:

«¡Vaya mi pájaro preso
a buscarme arena fina!».

MADRE:

«Yo voy con mi niña hermosa».

NARRATORS:

Le dijo la madre buena:

MADRE:

«¡No te manches en la arena
Los zapaticos de rosa!».

NARRATORS:

Fueron las dos al jardín
por la calle del laurel:
La madre cogió un clavel
y Pilar cogió un jazmín.

Ella va de todo juego,
con aro, y balde, y paleta:
El balde es color violeta:
el aro es color de fuego.

Vienen a verlas pasar:
nadie quiere verlas ir:
la madre se echa a reír,
y un viejo se echa a llorar.

El aire fresco despeina
a Pilar, que viene y va
muy oronda.

PILAR:

«¡Di, mamá!
¿Tú sabes qué cosa es reina?».

NARRATORS:

Y por si vuelven de noche
de la orilla de la mar,
para la madre y Pilar
manda luego el padre el coche.

Está la playa muy linda:
todo el mundo está en la playa:
lleva espejuelos el aya
de la francesa Florinda

Está Alberto, el militar
que salió en la procesión
con tricornio y con bastón,
echando un bote a la mar.

¡Y qué mala, Magdalena
con tantas cintas y lazos,
a la muñeca sin brazos
enterrándola en la arena!

Conversan allá en las sillas,
sentadas con los señores,
las señoras, como flores,
debajo de las sombrillas.

Pero está con estos modos
tan serios, muy triste el mar:
¡Lo alegre es allá, al doblar,
en la barranca de todos!

Dicen que suenan las olas
mejor allá en la barranca,
y que la arena es muy blanca
donde están las niñas solas.

Pilar corre a su mamá:

PILAR:

«¡Mamá, yo voy a ser buena:
déjame ir sola a la arena:
allá, tú me ves, allá!».

MADRE:

«¡Esta niña caprichosa!
No hay tarde que no me enojes:
anda, pero no te mojes
los zapaticos de rosa».

NARRATORS:

Le llega a los pies la espuma:
gritan alegres las dos:
y se va, diciendo adiós,
la del sombrero de pluma.

¡Se va allá, dónde ¡muy lejos!
Las aguas son más salobres,
donde se sientan los pobres,
donde se sientan los viejos!

*Se fue la niña a jugar,
La espuma blanca bajó,
y pasó el tiempo, y pasó
un águila por el mar.*

*Y cuando el sol se ponía
detrás de un monte dorado,
un sombrerito callado
por las arenas venía.*

*Trabaja mucho, trabaja
para andar: ¿qué es lo que tiene
Pilar que anda así, que viene
con la cabecita baja*

*Bien sabe la madre hermosa
por qué le cuesta el andar:*

Madre:

*«¿Y los zapatos, Pilar,
los zapaticos de rosa?».*

*«¡Ah, loca! ¿en dónde estarán?
¡Di, dónde, Pilar!».*

Mujer:

*«Señora»,
Dice una mujer que llora:
«¡Están conmigo: aquí están!».*

*«Yo tengo una niña enferma
que llora en el cuarto oscuro.*

*y la traigo al aire puro
a ver el sol, y a que duerma.*

*«Anoche soñó, soñó
con el cielo, y oyó un canto:
me dio miedo, me dio espanto,
Y la traje, y se durmió.*

*«Con sus dos brazos menudos
estaba como abrazando;
y yo mirando, mirando
sus piececitos desnudos.*

*«Me llegó al cuerpo la espuma,
alcé los ojos, y vi
esta niña frente a mí
con su sombrero de pluma».*

Pilar:

*«¡Se parece a los retratos
tu niña!» dijo: «¿Es de cera?
¿Quiere jugar? ¡Si quisiera!…
¿Y por qué está sin zapatos?*

*«Mira: ¡la mano le abrasa,
y tiene los pies tan fríos!
¡Oh, toma, toma los míos;
Yo tengo más en mi casa!».*

Mujer:

*«No sé bién, señora hermosa,
lo que sucedió después:*

¡Le vi a mi hijita en los pies
los zapaticos de rosa!».

NARRATORS:

Se vio sacar los pañuelos
a una rusa y a una inglesa;
el aya de la francesa
se quitó los espejuelos.

Abrió la madre los brazos:
Se echó Pilar en su pecho,
y sacó el traje deshecho,
sin adornos y sin lazos.

Todo lo quiere saber
de la enferma la señora:
¡No quiere saber que llora
de pobreza una mujer!

MADRE:

«¡Sí, Pilar, dáselo! ¡y eso
también! ¡Tu manta! ¡Tu anillo!».

NARRATORS:

Y ella le dio su bolsillo:
le dio el clavel, le dio un beso.

Vuelven calladas de noche
a su casa del jardín:
Y Pilar va en el cojín
de la derecha del coche.

Y dice una mariposa
que vio desde su rosal
guardados en un cristal
los zapaticos de rosa.

—JOSÉ MARTÍ (1853–1895)

8

OTHER RESOURCES

8.1 Lyrics for Songs in the Lower Grades

El botón de Martín

The first time we sing the song with gestures. The second time, we sing the song without singing the word *botón* and the onomatopoeia (*ton, ton, tin, tin*); instead, we clap to the silent (*botón*, Martin, etc.). We then sing it using a natural rhythm. Rosa León sings this popular children's song and it is easy to find on YouTube.

> *Debajo de un botón, ton, ton*
> *que encontró Martin, tin, tin*
> *había un ratón, ton, ton*
> *¡ay! que chiquitín, tin tin*
>
> *¡Ay! que chiquitín, tin tin*
> *era aquel ratón, ton, ton*
> *que encontró Martin, tin, tin*
> *debajo un botón, ton, ton.*
>
> *Es tan juguetón, ton, ton*
> *el señor Martín, tin, tin,*
> *que guardó el ratón, ton, ton,*
> *en un calcetín, tin, tin*
>
> *En un calcetín, tin, tin*
> *vive aquel ratón, ton, ton*
> *que metió Martín, tin, tin*
> *el muy juguetón, ton, ton.*
>
> (canción española[1])

---
1 See www.youtube.com/watch?v=duhSUtPcvYU.

¡QUE LLUEVA!

This song is excellent for transitions in grades 1 and 2.

Que llueva, qué llueva,
el sapo está en la cueva,
los pajarillos cantan,
las nubes se levantan,
que sí,
que no,
que caiga un chaparrón,
con azúcar y turrón.
    (oral tradition)

LOS POLLITOS

Muy popular, esta canción es apropiada para los más pequeños acompañada de gestos.

Los pollitos dicen «pío, pío, pío»
cuando tienen hambre,
cuando tienen frío.

La gallina busca,
el maíz y el trigo
les da la comida,
y les presta abrigo

Bajo sus dos alas,
acurrucaditos
hasta el otro día,
duermen los pollitos.
pío, pío, pío (bis)
    (tradicional)

A BELÉN VA UNA BURRA

Grade 2. Children love this Christmas carol. I use a tambourine, and a little donkey for the children to ride. First I teach the song without the chorus, and then I chose three children to sing as the chorus without our help.

Hacia Belén va una burra,
rin, rin,

Chorus: yo me remendaba,
yo me remendé,
yo me eché un remiendo,
yo me lo quité,

cargada de chocolate.
Lleva su chocolatera,
rin, rin,

Chorus: yo me remendaba,
yo me remendé,
yo me eché un remiendo,
yo me lo quité,

su molinillo y su ágape.

María, María
ven acá corriendo
que el chocolatillo
se lo están comiendo.

María, María
ven acá volando
que el chocolatillo
se lo están llevando.
    (popular)

El coquí

Can be presented with a rain stick.

El Coquí, el coquí a mi me encanta,
es tan lindo el cantar del coquí.
Por las noches al ir a acostarme,
me adormece cantandome así:
coquí, coquí, qui, qui, qui (Bis)
(popular, Puerto Rico[2])

Arroz con leche

Recommended song during transitions or acted with the fingers.

Arroz con leche,
me quiero casar,
con una señorita de la capital.
Que sepa coser,
que sepa bordar,
que sepa abrir la puerta,
para ir a pasear.

Con esta sí.
con este no,
con esta señorita,
me caso yo.
(tradicional)

Tengo tres cabritillas

Paloma del palomar
que el amor vas a buscar.

Tengo tres cabritillas
ay remerreme ré, (bis)

Arriba en la montaña
ay remerreme ré, (bis)
Arriba en la montaña,
aire, airé.

Una me da la leche
ay remerreme ré (bis)

otra me da la lana
ay remerreme ré,
otra me da lana,
aire airé.

Otra me da manteca
ay remerremeré, (bis0

pa toda la semana,
ay remerremeré, (bis)
aire, airé.
(popular)

---

2 See www.youtube.com/watch?v=3nYNxvimsGM
&feature=related.

Los peces en el río

This is a Carol with a bit of Flamenco favor from the oral tradition, appropriete for lower grades. A tambourine, castanets and guitar are ideal instruments for this piece!

La Virgen se esta peinando
entre cortina y cortina.
sus cabellos son de oro
el peine de plata fina.

Pero mira como beben
los peces en el río.
pero mira como beben
por ver a Dios nacido.

Beben y beben
y vuelven a beber.
los peces en el rio
por ver a Dios nacer.

La Virgen esta lavando
y en el romero tendiendo
los angelitos cantando
y el romero floreciendo.

Pero mira como beben
los peces en el río,
pero mira como beben
por ver a Dios nacido.

Beben y beben
y vuelven a beber,
los peces en el río
por ver a Dios nacer.

(popular)

San Serenín

An excellent song for grade 1. The teacher acts out the professions and when the song says, «*hacen asi los zapateros*», the teacher calls on a student, who also needs to do the gestures of the profession. Then we all join in with *Así, así, así. Así me gusta a mí.*

San Serenín, de la buena, buena vida.
Hacen así.
Hacen los zapateros, así, así, así.
Así me gusta a mí.

San Serenín, de la buena, buena vida.
Hacen así.
Hacen los panaderos, así, así, así.
Así me gusta a mí.

San Serenín, de la buena, buena vida.
Hacen así.
Hacen los carpinteros, así, así, así.
Así me gusta a mí.

San Serenín de la buena, buena vida.
Hacen así.
Hacen los artistas, así, así, así.
Así me gusta a mí.
San Serenín de la buena, buena vida.

Hacen así.
Hacen los policías, así, así, así,
Así me gusta a mí.
San Serenín de la buena, buena vida.

Hacen así.
Hacen las secretarias, así, así, así
Así me gusta a mí.

(oral tradition)

Ya vienen los reyes

Villancico

Ya vienen los reyes
por el arenal;
ya le traen al Niño
ofrenda real.
Pampanitos verdes
hojas de limón,
la Virgen María,
Madre del Señor.
Oro le trae Melchor,
incienso Gaspar,
y olorosa mirra
el rey Baltasar.
Pampanitos verdes,
hojas de limón,
la Virgen María,
Madre del Señor.

(popular)

Cú, Cú cantaba la rana

*Cú cú, cú cú,
cú cú, cú cú.*

*Cú cú cantaba la rana.
Cú cú debajo del agua.*

*Cú cú paso un caballero.
Cú cú con capa y sombrero.*

*Cú cú paso una señora.
Cú cú con traje de cola.*

*Cú cú paso un marinero.
Cú cú vendiendo romero.*

*Cú cú le pidió un ramito.
Cú cú no le quiso dar.
Cú cú y se echó a llorar.*

(tradicional)

Sabes Coles cultivar

*Todos de pie la maestra comienza
girando los puños unos contra otro.*

> ¿Sabes coles cultivar?
> A la moda, a la moda,
> ¿sabes coles cultivar
> a la moda del lugar?

*En la siguiente estrofa cuando decimos
manos damos palmas.*

> Las plantamos con las manos
> a la moda, a la moda,
> las plantamos con las manos
> a la moda del lugar.

Con los pies marcamos el ritmo:

> Las plantamos con los pies,
> a la moda, a la moda,
> las plantamos con los pies
> a la moda del lugar.
>
> las plantamos con los codos…
> las plantamos con la nariz…
> las plantamos con la cabeza…
> (etc.)

(popular)

Con real y medio

Se puede presentar con ilustraciones o figuritas de animales.

> Con real y medio (bis)
> compré una pata.
> La pata tuvo un patito,
> tengo la pata tengo el patito,
> siempre me queda mi real y medio.
>
> Con real y medio (bis)
> compré una burra.
> Tengo una burra tengo un burrito,
> tengo una pata tengo un patito,
> siempre me queda mi real y medio.
>
> Con real y medio (bis)
> compré una gata, chiva, mona,
> (etc.)

—Oscar Chávez[3]

---

3 See www.cuandoerachamo.com/con-real-y-medio-canciones-infantiles.

A LA NANITA NANA

*A la nanita nana
nanita ea, nanita ea,
mi Jesús tiene sueño,
bendito sea, bendito sea.*

*Pajarillo que cantas en la laguna,
no despiertes al niño
que está en la cuna.*

*Calla mientras la cuna se balancea
a la nanita nana, nanita ea.*
  (popular)

PIMPÓN

*Pimpón es un muñeco
muy guapo y de cartón.
Se lava la carita
con agua y jabón.
Se desenreda el pelo
con peine de marfil,
y aunque se dé tirones
no llora ni hace así.
Cuando las estrellas
comienzan a salir,
Pimpón se va a la cama
se acuesta, y a dormir a dormir.*
  (popular)

SUBE UNA HORMIGUITA

*Sube una hormiguita
sube una hormiguita,
baja un elefante
baja un elefante*
  (popular)

Other Resources

8.2 Reenacting Songs for the Lower Grades

Los tres alpinos

Los Tres Alpinos se puede introducir como un juego de dedos una vez sentados en sus sillas. Los tres alpinos serán tres dedos de una mano. El alpino más pequeño será el meñique. El rey, el pulgar y la princesa, el otro meñique o el índice. Cuando los alumnos aprenden varias de las estrofas, entonces se puede actuar con disfraces.

*Eran tres alpinos
que venían de la guerra, (bis)
ría, ría, cataplán,
que venían de la guerra.*

*El más pequeño
traía una rosa (bis)
ría, ría, cataplán,
traía una rosa.*

*La hija del rey
le vio de su ventana (bis)
ría, ría, cataplán,
le vio de su ventana*

*Princesa —Oh, bello alpino,
regálame tu rosa (bis)
ría, ría, cataplán,
regálame tu rosa.*

*Alpino — Te la daré
si te casas conmigo (bis)
ría, ría, cataplán,
si te casas conmigo.*

*Princesa — Para casarme
has de hablar con mi padre (bis)
ría, ría, cataplán,
has de hablar con mi padre.*

*Alpino — Oh, buen señor,
me caso con su hija (bis)
ría, ría, cataplán,
me caso con su hija.*

*Rey — Bello alpino
Mi hija será tuya (bis)
ría, ría, cataplán,
mi hija será tuya.*

*Los tres alpinos
han vuento de la guerra (bis)
ría, reia, cataplán,
han vuelto de la guerra.*

(oral tradition)

El burro enfermo

La clase forma un semicírculo y se eligen a cinco médicos y a un burro. El burro estará en el centro del círculo sentado en una silla y llevará una máscara o un disfraz de burro. Los cinco doctores estarán en el círculo llevando túnicas blancas y si se quiere, se pueden hacer unos estetoscopios con goma negra y cartulina plateada. Cada médico llevará el remedio consiguiente. Todos cantan la primera estrofa y el primer médico se acercará al burro trotando y siguiendo el ritmo de la canción, le pondrá una bufanda blanca.

> *A mi burro, a mi burro*
> *le duele la garganta,*
> *el médico le manda*
> *una bufanda blanca.*

(El médico se acerca y le pone la bufanda.)

TODOS CANTAN: ¡Mi burro enfermo está !
  (bis)

(El médico vuelve a su sitio en el semicírculo. Cuando termina la música el burro rebuzna):

BURRO: Iooo, Iooo

(Cantamos la segunda estrofa y el segundo médico sale y haciendo lo mismo que el anterior, pone al burro una gorrita negra.)

> *A mi burro, a mi burro*
> *le duelen las orejas,*
> *el médico le manda*
> *una gorrita negra.*

(El segundo médico se acerca, y le pone una gorrita negra.)

TODOS: ¡Mi burro enfermo está
  mi burro enfermo está!

(El médico vuelve a su sitio en el semicírculo)

BURRO: Iooo, iooo.

(Tercera estrofa igual que las anteriores)

TODOS : A mi burro, a mi burro,
  le duelen las pezuñas,
  el médico le ha dada zapatos de gamuza.

(El médico le pondrá unos zapatos de fieltro.)

TODOS: ¡Mi burro enfermo está ! *(bis)*

(El médico vuelve a su sitio en el semicírculo).

BURRO: *Iooo. Iooo.*

(El quinto médico se acercará llevando en cada mano un limón y una cuchara y pretenderá dar una cucharada de «medicina» al burro.)

TODOS: *A mi burro, a mi burro*
  le duele el corazón,
  el médico le ha dado
  jarabe de limón.

TODOS: *¡Mi burro enfermo está! (bis)*

(El médico vuelve a su sitio en el semicírculo, y finalmente todos cantan):

  A mi burro, a mi burro
  ya no le duele nada
  ¡mi burro alegre está,
  mi burro alegre está!

(El burro saltará de su silla contento y todos terminamos la historia con un fuerte rebuzno de toda la clase):

CLASE: *IOOO, IOOO, IOOO.*

  (oral tradition; adapted by Elena Forrer)

Estaba una pastora

This song has been adapted from the oral tradition for the classroom. We need a shepard, some goats, a cat, an old-fashioned milk pail, and some costumes for the actors. The class sings the song while the Shepard skips around and sits next to the goats to milk them. Skipping, the cat approaches the milk pail and the "basket with the cheese," and the Shepard warns him. The cat leaves. Then the shepard takes the basket and leaves for the market, to the other side of the room. The cat approaches the basket with the cheese and eats the cheese. When the Shepard returns, she chaises the cat around the room, until the cat finds his desk.

Estaba una pastora
larán, larán, larito,
estaba una pastora
cuidando un rebañito. (Bis)

Con leche de sus cabras
larán, larán, larito,
con leche de sus cabras
hacía un buen quesito. (Bis)

El gato la miraba
larán, larán, larito,
el gato la miraba
con ojos golositos. (Bis)

Si incas la uña
larán, larán, larito,
si incas la uña
te cortaré el rabito,
te cortaré el rabito.

La pastora ha salido
larán, larán, larito,
la pastora ha salido
con su cesta tempranito,
con su cesta tempranito.

El gato muy goloso
larán, larán, larito,
el gato muy goloso
se comió el quesito,
se comió el quesito.

La pastora ha vuelto,
larán, larán, larito,
la pastora ya ha vuelto
y persigue al gatito
y persigue al gatito.

(oral tradition; adapted by Elena Forrer)

Other Resources

Tan, tan

This song can be performed during the time of the "Three Kings." We can choose a child to be the angle that will carry a star, and "Three Kings." The song begins with the angel leading with the star and the three kings following the angel. When each king is named in the song, they can bow while presenting the offerings. Then, they depart without the gifts. Since this is a very special celebration in the Hispanic World, I often bring a treat for the children—the special gift of gold could be golden foil-covered chocolate coins. The gift of the incense, seashells; and the mirth, glitter. I tell the children that kings only arrive if the children are asleep. Soon after, they all close their eyes and wait for their gift from the kings while singing. The actors will have costumes, capes and crowns. The music is easy to find; see www.aplicaciones.info/villan/villano3.htm).

Tan, tan, van por el desierto
Tan, tan, Melchor y Gaspar,
Tan, tan, les sigue un reycito que todos le llaman el rey Baltasar.

Tan, tan, vieron una estrella,
Tan, tan la vieron brillar,
Tan, tan, pura y tan bella que todos la siguen pa ver dónde va.

Tan, tan Melchor lleva oro
Tan, tan, mirra Gaspar,
Tan, tan, Baltasar incienso para todo un rey, un rey celestial.

Tan, tan, van por el desierto
Tan, tan, Melchor y Gaspar,
Tan, tan, les sigue un reycito que todos le llaman el rey Baltasar.

(oral tradition; adapted by Elena Forrer)

Illustration by a student in grade 4

Pedrito conejo (Peter Rabbit)

The class follows a choral recitation or sings the lyrics while students act out the story.

Characters: Pedrito, mamá conejo, los hermanos de Pedrito, don Fermín, y los pájaros. The class can be staged with different "stations": On one side, the house with mama conejo, in the other side, the garden of Don Fermin. Close to the gaden of Don Fermin, another station with a net and some birds.

(Mamá conejo appears with a basket, ready to leave the house. She looks at the three bunnies and the class repeats.)

CHORUS	—*Pedrito conejo al monte se escapó, su mamá le dijo:*
MOTHER	—«*no te vayas no*».

(Mamá conejo leaves with her basket. The three bunnies follow a pad while Pedrito takes a different way. Don Fermin appears working with a rake in his garden.)

El pillo corrió al jardín de don Fermín,
y de rábanos y coles se dio un festín.

(Pedrito eats some carrots and cabbage and don Fermin sees Pedrito and runs after him with his rake running around the classroom.)

CHORUS: *Don Fermin enojado*
corrió y le persiguió,
y Pedrito asustado en las redes cayó.

(Pedrito it's trapped. The birds help him to escape.)

CHORUS : *Los pájaros buenos le ayudan a escapar,*
y de vuelta a su casa acaba de llegar.

(When Pedrito arrives tired, mother and bunnies are celebrating a feast.)

CHORUS: *Los buenos conejos celebrando están,*
una rica cena de tortas y pan.
Pedrito en su cama malito está,
y mamá conejo sopitas le da.

(adapted by Elena Forrer)

El carbonero

Recommended for grade 3, with as many as ten *carboneros*. Each student carries a sack with *carbón*. In a line, the *carboneros* approach with rhythmic steps toward the front of the class, carrying the sack as the class sings:

Madre, mi carbonero no vino anoche
y le estuve esperando hasta las doce.

Next, holding their hands close to their mouth, the ten students shout as if selling the charcoal:

¡Carboon, carbooon!

As the song progresses, they drop their sacks on the floor and choose (or are assigned) a partner, and each ten pair of students skip around each sack.

Madre, mi carbonero vino de Vélez
y en el sombrero trajo cuatro claveles.
Carbón, carbón de encina y picón,
carbón de encina, picón de olivo,
niña bonita, vente conmigo

After this stanza has been sang, then the first dancers pick up their sack, and all follow in a line departing through the audience.

Lleva mi carbonero en el sombrero,
un letrero que dice: por ti me muero.
Carbón, carbón de encina y picón,
carbón de encina, picón de olivo,
niña bonita, vente conmigo.

(popular[4])

Estaba la pájara pinta

(Recommended for grade 2)

Estaba la pájara pinta
sentada en el verde limón;
con el pico picaba la rama,
con la rama cortaba la flor.
Ay, ay, ¿dónde estará mi amor?
(bis)

Me arrodillo a los pies de mi amante,
me levanto fiel y constante.
Dame una mano,
dame la otra;
dame un besito sobre tu boca.
Daré una media vuelta,
daré una vuelta entera.
Con un pasito atrás,
Haciendo una reverencia;

Pero no, pero no, pero no,
porque me da vergüenza;
Pero sí, pero sí, pero sí,
pero sí porque te quiero a ti.

(popular)

---

4 See www.youtube.com/watch?v=gpjlfNtT5uw.

Estaba el señor don Gato

(Don gato sits comfortably in the middle of the class while the students sing in a circle.)

> *Estaba el señor don Gato*
> *sentadito en su tejado,*
> *marramiau, miau, miau,*
> *sentadito en su tejado.*

(He reads a letter.)

> *Ha recibido una carta*
> *por si quiere ser casado,*
> *marramiau, miau, miau, miau,*
> *por si quiere ser casado.*

(A female cat appears with in pink hat.)

> *Con una gatita blanca*
> *hija de un gato pardo,*
> *marramiau, miau, miau, miau,*
> *hija de un gato pardo.*

(He falls from the roof.)

> *Al recibir la noticia*
> *se ha caído del tejado,*
> *marramiau, miau, miau, miau,*
> *se ha caído del tejado.*

> *Se ha roto seis costillas*
> *el espinazo y el rabo,*
> *marramiau, miau, miau, miau,*
> *el espinazo y el rabo.*

(The six students carry the cat around.)

> *Ya lo llevan a enterrar*
> *por la calle del pescado,*
> *marramiau, miau, miau, miau,*
> *por la calle del pescado.*

(Someone else carries a basket with sardines made of paper. The cat smells the sardines and revives.)

> *Al olor de las sardinas*
> *el gato ha resucitado,*
> *marramiau, miau, miau, miau,*
> *el gato ha resucitado.*

(Don gato dances in jubilation with the female cat.)

> *Por eso dice la gente*
> *siete vidas tiene un gato,*
> *marramiau, miau, miau, miau,*
> *siete vidas tiene un gato.*
>
> (oral tradition)

Other Resources

8.3 Games for Lower, Middle, and Upper Grades

¿Lobo estás listo?

Seven or eight children are asked to come to the front of the classroom and form a circle. One of them is chosen to be "Lobo," who will be outside the circle. Next to *el Lobo* we could have some clothes. For instance: a hat, a scarf, a big shirt, or gloves. The children in the class and in the circle sing the following popular tune, easily found online:

> *Jugando al escondite en el monte*
> *amaneció. El cuco cantando el miedo nos quitó.*
> *El cuco cantando el miedo nos quitó.*

(Then the children from the circle ask the wolf...)

> *¿Lobo estás listo?*
> *—No, me estoy poniendo la bufanda...*

(The children repeat the song and at the end, they ask again...)

> *¿Lobo estás listo?*
> *—No. Me estoy poniendo el sombrero...*

(The students move around the circle while the class sings, until "Lobo" is ready with all the clothes. Then he responds...)

> *Sí, estoy listo.*

The children run back to their desks before lobo reaches their seats first. This game has been adapted to a small classroom space in this manner; however, if it is played outside, the game can be freely played until Lobo catches one of the children, who then gets to be Lobo.[5]

(popular; adapted by Elena Forrer)

---

5 Music: www.youtube.com/watch?v=BoRAlduWvWc.

Antón Pirulero

This game begins with the children seated in a circle. A child is chosen to be the director, or "Antón Pirulero." The teacher then assigns imaginary instruments to each child or lets the children choose their own.

All will begin singing Antón Pirulero, acting along with their instruments as though in a symphony, except for Antón Pirulero, who instead acts like a conductor, moving his hands and arms along with the rhythm of the song. After a short while, Antón Pirulero chooses a moment to imitate the instrument of a particular child.

The chosen child should begin trading movements with Antón Pirulero (using a faster or slower tempo, for example) and then all of the children should begin to imitate this instrument and rhythm. If any of the children are distracted and do not change their movements on time with Anton, then they are out of the game and go to sit at their desks.

The goal is to be attentive and to immediately change one's instrument for the new one by following the director's movements. This game also serves as an opportunity to review the names of the instruments by asking the students:

¿Qué instrumento tocas tú?

It can also be played with professions (see: http://enlaermita.tripod.com/juegos.htm).

Canción:
Antón, Antón
Antón Pirulero.
Cada cual, cada cual,
cada cual a su juego
y el que no y el que no lo aprenda,
pagará, pagará una prenda.
(popular)

AL PAVO PAVITO PAVO (THE TURKEY GAME)

During Thanksgiving time, we play this lovely singing game in grades 1 and 2. The teacher chooses six volunteers to come to the front of the class and form a circle. The desks in the first row can be moved so there is enough space to play the game. One child is chosen to be *el pavo,* who is then blindfolded and stands with the teacher at the center of a circle of the other five children. Those children begin skipping around el pavo in a circle, singing…

> *Al pavo pavito, pavo*
> *al pavo pavito sí,*
> *este pavo se ha perdido*
> *y el pavero no está aquí.*
> *Uno.*

Next, the children change directions and sing this verse…

> *Al pavo pavito, pavo*
> *al pavo pavito sí,*
> *este pavo se ha perdido*
> *y el pavero no está aquí.*
> *Dos.*

The children again change directions and sing this verse…

> *Al pavo pavito, pavo*
> *al pavo pavito, sí*
> *este pavo se ha perdido*
> *y el pavero no está aquí.*
> *Tres.*

Then the children stop skipping and the teacher rotates *el pavo* so he is a bit disoriented and the children begin skipping around the circle again as described previously.

Next, while still blindfolded, *el pavo* needs to reach out toward one of the children in the circle. The children must be very quiet so that they do not give away their identity to *el pavo*. When *el pavo* has chosen a child, the teacher helps place her or his hand on top of the child's head; tapping gently on the child's head, he or she says to *el Pavo*…

> —*Una, dos y tres. ¿Quién es?*

If *el pavo* guesses the child's name correctly, that child becomes the next *el pavo*. If this child does not guess correctly, then another child is selected from the circle to be *el pavo,* and a new child is called from the rest of the class to join the circle. The first *el pavo* sits down, and the game continues.

(popular; adapted by Elena Forrer)

VERBENA

This game begins with the children forming a circle holding hands. The first child next to the teacher, without letting go, will duck under the arm of the child in front of her or him. The other children will do the same until they have all made a knot. It is always advisable in all the movement games to teach the song first so the class can play the game correctly.

> *Verbena, verbena,*
> *la casa se te quema.*
> *¿Por dónde? ¿por dónde?*
> *Por la casa del conde.*
> *-Señora María,*
> *¿tiene usted una cuerda?*
> *-Sí, pero está*
> *llena de nudos.*
> *-Pues vamos*
> *a deshacerla.*
> *Verbena, verbena,*
> *la casa se te quema…*
> *(etc.)*
>
> (popular)

EL ANILLO

The group sings the Mexican song «*El florón está en las manos*». Meanwhile, the children wait at their desks with the palms of their hands close together. Then, the teacher carries a ring and the children begin to sing as the teacher passes his or her hand between the palms of each child. At some point, the teacher drops the ring into one of the children's palms.

El florón está en las manos,
en las manos, en mis manos está el florón.
Quien acierte el que lo tiene el que lo tiene,
que se quede de plantón.

When they have finished, the children ask:

—¿*Mary tienes tu el anillo?*

And Mary responds:

—*No, no tengo el anillo.*

The students who guess correctly get to pass the ring next.

If the classroom has many students, the class can be divided and use two rings instead of one.

(popular; adapted)

Estoy pensando en un número...

This game is recommended for grades 1 and 2. It begins when the teacher says:

Estoy pensando en un número entre 10 y 20. ¿Qué número es?

The students in class have six opportunities to guess the number. Each time a student says a number, the teacher writes the number on the board. Those who guess the number come to the front and think of a new number. They conduct the game by asking classmates to guess the new number. The guessed numbers are written with a yellow chalk. This a good game during transitions.

¿Dónde está el osito?

This is a favorite game in grade 1. For this game we need three baskets: One small, one medium and one large, preferably the same shape. We call two volunteers: one comes to the front and the other leaves the room. The first volunteer hides a little bear, or *el osito*, in one of the three baskets. When the second child comes into the classroom we all sing:

> *Tengo un osito*
> *muy chiquitito,*
> *tiene bigotes,*
> *ojos grandotes;*
> *come frambuesas*
> *tintirimbesas.*
> *come melón,*
> *Tintirinbón.*

The child has only one guess. Those who guess correctly then hide *el osito*, and a different student leaves the classroom. If that student does not guess correctly, another two students begin all over again.[6]

If you cannot find this song, you can adapt a different song. Alter the class has finished singing, they all ask in unison:

> —*¿Dónde está el osito, en la cesta grande,*
> *en la cesta mediana,*
> *o en la cesta pequeña?*
> (adapted by Elena Forrer)

Las tres calabazas

During Halloween, we can adapt this game with three little flan pumpkins in three different sizes and a little coin to hide inside or under the pumpkins. We sing:

Calabaza, calabaza, ¿dónde estás?
Si no encuentras la moneda, calabaza serás.

(Elena Forrer)

---

6 «Tengo un Osito»; www.silvitablanco.com.ar/canciones/video-tengo-un-osito.htm.

Juego-canción: El burrito Pepe

One child rides the felt-cardboard donkey, Pepe. The others sing the song (see footnote) as the child trots between the rows in the classroom. When the class sings «*deja su carguita*», the trotting child leaves the donkey Pepe on the closest table and trots back to his or her seat. The song begins again with the student that has el burrito.

(Un niño monta al burrito Pepe hecho de cartón. Todos cantan la canción indicada abajo, mientras el niño trota por toda las filas de clase. Cuando decimos: «deja su carguita» el niño que monta el burrito, deja el burrito encima de la mesa del niño que le quede más cerca y vuelve trotando a su asiento. Comienza de nuevo la canción con el niño nuevo, trotando por las filas con el burrito, hasta que se vuelve a repetir «deja su carguita» en otro pupitre de la clase.[7])

Ratón que te pilla el gato

This is a circle game. A small group of students form a circle in front of the classroom. One is designated the cat, and the other, the mouse. The cat waits inside the circle while the cat stays outside. Holding hands, the students sing the song in their places, while the mouse moves "between the gates." When the song ends, the cat enters the circle and asks two questions. The students now point the cat the to "gate" where the mouse left. Now the cat leaves the circle to chase the mouse, running in and out the circle and using the same "gates" the mouse used.

Juego de corro. Entre ellos se elije un gato y un ratón. El ratón se queda dentro del círculo y el gato fuera. Con las manos enlazadas todos cantan mientras el ratón sale fuera por una de las «puertas»:

Canción
*Ratón, que te pilla el gato,
ratón, que te va a pillar.
Si no te pilla esta noche,
mañana te pillará.*

(popular[8])

Cuando termina la canción entra el gato en el círculo y pregunta:

— *¿Por dónde salió el ratón?*
— *Por aquella puerta. (Responden apuntando el lugar por donde salió el ratón.*

El gato ahora saldrá fuera del círculo persiguiendo al ratón, entrando y saliendo por las mismas «puertas» hasta que alcanza al ratón.

---

7   See Castañeda and Joven, *Cantemos con los niños.*

8   See www.doslourdes.net/JUEpopratonquetepillaelgato.mp3.

Other Resources

Pase Misí, Pase Misá / La Víbora de la mar

This popular tune is often used as a game with gates. The goal is for the children to pass under the "gates" quickly. When the last words *se quedarán* are sung, the gates close, and the child trapped needs to choose between two colors without letting the rest of the children hear the choice. Then, the child moves behind one of the children forming "the gates," who has that color. In the end, two lines are formed in the "two gates." The children from each line pull, until one of the lines crosses to the other side.

Since this game can get a bit loud, the following version was adapted for my class. Each row holds hands. Standing between their desks, they move quickly back and forth while singing «*pase misí, pase misá*». When we say «*por la puerta de Alcalá*», the children stop holding hands, turn around, and hold hands again. This time, however, they raise their hands to form "gates." When we sing, «*Los de adelante corren mucho, los de atrás se quedará*», the child at the end of each row passes in and out of the gates and joins the last child holding hands. The whole row moves a step toward the left or right until all the children have had an opportunity to move through the gates. This game is particularly good when the children in lower grades need to move and you have little space in the classroom.

Pase misí, Pase misá
por la puerta de Alcalá.
Los de adelante corren mucho
los de atrás se quedarán.

(popular, Spain)

A la víbora, víbora de la mar,
de la mar por aquí pueden pasar.
Los de adelante corren mucho
y los de atrás se quedarán,
tras, tras, tras, tras.

Una Mexicana que fruta vendía:
ciruela, chabacano, melón y sandía.
Será melón, será sandía,
será la vieja del otro día
día, día, día, día.

El puente está quebrado
que lo manden componer
con cáscaras de huevo
y pedazos de oropel
pel, pel, pel, pel.

(traditional, Mexico)

Dónde Están las llaves

This is a traditional game for professionals adapted for the classroom. We choose two children; one hides a key and the other steps out of the classroom. The child with the key hides it somewhere in the classroom (we avoid places such as inside their desks, baskets with lunches or the teacher's table). When this is done, the other child reenters the classroom and tries to find the key. The first time the class sings, «*Dónde están las llaves*» in a normal tone of voice; but the second and the third time, the children's voices can become louder when the child approaches the key and softer if farther from the key. After the song is sung three times, any student who has not found the key is asked to do something in front of the class—for instance, count in Spanish or sing a song.

> *Dónde están las llaves,*
> *matarile, rile, rile.*
> *Dónde están las llaves,*
> *matarile, rile, ron, chimpón.*
>
> *En el fondo del mar,*
> *matarile, rile, rile.*
> *En el fondo del mar,*
> *matarile, rile, ron, chimpón.*
>
> *Quién irá a buscarlas,*
> *matarile, rile, rile.*
> *Quién irá a buscarlas,*
> *matarile, rile, ron, chimpón.*
>
> (oral tradition;
> adapted by Elena Forrer)

Con La zapatilla por detrás

A student is chosen to be "it" and to carry *la zapatilla*. The student is given a slipper and the class begins to sing the following popular tune. When the children reach the line (*mirar para abajo*), they should put their heads down on their desks and close their eyes. The student who is "it" will walk quietly around the room and place the slipper behind someone's chair before returning to the front as quickly as possible. When selected, students must grab the slipper and try to reach the first child's desk first. The name changes according to each child chosen to carry la zapatilla.

> *Con la zapatilla*
> *por detrás,*
> *tris, tras.*
> *Ni la ves,*
> *ni la verás,*
> *tris, tras.*
> *Mirar para arriba,*
> *que caen judías.*
> *Mirar para abajo,*
> *que caen garbanzos.*
> *A callar, a callar,*
> *que «Mary» va a pasar.*
>
> (popular, Spain;
> adapted by Elena Forrer)

Other Resources

VOCABULARY GAME: FOOD, CLOTHES, PARTS OF THE HOUSE...

This is a practical game for grades 5 and 6, but it can be adapted for grades 3 and 4. First ask each student to draw six vocabulary cards with, for example, the topic of clothing recently used for homework. Next, divide the students into groups of four. Have each student select five (or six) cards from their stack. It is very important for each group to have five or six cards. Each player will hold the cards without showing the illustrations, but everyone knows all the vocabulary covered. The game begins when the first student asks another in the same group:

¿Por favor Rose, tienes tú los pantalones?

If "Rose" has the picture of that item, she should give the card to the person who asked. Then, the first player will respond:

Gracias.

Any student who forgets to say «*gracias*» loses a turn. Now it is Roses's turn to ask. If Rose does not have «*los pantalones*», she says:

No, yo no tengo los pantalones.

That student now looses a turn and Rose gets a turn to ask someone else:

¿Por favor tienes tú la camisa?
Sí, yo tengo la camisa.
Gracias.

Rose will continue the game until someone does not have the item asked for, or until she forgets to say «*por favor*» and «*gracias*». Those who forget to say «*gracias*» or «*por favor*» lose a turn and the one who asked gets to ask again.

This is a very dynamic game if the students are acquainted with the vocabulary covered. The conversation must always take place in the foreign language, and we can add penalties for speaking English. The object of the game is to obtain as many cards as possible from the other players, always with «*por favor*» and «*gracias*». This game facilitates conversation while reinforcing vocabulary. While this game is excellent for grade 6, it could be played in other grades. For instance, in grades 3 or 4, we can play with fruits or vegetables. The children make four or five cards. each with an illustration, and play with their desk partners instead of in groups of four.

—ELENA FORRER

Tic Tac Toe

This is a great game for conjugating verbs and for forming sentences. In the middle grades, it can be played for vocabulary reinforcement with vocabulary words (family, parts of the house, etc.).

On the board, the teacher writes nine verbs in the infinitive in each space of the chart. The class is divided in half and designated "O" and "X."

The first student must conjugate a complete sentence with the chosen verb. If the sentence is correct, the teacher marks an X on the verb. The next student from the other group now forms a sentence. If that sentence is correct, the teacher marks the verb with "O." The winner is the first group to reach three X's or three O's in any direction.

For instance:

(Salir)	Estudiar	(Pintar)
Cantar	Es✗ribir	Correr
Co✗inar	Comer	Visitar

The first player in group "O" gets to chose first. For instance, «*estudiar*». If «*estudiar*» is chosen, the student needs to form a sentence such as «*Nosotros estudiamos en la escuela*». Then the turn moves to a student in "X" group, who might say, «*Ellos escriben en su cuaderno*» until there are three X's or three O's in a row.

For new students or those who tend to need more help, I allow them to say, «*Paso mi turno*». Now the next student in that group takes a turn.

This game can be adapted for practice in past tense or with other vocabulary topics.

Other Resources

SIETE ARRIBA

This game can be played in all grades for vocabulary reinforcement. We can begin in grade 2 with little figurines of animals, and in grade 3 with cards of fruits and vegetables or other foods. We call seven students to the front, and each will carry one of the animal cards. The others remains seated. The teacher instructs:

Cabezas abajo pulgares arriba.

All the seated children now put their heads down with their thumb up. While the teacher sings a song or plays an instrument such as a lyre, each child in the front moves around the classroom searching for a child. The student pushes the thumb of the child down and returns to the front with the rest of the children. Once all of the seven children have finished and stand at the front, the teacher says:

Cabezas arriba.

Now seven seated children stand. One by one, they all need to guess which "animal" has pushed their thumb down. Following this example:

¿Es el caballo?
—No. No es el caballo.

Any child who is not ready to answer may say:

Paso mi turno.

And we wait until the student is ready to respond. They get only one turn to ask. If the child now standing guesses correctly which animal has pushed his or her thumb, they trade places, and the student who guesses correctly goes to the front.

(popular game adapted for the language lesson by Elena Forrer)

San serenín

Although this song talks about a grade 3 topic, in my opinion it belongs in grade 2 for the imitation and level of difficulty. When we begin the song, we move our hands around each other forming quick circles, and when we name a profession, the children imitate the profession. The child who makes a mistake must sit down.

San Serenín, de la buena, buena vida.
Hacen así, así los zapateros,
así, así, así.
Así me gusta a mí.

San Serenín, de la buena, buena vida.
Hacen así, así los panaderos,
así, así, así.
Así me gusta a mí.

San Serenín, de la buena, buena vida.
Hacen así, así los carpinteros,
así, así, así.
Así me gusta a mí.

San Serenín de la buena, buena vida.
Hacen así, los doctores,
así, así, así.
Así me gusta a mí.

San Serenín de la buena, buena vida.
Hacen así, los policías,
así, así, así.
Así me gusta a mí.

San Serenín de la buena, buena vida.
Hacen así.
Hacen los artistas, así, así, así
Así me gusta a mí.
    (directores de orquesta, violinistas, pianistas; popular)

Other Resources

Bingo/ Lotería Tercer Grado

Se distribuyen para cada alumno un papel tamaño folio pegado a una cartulina. El folio contendrá una cuadrícula con veinticuatro espacios. Cada alumno escribe su nombre en su cartón y escoge al azar, un espacio o dos en blanco, que será «el espacio libre». La maestra preparará alrededor de sesenta tarjetas con ilustraciones de todos los temas cubiertos en la clase como la ropa, el cuerpo humano, objetos de la casa y clase, frutas, verduras, comida, etc. Una vez distribuidas por toda la clase las tarjetas, los alumnos comenzarán a ilustrar sus casillas con las ilustraciones sin que se repitan. Por ejemplo, no puede haber dos ojos o dos lápices. El juego comienza con las siguientes reglas:

La maestra saca una tarjeta y repite dos o tres veces el objeto. Si el alumno no comprende lo que se dice, entonces levanta la mano para que la maestra muestre la tarjeta. Esto evita conmoción y al mismo tiempo ofrece una oportunidad a los alumnos que comprendieron.

Se pide a los alumnos que utilicen un lápiz de un color específico y se determina que cada vez que la maestra nombra un objeto, ellos marquen la casilla con una determinada marca, como un círculo o una estrella. Así, se evitan los papeles, las nueces o piedras que se caen o mueven y es otra vez usable, ya que se cambia el color o la marca en cada juego.

Gana el alumno que completa varias filas o líneas, o la cuadrícula completa según se determine. La maestra escribirá en la pizarra el nombre del ganador junto con tiza amarilla y junto a una estrellita. En mi experiencia, el alumno no necesita un «premio» material.

—Marta Nañez

¡Alto! (A Vocabulary Game)

This game is recommended for grades 7 and 8 and reinforces vocabulary. The students can play in pairs.

After distributing paper to the class, the students draw four or more vertical columns on their paper and leave a small column for adding points. Each category can have several or just one topic. For instance:

1) Food & Drinks	1) Months 2) Adjectives	Verbs: AR/ER/IR	1) Spanish-speaking countries & cities	TOTAL

The game starts with a random letter from the alphabet such as "C"; for each category the students must supply a vocabulary word, which earns a point. In this case we can write:

Carne   Corto   Comer   Caracas = 4 points

The first student to shout «¡Alto!» wins that particular row and the other students are not allowed to continue writing; they have to "freeze." The students who have supplied one word in each column earn four points; however, those who are first to call «¡Alto!» earn double points (in this case, 8 points) and write 8 points under "total." Those who have responded with more than one vocabulary word, but have also managed to complete the row, earn double the points. For instance, in the example from before, if the other students manage to complete three words in each category, they will add only 3 points to heir total. Only the first person (or pair if they are working in pairs) who has completed one word in each category has «¡Alto!».

Carne, café......Corto......Correr, comer......Caracas, camisa......   14 points

The upper grade classes love this game. They become very engaged with vocabulary and, by playing in partners, have the opportunity to help each other with vocabulary. It is important to alternate and change categories; for instance: clothes, anatomy, parts of the house, places to go (*montañas, lago, playa*, etc), and any other topic covered in class.

(adapted for the class by Elena Forrer)

8. 4 CULTURAL TOPICS AND OTHER PRESENTATIONS

THE DAY OF THE DEAD IN MEXICO

The Day of the Dead is a strong tradition throughout most of Mexico. It is celebrated on November 1 and is dedicated to the souls of young children, and November 2 is dedicated to adults. This celebration has its roots in Aztec beliefs about the transition of the soul after death. It was believed that all souls would go to Mictlan, a place prepared by the Gods where they could await the day when they could come back and visit their relatives on Earth.[9] Knowing the traditional hospitality of the Mexican people, they of course prepare for this visit with no sorrow or pain in their hearts, but mainly as a way of honoring and remembering their loved ones.

According to this belief, souls of the dead will come to visit and "share" their favorite food with the family. The family sometimes keeps vigil and prayer through the night, and while some do it at home, in many small towns people get together in the cemetery. There they clean and prepare the tombs and bring food as well as their instruments to pray and sing together.

At home, families prepare a special altar for the dead, which features pictures of deceased relatives, friends, and their favorite foods, such as mole, rice, chocolate, and even beer and tequila for the adults. Days before the actual date, markets and streets are covered by impressive heaps of striking yellow and orange marigolds, still called *Cempasuchitl* ("flower of the dead"), as they were in the Nahuatl language, as well as other colorful seasonal flowers. People adorn the altar by adding flowers, incense, water in case they are thirsty, and salt for the journey. They may even make a path of marigold petals all the way from the door to the altar, so the souls don't lose their way.

The altar, or *ofrenda* (offering), should always include the favorite food and objects of the person being honored, as well as the four elements in nature:

---

9 See http://en.wikipedia.org/wiki/Mictlan.

- Earth, represented by the food itself;
- Wind, which is represented mainly by the subtle movement of elaborate pictures cut from colorful tissue paper, as well as the copal, or incense, used in the celebration, which is related to this element;
- Water, as we have said, to quench their thirst after the long journey;
- Fire, a candle for each of the souls being honored, and extras for all the souls that may have been inadvertently forgotten.

What both children and adults really look forward to is the skeletons and sugar skulls that are so popular during this time. Skulls are made primarily of a sugar paste and decorated with colored sugar and shiny paper. There is a space on the forehead for the name of the skull. In that way, people usually buy a sugar skull with their friends' names, so that they may eat them as candy. Although the traditional skulls are made of sugar and may be beautifully decorated, today one can also find skulls made of chocolate and amaranth.

There are also versions of whole skeletons made of papier-mache, portraying Death herself in human costume and performing diverse human activities such as cycling, dancing, working in the fields, and so on. There is a huge tradition of depicting Death in its various forms at this time, and some galleries and museums dedicate whole sections to showcase the creations made by a number of artists, especially in Mexico City.

Finally, the tradition would not be complete without the basic food used for celebrations in all corners of the world: a special kind of bread, the bread of the dead, is prepared on this day, with little representations of bones on top. The recipe for this bread is very special and it is baked only at this time of the year.

On the day of the dead, newspapers usually publish *calaveras*, or poems and rhymes, written especially about the death of living politicians and celebrities. These usually express a form of scorn toward the kind of lives they have led, as if they were already caught by death, though they are still alive.

La calavera tiene hambre,
¿no hay un pedazo de pan por ahí?
No se lo acaben todo,
déjenme la mitad.
Chile con huevo,
chile con pan,
la calavera quiere cenar.[10]

To celebrate the Day of the Dead at school, I usually prepare an altar for the whole school in the auditorium. One can also prepare individual altars in select classrooms, especially in the upper grades.

The main items to be included in the altar could be: cut-out tissue paper, candles, flowers, and pictures or even just a card with the name of the deceased. Other items can include bread, food, water, salt, and sugar skulls.

It is advisable to offer all the students the space to put up either a picture or a name, since this provides an opportunity to share and heal together. Many children like to bring pictures of their pets, and that is okay, too. Another good idea is to have them make a single card with all the names they wish to remember. It is also a good time to speak about the Monarch butterflies, which fly all the way from northern US to a small town in Mexico, in Michoacán, right at this time of the year. Millions of butterflies completely cover the forest. The ancient peoples of Mexico believed that these were the spirits of the dead. Some of my grade 7 students have made cards with butterflies to honor their loved ones who have passed.

On the day of the celebration, I have one class at a time come to the *ofrenda* to set up their pictures. They look silently at the whole *ofrenda*, and then they sit and I explain briefly and according to their age, each of the elements in it. Next, they tell us who they brought and how they were related to them. One representative from the class is allowed to light a tall candle and place it on the altar. We sing a short song that I have previously taught and they leave. This takes just 15 minutes or so. At the end of the day, the altar looks full and beautiful, ready for the whole school to gather. I might give a short presentation, dedicate the altar to some member of the community, and tell a story (I recommend «*Francisca y la muerte*», by Onelio Jorge Cardoso). We sing the song together and finish with artistic presentations.

—NORA HILDAGO

---

[10] See www.dayofthedead.com.

Día de los Muertos

El día de los muertos se celebra el uno y el dos de Noviembre. Nuestra escuela prepara un altar en memoria de Hilary. El altar tiene flores, semillas, frutas, agua, velas, papel picado e incienso. Hay muchas fotos de familiares y amigos y una foto grande de Hilary. ¡Hoy es una fiesta!

Rendering by Justine Lippens (San Francisco Waldorf School)

This is the song I use:

*A las almas que se han ido
las queremos recordar
una flor y una vela
les llevamos al altar
y nuestra luz
queremos enviar
el amor unidos
nos ha de guardar.*
—Nora Hidalgo

Día de los Muertos

*Estaba la muerte un día
sentada en un arenal,
comiendo tortilla fría
pa'ver si podía engordar.*

*Estaba la media muerte
sentada en un tecomate,
diciéndole a los muchachos:
vengan, beban chocolate.*

*Estaba la muerte seca
sentada en un carrizal,
comiendo tortilla dura
y frijolitos sin sal.*

(traditional folklore)

Las posadas

During the Christmas season in Mexico, children experience the joy and anticipation of the birth of Baby Jesus. According to tradition, from December 16 to 24, families and friends gather to celebrate Las Posadas. *Posada,* literally "inn," is a celebration that refers to the time when Mary and Joseph went from inn to inn asking for lodging in Bethlehem. Nowadays, very few people in Mexico do this every night, but every child gets to participate in at least one Posada during the week before Christmas.

The tradition begins with a recitation of the litany while someone carries clay figures of Mary on the donkey with Joseph by her side and the Angel Gabriel leading the way. Half of the people stand outside the door while the other half go inside the house. The people outside sing, asking for lodging, while the ones inside keep saying that they cannot open. At the end of the singing, the people "inside" recognize Joseph and Mary and let them in, and the whole party goes on to break a piñata. The piñata is usually stuffed with sugar cane pieces, peanuts, apples, tangerines, *tejocotes* (a small fruit), jicama, and candy. The children also receive small baskets with special treats. Afterward, there is usually a dinner with traditional Christmas food and fruit punch.

At school I usually have a piñata for the fourth grade. We prepare by learning the songs "asking for lodging" and the song for hitting the piñata. I choose one of the upper grades to be the people who will actually "let us in"; we try to keep it a secret.

On the day of the Posada, we set out, hopefully with someone playing a guitar as we sing, and we visit as many classes as possible. They are all prepared to say "No, you can't stay here." One of the children carries the clay figures on a tray and stands at the door when we reach a class. When we finally get to our destination, that class will sing for us the welcome verse, and they will usually share hot chocolate and cookies with us. Then we break the piñata. Days earlier, I explained to them all about the contents of the piñata, especially since I include *caña de azúcar.* They love to see how I chop the tall stalks in front of them in class and show them how to peel and chew it. I try to include Mexican items inside, such as sugar cane and peanut candies. I also show them how I blindfold them and how to hit the piñata. This is by far their favorite celebration!

—Nora Hidalgo

Outside/Inside

(A fragment of the song for «*Las posadas*»)

En el nombre del cielo
os pido posada
pues no puede andar
mi esposa amada.

Aquí no es mesón
sigan adelante
yo no puedo abrir
no sea algún tunante...

Song to hit the piñata

Dale, dale, dale
no pierdas el tino
porque si lo pierdes
pierdes el camino.
Una, dos, tres!

(tradición oral, compiladora Nora Hidalgo)

Diálogo de Simón Bolívar y George Washington

This presentation could be prepared with several grades. The main dialogue can be carried by two eighth graders and the grade 8 class. Other grades can prepare different activities, such as the song «*Marcha Panamericana*». For this song, the class could make flags representing all the Latin-American countries and then sing as they march with the flags. Another class could sing or recite a poem or song to Simón Bolivar or to George Washington. We begin the representation with a dark stage with only Simón Bolívar and George Washington illuminated as they speak.

> WASHINGTON: Good morning Sir. What is your name?
>
> BOLÍVAR: *Mi nombre es Simón Bolívar: yo soy de Sudamérica y nací en Caracas, la capital de Venezuela.*
>
> WASHINGTON: It is a pleasure to find you here Mr. Bolivar. I am George Washington. I was born in North America in the state of Virginia.
>
> BOLÍVAR: *El placer es mío Sr. Washington.*
>
> (They shake hands.)
>
> WASHINGTON: My parents died when I was young, but I became successful and accomplished my vision—to declare freedom from the colonies. I was one of the founding fathers of the great nation of United States of America.
>
> BOLÍVAR: *Mis padres también murieron cuando era joven. Desde niño me interesó la política y quise liberar a mi pueblo del poder de España. Por eso en mi tierra me llaman El Libertador.*
>
> AUDIENCE: «¡*El Libertador! El Libertador!*».
>
> (poem by grade 8, «*A Simón Bolívar*», by Llorens Torres.[11])

---

11 A Simón Bolivar, 7.3. "Poetry in the Upper Grades," p. 302.

Other Resources

A SIMÓN BOLIVAR

Político, militar, héro, orador y poeta.
Y en todo grande. Como las tierras libertadas por él,
que no nació hijo de patria alguna
sino que muchas patrias nacieron hijas de él.

Tenía la valentía del que lleva una espada,
tenía la cortesía del que lleva una flor,
y entrando en los salones arrojaba la espada,
y entrando en los compates arrojaba la flor.

Los picos del Ande no eran más a sus ojos,
que signos admirativos de sus arrojos.
Fué un soldado poeta. Fué un poeta soldado.

Y cada pueblo liberatado, era una hazaña del poeta
y era un poema del soldado.
Y fué crucifado!
—LUIS LLORENS TORRES (1876–1944)

BOLÍVAR: *Sí. A lo largo de mi vida viajé por otros países y abracé los ideales de la Revolución francesa: ¡Libertad, igualdad y fraternidad!*

(class 8, from the audience: «*¡Libertad, igualdad y fraternidad!*».)

WASHINGTON: Those ideals were also very important for me. I was also present in France during the French Revolution. Freedom of expression, freedom of religion and independence from England was the purpose of my life.

(Optional Poem in English about George Washington)

WASHINGTON: *Hoy many nations did you liberated Mr. Bolívar?*

BOLÍVAR: *Yo luché por la independencia de:* – Colombia – Venezuela – Ecuador – Perú – Bolivia.

(song: «*Simón Bolívar, Simón, caraqueño*»[12])

---

12 See www.musica.com/letras.asp?letra=843704; www.youtube.com/watch?v=iuZDhxRaNwo.

WASHINGTON: Mr. Bolívar, my congratulations sir; but tell me, did you enter into combat?

BOLÍVAR: *Sí. Fui político, escritor, poeta y general de caballería en la batalla de Boyacá. Luché por la libertad de los pueblos panamericanos.*

WASHINGTON: I also was a thinker and a general. I fought in the battle of Potomac. I addressed the congress in my famous speech "The Creation of the American State"

BOLÍVAR: *Ya veo que los dos compartimos los mismos principios. Yo también presenté mis ideas en el discurso: «La Carta de Jamaica» y «El pensamiento boliviano».*

WASHINGTON: (Getting closer to Bolivar) My dear friend Bolívar, it will be an honor to shake your hand.

BOLÍVAR: *Con mucho gusto señor Washington. ¡Por la libertad y la igualdad de los pueblos!*

WASHINGTON: For the freedom and equality of the nations!

(Song or «*Marcha Panamericana*», Rodolfo Sciammarella[13])

---

13 See http://www.youtube.com/watch?v=29gmaTrIS2Y.

Other Resources

FRIDA KAHLO

This presentation was part of the festival for *Día de Los Muertos*. It was presented and reenacted by grade 8.

Weeks before the event, the class learned the popular Mexican song «*La Llorona*». The class became familiar with the life of Frida Kahlo. Before the event, the students read small texts about her life and became acquainted with her paintings. The students also learned many new vocabulary words from the readings and wrote an essay in Spanish on their books.

For the event, we prepared the questionnaire presented below and eleven students were assigned to read and memorize each a question. Another student was assigned to impersonate Frida. She also had to memorize the answers.

On a large canvas, we recreated the typical background of one of Frida's famous self-portraits, depicting jungle leaves. The student portraying Frida, sat stoically in front of the canvas, reenacted as a "living tableaux."

In front of the audience we placed on a platform, and on the riser, the easel with the canvas for the portrait of Frida. On the other side of the platform, we placed an altar for the school, but also in her honor. The rest of the students were seated in the audience but close to the platform. The hall was dark, illuminated only by the candles for the altar and a light focusing in the portrait of Frida. Frida sat frozen in front, illuminated as a focal point.[14]

The students in eighth grade accompanied by a guitar, began to sing the first part of the Mexican song «*La Llorona*». Frida in front sat frozen, until the class finished the first part of the song. Then, the class quietly began to hum the song, while one by one, the eleven students began

---

14 Pastel of Frida Kahlo by Malin Reedijk from the Portland Waldorf School, class of Sra. Chacón.

to ask Frida questions. Static until now, Frida became alive and began to respond. The student reenacting Frida, had to memorize the answers and also reenact the responses with gestures on the stage. When the questions and answers were completed, the student's sang the second part of *La Llorona*, while Frida sat again reenacting her portrait. The following questions summarize the main events in her live. When the questions were concluded, the class sang the second part of the song *La Llorona*. (This song can be found easily on the Internet.)

QUESTIONS

1. ¿Quién eres?

    «*Soy Frida, Frida Kahlo. Mi nombre significa paz*».

2. ¿De dónde eres?

    «*Soy de México. Mi padre es de origen alemán y mi madre es mexicana*».

3. ¿Qué te pasó de niña?

    «*A los seis años contraje la enfermedad de polio y como resultado tengo una pierna deforme. Por eso siempre llevo faldas largas*».

4. ¿Después, tuviste un accidente?

    «*Sí tuve un accidente de autobús. Yo tuve heridas muy serias principalmente en la espalda y en el cuello y como consecuencia, no pude tener hijos*».

5. ¿Pudiste caminar después del accidente?

    «*No, no pude caminar durante meses. Poco a poco me recuperé y pude caminar, pero tuve muchos relapsos y mucho dolor*».

6. ¿Cuándo empezaste a pintar?

    «*Empecé a pintar después del accidente*».

7. ¿Por qué pintaste tantos retratos tuyos?

    «*Pinté frecuentemente mi retrato, porque paso mucho tiempo sola y así expreso mi dolor y mi amor por la cultura mexicana*».

8. ¿Qué te gusta pintar?

    «*Me gustan los colores y los temas de la cultura mexicana*».

9. ¿Te casaste?

    «*Sí. Me casé con el pintor mexicano Diego Rivera. Él y yo tuvimos una relación turbulenta porque los dos tenemos un temperamento fuerte*».

10. ¿Te gusta la política?

    «*Sí. Mi vida no es nada sin la pintura y la política. ¡Soy amiga del comunismo y de los políticos rusos!*»

11. ¿Cómo fue tu muerte?

    «*Mi muerte… tuve tantas enfermedades… mi fin fue corto y triste. Como dijo mi esposo Diego Rivera: El día más triste de mi vida…*».

—ELENA FORRER

Popol Vuh: Escenas sobre el mito Maya de la creación

Adapted for young students by Elena Forrer from the Maya myth

Escena Primera

(Escenario decorado con mazorcas de maíz. Decoraciones mayas en el a los lados del escenario. Los dos narradores se situarán a cada lado del escenario.)

> Narrador 1: *Quiero contarte la historia de los pueblos Mayas que vive en el campo. Quiero hablarte sobre el espíritu del maíz, que alimenta sus cuerpos. Estas mazorcas (tomando una mazorca) que crecen en cada cosecha, representan un milagro. Por eso las gentes purifican sus campos con incienso antes de plantarlas.*

(Los músicos acompañan con melodías tradicionales Mayas. Sale el otro narrador.)

> Narrador 2: *Meses después, recogen las cosechas. Los mayas creen que el maíz tiene vida y alma.*

(Música. Los bailarines salen al escenario. Pueden recitar una poesía Quiché o bailar una danza maya con cestos de maíz sobre sus cabezas. Terminado el baile o la poesía, un estudiante depositará una cesta con mazorcas en el escenario. Dos estudiantes traen una pantalla hecha con tela de lienzo, que iluminará las siluetas de los dioses en sombras agrandadas por medio de la luz de una lámpara,— como en un teatro chino de sombras—. Los dioses serán alumnos. Los dioses se moverán detrás del teatro de sombras mientras los narradores hablan.)

> Narrador 1: *En el principio había silencio. No había pájaros. No había peces.*
> *No había animales en las montañas y no había gente.*
> *Todo estaba en tinieblas. Solo el dios creador Tepeu se movía con luz propia en el agua.*
> *Tenía plumas verdes y azules y por eso también se llamaba la serpiente emplumada.*
> *El otro dios creador, Gucumatz o «Corazón del cielo» también existía.*
> *Un día, los dioses de la creación, decidieron crear vida.*

(Los dos dioses se moverán con movimientos detrás de la pantalla de tela o en el escenario representando las palabras de narrador.)

> Narrador 2: *Juntaron sus pensamientos y unieron sus palabras y pintaron mapas en el cielo. Planearon la creación de árboles y la creación del hombre.*
> *Hicieron el día, la noche y la vida.*

Dioses: *¡Qué sea todo hecho! ¡Qué el vacio se llene! ¡Qué el agua se separe de la tierra! ¡Qué así sea!*

Narrador 1: *En un instante la tierra se hizo.*
Aparecieron entre la niebla, las montañas y el agua corriendo en los ríos.

(Los dioses salen fuera del teatro de sombras enfrente de la audiencia.)

Serpiente Emplumada: *¿Sólo hay silencio entre los árboles?*
No hay nadie que los guarde?

Narrador 2: *Después crearon animales y los espíritus y guardianes de las montañas.*
También crearon El ciervo, los pájaros, pumas, jaguares y serpientes.

(Aparecen por un lado del escenario los animales. Los estudiantes descalzos, llevarán máscaras y túnicas.)

Corazón del cielo: *Tú ciervo, dormirás en los bosques comerás del pasto y te multiplicarás. Tú pájaro, vivirás en los árboles y harás nidos.*

(Baile del venado. Los alumnos pueden llevar cascabeles en los tobillos.)

Narrador 2: *Después, los dioses terminaron la creación de los animales y quisieron que ellos pronunciaran sus nombres.*

Serpiente emplumada: *Ahora animales, llamarnos por nuestros nombres.*

(Los animales sólo emiten sonidos.)

Serpiente Emplunada: *No pueden decir nuestros nombres. Esto no está bien. Porque no les es posible hablar, serán cambiados. Vivirán en las montañas, en los árboles y en los pastos pues no les es posible adorarnos.*

Corazón de cielo: *Crearemos otros seres que sean capaz de invocarnos. Este es su destino.*

Escena Segunda

(Música instrumental o tambor.)

Narrador 1: *Entonces los dioses visitaron a la abuela del ocaso y del sol para pedirla consejo.*

(Los dioses, fuera de la pantalla viajan por el escenario en busca de la abuela. La abuela aparecerá sentada sobre un trono junto a un telar y rodeada de luz.)

Dioses: *Abuela del ocaso y de la luz, necesitamos tu consejo.*
Queremos que el hombre repita nuestros nombres y nos adore por ser sus creadores.

Abuela: *Echa la suerte con los granos de maíz y las semillas de tzité y sabrás si puedes modelar al hombre con madera.*

(*Los dioses bajan a la tierra y echan la suerte.*)

Dioses: *Maíz, tzité danos tu suerte para que la criaturas de madera juntas puedan ser creadas.*

Abuela: *Así será. Las criaturas de madera hablarán.*

(*Aparecen en la pantalla de sombras los hombres creados de madera y de barro con máscaras y sin expresión. Todos vestirán igual y tendrán el mismo color. Se moverán como marionetas por la pantalla. Efectos de sonido.*)

Narrador: *Se fueron multiplicando. Tuvieron hijos e hijas pero no se acordaron de sus creadores porque no tenían mentes y almas.*
No tenían expresión y sus manos no tenían fuerza.
Por eso no pensaron en sus creadores.
Entonces los dioses bajaron y destruyeron las figuras de barro que había sobre la tierra.

(*Los dioses bajan y destruyen las figura en sombras. Corazón de cielo aparecerá enojado.*)

Corazón del cielo: *Enviaré sobre la tierra una inundación que cubrirá todo.*

Narrador 2: *Durante muchas noches y días llovió hasta que la tierra quedó cubierta de agua.*
Los animales se dispersaron por las cumbres en busca de refugio.

(*Palos de lluvia y tormenta. Todo se queda en silencio.*)

Escena tercera.

Narrador 1: *Había nubes y el ocaso cubría la tierra.*
No había sol y la luna no tenía cara.
Pero existía un ser que se llamaba Vacub-Caquix que era falso y vanidoso.

(*Sale al escenario, fuera de la pantalla un personaje «luciférico», ricamente vestido en colores negro y plata, con plumas negras con detalles esmeralda.*)

Vacub: *Ahora yo seré el más poderoso de todos los seres creados.*
Yo soy el sol, la luz y la luna. Magnífico es mi esplendor.
Gracias a mí, el hombre caminará sobre la tierra.
Yo puedo ver muy lejos.

Narrador 2: *Vacub habló.*
Pero él no era realmente el sol, el presumía de sus plumas y sus riquezas.
No podía ver todo el mundo.
No podía ver las estrellas y ser el sol y la luna porque su luz no le había iluminado.

Narrador 1: *Corazón de cielo preocupado mandó a dos de los dioses jóvenes a destruir a Vucub.*

(Aparecen en el escenario dos dioses. Los dioses llevan unas mazorcas de maíz a modo de espadas. Lucharán contra Vucub. Ruido de tambores.)

Narrador: *En un instante surgieron en el cielo el sol y la luna.*
Ellos vivieron en el cielo.

(Aparecen los dioses representando el sol y la luna.)

Escena cuarta

(Aparecen los dioses Corazón del cielo y Serpiente emplumada.)

Corazón del cielo: *¡Qué el hombre aparezca y llene la faz de tierra!*

Narrador 1: *Entonces llegaron los animales. Llegaron el gato, el coyote,*
el loro y el cuervo y señalaron a los dioses la comida que era el maíz.
Entonces modelaron de maíz al hombre.
Crearon cuatro figuras. Y pudieron hablar.

(Los dioses recogerán la cesta de maíz depositada al principio de la obra en el centro del escenario y modelarán el maíz. Aparecen de un lado del escenario dos hombres sin máscaras. Aquí la obra puede terminar con las palabras del narrador.)

Narrador 2: *Grande fue su sabiduría.*
Ellos podían ver muy lejos: el arco del cielo y la faz de la tierra.

Hombres: *Mira el arcoíris del cielo, Balam. Nuestros ojos pueden verlo todo.*

BALAM: *Daremos gracias a los dioses por nuestra felicidad y nuestros conocimientos.*

NARRADOR 2: *Pero los creadores, no escucharon esto con placer. Y dijeron:*

SERPIENTE EMPLUMADA: *No es bueno que nuestras criaturas conozcan todos los misterios del cielo y la tierra.*
¿Qué haremos ahora?
Tienen que acaso ser ellos dioses?

CORAZÓN DEL CIELO: *Comprobaremos sus deseos.*
Ellos no pueden ser iguales a nosotros.

NARRADOR 2: *Entonces Corazón del cielo cegó sus ojos con una niebla que sopló en ellos.*
Sus ojos se cubrieron y no pudieron ver de lejos.
De esta forma el conocimiento del universo quedó destruido y sólo pudieron ver lo que era real.

NARRADOR: *Pero los dioses no pudieron velar del todo sus ojos.*
La gente maya cree por la noche durante el sueño sus ojos vuelven a ver el mundo y pueden viajar hacia los dioses y ver el maíz sagrado y lo que ven en maravillosos colores que son capaces de recordar.
Y los dibujos y colores que aparecen en los tejidos, creen que representan su visión divina tal como aparece en sus sueños.

BIBLIOGRAPHY

INTRODUCTIONS TO THE CHAPTERS

Castañeda, María Inés, and Joven, Vicente. *Cantemos con los niños*. Bogota: Cooperativa editorial magisterio, 2000.

Forrer, Elena, et al. *Senderos: Teaching Spanish in Waldorf Schools* Fair Oaks, CA: AWSNA, 2000.

Glöckler, Michaela, Stefan Langhammer, and Christof Wiechert. *Education – Health for Life: Education and Medicine Working Together for Healthy Development*. Dornach: Medical and Pedagogical Sections at the Goetheanum, 2006.

Kellman, Janet, Betty Staley and Astrid Schmitt-Stegman. *Working Materials for the Class Teacher: Forming the Lessons of Grades One through Eight*. Fair Oaks, CA: AWSNA, 1996.

Kiersch, Johannes. *Language Teaching in Steiner Waldorf Schools*. Forest Row, UK: Fellowship Publications, 1997.

Moffat, Pelham. *Forward toward What?* Edinburgh, Rudolf Steiner Educational Association, 1976.

Oxford, Rebecca L. *Language Learning Strategies*. Scarborough, ON: Heinle ELT, 1990.

Querido, René. *Creativity in Education: The Waldorf Approach*. San Francisco: H. S. Dakin, 1987.

Steiner, Rudolf. *Balance in Teaching*. Great Barrington, MA: SteinerBooks, 2007 (this volume incorporates *Deeper Insights into Education* and is a complete translation of CW 302a).

———. *Faculty Meetings with Rudolf Steiner,* 2 vols.: 1919–1922 and 1922–1924. Hudson NY: Anthroposophic Press, 1998.

———. *Foundations of Human Experience*. Hudson, NY: Anthroposophic Press, 1996.

———. *The Genius of Language: Observations for Teachers*. Hudson, NY: Anthroposophic Press, 1995.

———. *A Modern Art of Education*. Great Barrington, MA: Anthroposophic Press, 2004.

———. *Practical Advice to Teachers*. Hudson, NY: Anthroposophic Press, 2000.

———. *The Renewal of Education*. Great Barrington, MA: Anthroposophic Press, 2001.

———. *Towards the Deepening of Waldorf Education: Excerpts from the Work of Rudolf Steiner: Essays and Documents*. Pedagogical Section of the School of Spiritual Science, 1991.

Stockmeyer, E. A. Karl. *Rudolf Steiner's Curriculum for Waldorf Schools: An Attempt to Summarize His Indications*. Stourbridge, UK: Steiner Waldorf Schools Fellowship, 2001.

Teaching Spanish in the Classroom with *Andando Caminos*

Lower Grades

Beskow, Elsa. *Pelle's New Suit*. Edinburgh: Floris Books, 1989.

Bravo-Villasante, C. *El libro de las Fábulas*. Valladolid, Spain: Editorial Miñon, 1985.

Jiménez, Juan Ramón. *Juan Ramón Jiménez para Niños*. Madrid: Ediciones de la Torre, 1986.

Jiménez, Juan Ramón, Federico Garcia Lorca and Rafael Alberti. *Mi Primer Libro de Poemas. Lengua Española: Ingreso*. Barcelona: Ediciones SM, 1958.

Medina, Arturo, ed. *El Silbo del Aire: Antología Lírica Infantil 1*. Lima: Editorial Vicens-Vives, 1985.

———. *El Silbo del Aire: Antología Lírica Juvenil 2*. Lima: Editorial Vicens-Vives, 1985.

Mistral, Gabriela. *Ronda de los Astros*. Barcelona: Espasa-Calpe, 1998.

Morales, Maria Luz. *Libro de la Poesía en Lengua Castellana* (España y América S. XII-XIX), vol. 1. Barcelona: Editorial Juventud, 1984.

———. *Libro de la Poesía en Lengua Castellana* (España y América S. XX), vol. 2. Barcelona: Editorial Juventud, 1984.

Pelegrín, Ana. *Poesía Española para Niños*. Madrid: Ediciones Alfaguara, 2005.

Sánchez Trincado, José Luis, and R. Olivares Figueroa. *Poesía Infantil Recitable*. Madrid: Compañía Literaria, 1996.

Seco, Manuel. *Gramática esencial de español: Introdución al estudio de la lengua*. Aguilar. Madrid, 1982.

Bibliography

Books to Support Preparation of the Mexican Fiesta
   (Contributed by Marcela Mejía Ronan)

Arcona, George. *Mayeros: A Yucatec Maya Family.* New York: HarperCollins, 1997.

Contreras, Kathleen. *Pan Dulce.* New York: Scholastic, 1995.

deRubertis, Barbara. *Cuenta con Pablo.* Minneapolis: Kane Press, 2005.

Gomez, Ignacio. *La Bella Hortelana.* New York: McGraw-Hill, 1997.

Herrera, Juan Felipe. *Calling the Doves / El canto de las palomas.* New York: Lee and Low Books, 2001.

Jordan, Helen J. *Cómo Crece una Semilla.* New York: Rayo/HarperCollins, 2006.

McMillan, Bruce. *Everything Grows: Raffi Songs to Read.* New York: Mcgraw-Hill, 1997.

Rius, Maria. *La Vida Bajo la Tierra.* Hauppauge, NY: Barrons, 1987.

———. *La Vida Sobre la Tierra.* Hauppauge, NY: Barrons, 1987.

Rius, Maria, and Josep Mª Parramon. *El Campo.* Hauppauge, NY: Barrons, 1986.

Rondon, Javier, and Marcela Cabrera. *El Sapo Distraido.* Editorial Ekaré, 1995.

Swamp, Cacique Jake. *Gracias te Damos: Una ofrenda de los nativos Americanos al amanecer de cada dia.* New York: Lee and Low Books, 1996.

Torres, Leyla. *El Sancocho del Sábado.* New York: Scholastic, 1995.

Zamorano, Ana, and Julie Vivas. *A comer!* New York: Scholastic, 1999.

Middle and Upper Grades

Barlow, Genevieve, and William N. Stivens. *Leyendas Mexicanas: A Collection of Mexican Legends.* Lincolnwood, IL: National Textbook, 1992.

Bravo-Villasante, Carmen. *Romancero.* Madrid: Montena, 1989.

Darío, Rubén. *Antología Poética: Introducción Francisco Abad Nebot.* Madrid: Editorial EDAF, 1990.

Día de los Muertos. Sacred Gifts: Precolumbian Art and Creativity November 1995. The Mexican Museum. San Francisco.

Diaz-Pimienta, Alexis. *En un lugar de La Mancha.* Havana: Editorial Gente Nueva, 2006.

Díaz-Plaja, Guillermo. *Lengua y literatura Enseñanza Media.* Murcia, Spain: Ediciones La Espiga, 1967.

Forrer, Elena, and E. Silvestry. *Aventuras de aquí y de allá*. A & A Printing, self-published.

García Viñó, Manuel and Pepi Sánchez. *Juan Ramón Jiménez para niños*. Madrid: Ediciones de la Torre, 2005.

Goetz, Delia, Sylvanus G. Morley and Adrián Recinos. *Popol Vuh: The Sacred Book of the Ancient Quiché Maya*. Norman, OK: University of Oklahoma, 1950.

Lengua española: Primer curso. Edelvives. Zaragoza, Spain: Editorial Luis Vives, 1957.

Lengua española: Segundo curso. Edelvives. Zaragoza, Spain: Editorial Luis Vives, 1958.

Lengua y literatura: Cuarto curso. Madrid: Ediciones S.M. Editorial Luís Vives, S.A. 1958.

Martí, José and Lulu Delacre. *Los zapaticos de Rosa*. Lyndhurst, NJ: Lectorum Publications, 2009.

Medina, Arturo. *El silbo del aire: Antología lírica juvenil* (2). Barcelona: Vicens-Básica, 1985.

Morales, María Luz. *Libro de la poesía en lengua Castellana (España y América, vol. 1)*. Barcelona: Editorial Juventud, 1984.

Noguez, Susan A., and Emily Boyd. *Realidad y Fantasía*. Logan, IA: AMSCO School Publications, 1984.

Pelegrín, Ana. *Poesía Española para Jóvenes*. Madrid: Ediciones Alfaguara, 1997.

Saravia, Albertina. *Popol Wuj: Antiguas historias de los indios quichés de Guatemala: Illustradas con dibujos de los códices Mayas*. México City: Editorial Purrúa, 1997.

Valmaseda Santillana, Martin. *Segundo Curso de bachillerato*. Madrid: Ediciones SM, 1958.

Wood, Tim. *The Aztecs*. New York: Viking Juvenile, 1992.

Zarate, Christina. *Día de los Muertos: A User's Guide*. Program of Latino History and Culture, Smithsonian National Museum of American History (download at http://latino.si.edu/dayofthedead/DODManual.pdf).

www.ingramcontent.com/pod-product-compliance
Lightning Source LLC
Chambersburg PA
CBHW080803020526
44114CB00046B/2758